The Personal Computer

TIME LIFE ®

Other Publications:
AMERICAN COUNTRY
VOYAGE THROUGH THE UNIVERSE
THE THIRD REICH
THE TIME-LIFE GARDENER'S GUIDE
MYSTERIES OF THE UNKNOWN
TIME FRAME
FIX IT YOURSELF
FITNESS, HEALTH & NUTRITION
SUCCESSFUL PARENTING
HEALTHY HOME COOKING
LIBRARY OF NATIONS
THE ENCHANTED WORLD
THE KODAK LIBRARY OF CREATIVE PHOTOGRAPHY
GREAT MEALS IN MINUTES
THE CIVIL WAR
PLANET EARTH
COLLECTOR'S LIBRARY OF THE CIVIL WAR
THE EPIC OF FLIGHT
THE GOOD COOK
WORLD WAR II
HOME REPAIR AND IMPROVEMENT
THE OLD WEST

This volume is one of a series that examines various aspects of computer technology and the role computers play in modern life.

UNDERSTANDING COMPUTERS

The Personal Computer

BY THE EDITORS OF TIME-LIFE BOOKS
TIME-LIFE BOOKS, ALEXANDRIA, VIRGINIA

Contents

7 PCs Proliferant
ESSAY Secrets of Word Processing

45 The Apple Alternative
ESSAY Wizards of Number-Crunching

87 Challenging the Mainframe
ESSAY A Universal Network

120 Glossary
121 Bibliography
125 Picture Credits
125 Acknowledgments
126 Index

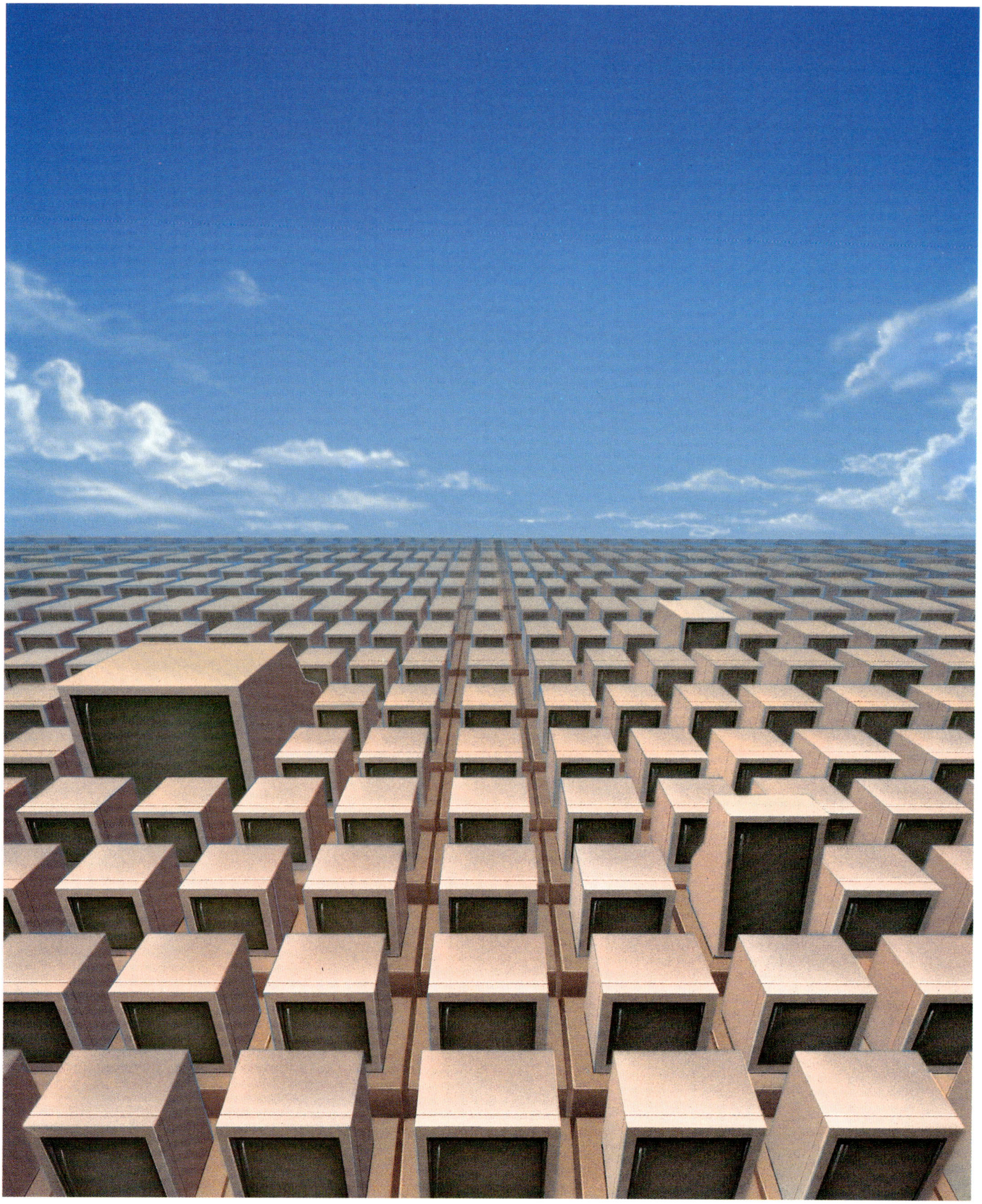

PCs Proliferant

Steve Jobs, quintessential Californian and the marketing whiz behind a new company called Apple Computer, was wearing a suit—his only suit, his first suit. It set him apart from the mostly T-shirt-and-jeans crowd of electronics hobbyists and company representatives that thronged San Francisco's Brooks Civic Auditorium on April 16, 1977, for the First West Coast Computer Faire. Many of Apple's competitors, including a few much larger companies, made do with simple displays identified by hand-lettered signs. In contrast, Jobs manned one of the most prominent and attractive exhibits on the floor. A rainbow-hued apple with a big bite missing, the firm's distinctive new logo, gleamed everywhere. Well-dressed staff members distributed brochures and ran demonstration programs—mostly games—on a cluster of sleek new computers about the size of typewriters. Some spectators, unconvinced that the entire machine actually fit inside a case so small, wanted to look under the counter on which it rested.

The computers on display were the first samples of the Apple II. For $1,298, the machine offered a four-kilobyte (4K) memory—enough to store about 4,100 characters of program instructions or data. (One kilobyte equals 1,024 bytes.) The computer was equipped with a built-in version of the programming language BASIC. Along with the keyboard, which was molded into the case, the Apple II came with two game-controller paddles. To store programs and data, the machine could be hooked up to an everyday audio-cassette recorder. For a monitor, it used a television set, black-and-white or color.

Eleven years later, on October 12, 1988, Steven Jobs introduced another new computer. No stranger to a suit by then, he stood alone on the stage of San Francisco's Symphony Hall before an invited audience of 3,000 educators, software developers, and reporters and unveiled NeXT, a $6,500 powerhouse of a computer built into a black one-foot cube. At five times the price of the first Apple II, Jobs's new machine had 2,000 times that machine's memory. It could perform most operations at least six times faster, and in other capabilities it far surpassed the Apple II. NeXT could, for example, hold several complex programs in memory simultaneously; the original Apple II could handle only one simple program at a time. Instead of borrowing a television screen, NeXT had its own high-resolution black-and-white monitor capable of producing images of exceptional clarity. A speedy, laser-sensitive storage disk archived data and programs. And while the Apple II had little more than a beep of a voice, NeXt incorporated a sound chip that could reproduce the strains of a string quartet.

YEARS THAT CHANGED THE COMPUTER WORLD
The time between the introductions of the Apple II and the NeXT encompassed the childhood, adolescence, and early adulthood of a new species of computer. Known variously as personal or desktop computers, microcomputers (they are built around integrated circuits called microprocessors), portables, luggables, and laptops, these machines have evolved from clever little devices of ques-

tionable utility into performers nipping at the heels of the mighty mainframes that were—along with their smaller but still expensive cousins, the minicomputers—the only data-processing machines to be had until the late 1970s.

Coincidentally, the personal computer stimulated a dynamic new business, one that offered the twin intoxications of fast-paced innovation and high-stakes corporate warfare. Hundreds of companies, large and small, anted up and joined the game. A few took home a substantial part of the pot; many more were cleaned out. Once just a gleam in eyes of hobbyists and eager entrepreneurs, the microcomputer precipitated wrenching change throughout the computer industry. These machines became indispensable to many businesses and spread the marvel of computing far beyond the field's traditional boundaries. In companies too small for a mainframe or a minicomputer, micros began handling inventory and accounting chores, freeing their owners from the drudgery of doing such jobs manually. In big corporations, managers impatient with the slow response of centralized data-processing departments brought in microcomputers to speed their daily work. Personal computers began to take root in home offices, where dedicated workers labored at night to complete tasks that overflowed the day. And all the while, rival manufacturers—many of them following the lead of Apple Computer—explored ways to make the ever-more-powerful systems more approachable to the average office or factory worker, who knew or cared little about the inner workings of these marvelous machines.

AN ENTREPRENEURIAL FRENZY

Before the close of the First West Coast Computer Faire three days after it opened, Jobs and company had secured orders for 300 Apple IIs, and by the end of the year, they had posted sales of $770,000. In 1978, revenues jumped past $7 million, then rocketed to $47 million the following year. Growth of such magnitude inevitably attracted the attention of the adventurers in the business world, who are always on the lookout for new ways to personal or corporate riches.

The man in the watchtower at IBM was William Lowe, director of the Boca Raton Laboratory in Florida. The outpost at Boca Raton had been established in 1968 to develop small minicomputers for the bottom of the company's product line. IBM intended that customers for these machines would become so hooked on Big Blue's products that they would stick with the company should they decide to acquire larger computers. By the time Lowe, a veteran of sixteen years with IBM, took over the lab in 1978, it had developed several minicomputers that appealed to businesses that lacked the means or need for mainframes.

In addition to keeping current projects on track, Lowe was determined to uncover new ways to bind neophyte computer users to IBM, and by mid-1980 he was convinced that he had found one in the kind of computer that Apple was producing. Surveying the personal-computer scene, Lowe beheld a rambunctious bazaar. In the words of Adam Osborne, a brash, opinionated columnist in the computer trade press, the microcomputer business was powered by "a multitude of entrepreneurs. By the thousands they are 'trying it,' and anything electronic that can happen will happen." Osborne contended that almost anyone could succeed in such an untapped, wide-open market.

And many did. More than 200 manufacturers were producing computers, and the number was climbing fast. Among their offerings were some machines that would soon disappear from view—the Sol from Processor Technology, the Z-1 from Cromemco, the Challenger from Ohio Scientific, and the Horizon from North Star, for example. But Lowe observed that other enterprises were widening their beachheads. Commodore International, an established calculator manufacturer, had introduced its own small computer, named the PET (for Personal Electronic Transactor). Like the Apple II, the PET came ready for hookup to a cassette recorder and a television set. It was equipped with 12K of memory, but following Commodore founder Jack Tramiel's philosophy of "going for the masses, not the classes," the PET cost only $595.

Tandy Radio Shack, a major retailer of electronic parts and gadgets, had already unveiled the second version of its TRS-80, a computer originally introduced a few months after the Apple II. The TRS-80 Model II, as it was called, had a 64K memory and was sold complete with keyboard and monitor. And like the Apple II, it was equipped with a floppy-disk drive to store data and programs. Not only were floppies easier to use and faster than tapes, they provided software writers with a convenient publishing medium.

With larger memories and a practical vehicle for software, personal computers had become more than instruments for playing games. Tandy touted its latest machine as a business computer, offering software to handle accounting, inventory, correspondence, and financial recordkeeping in small companies and the offices of professionals. Even more impressive was a milestone program named VisiCalc, a contraction of "visible calculator." Written for the Apple II in 1979 by Harvard Business School student Dan Bricklin and programmer Bob Frankston, VisiCalc was an electronic version of an accountant's paper spreadsheet, a ledger printed with rows and columns and used, among other things, for making financial forecasts. On a pencil-and-paper

A sleek new logo (above) ousted Apple Computer's old company emblem (right), a sketch of Sir Isaac Newton's apocryphal meditation under an apple tree, when the company made the leap from three men in a garage to a professionally run firm. One Apple executive later described the striped apple as "the symbol of lust and knowledge, bitten into, all crossed with the colors of the rainbow in the wrong order." It combined, he said, "lust, knowledge, hope, and anarchy."

spreadsheet, changing a number representing an assumption invariably led to time-consuming recalculation of numbers signifying conclusions. VisiCalc was a fresh breeze that ended spreadsheet drudgery by performing such arithmetic effortlessly. A year after VisiCalc's introduction, Apple attributed nearly a fifth of its 130,000 computer sales directly to the spreadsheet software.

Nationwide, sales of personal computers for the office would grow to $900 million by the end of 1980. But Lowe could see that no company had yet cornered the business market for the machines. Apple, the leading producer of small computers, was, like Commodore, selling largely to small businesses and professionals. Tandy had peddled more computers to businesses than Apple and Commodore combined. But the number of such sales was small, Tandy's share amounting to only 175,000. Of the 14 million small businesses in America, fewer than 10 percent were using personal computers. And inside the largest corporations, which employed more than half the nation's white-collar workers, fewer than three percent of all employees regularly used such computers.

Furthermore, IBM's competitors in mainframes and minicomputers had not yet set up stalls in the personal-computer bazaar—though many had considered the idea. At Digital Equipment Corporation (DEC), for example, engineer David Ahl had proposed in 1974 that the company produce an inexpensive version of its popular PDP-8 minicomputer. Ahl suggested pricing the machine at $5,000 or so and selling it principally to computer enthusiasts. Top management, however, torpedoed the idea on the grounds that an individual would be foolish to buy a computer when a relatively inexpensive dumb terminal would permit part-time access to a much more powerful computer.

Where DEC had feared to tread, IBM had forged ahead. In 1975, the Entry Level Systems unit, a group of about thirty computer developers at the Boca Raton lab, introduced the 5100 series. Intended for small businesses, the machine was a one-man minicomputer. It turned out to be a disappointment, not only for IBM, but for purchasers as well. Costing more than $10,000, the machines initially came without software. In a formula for frustration, IBM expected each 5100 buyer to hire independent programmers to make the computer perform useful tasks. In early 1978, Robert Hallock, owner of a fastener company near New York City, laid out $18,000 for one of the machines. Two years and additional thousands of dollars later, his computer had yet to become fully operational. A master of understatement, Hallock remarked to a reporter from the *Wall Street Journal:* "I certainly expected this to be done quicker."

Other manufacturers of large computers were also floundering. Hewlett-Packard, Data General, and Texas Instruments—to name a few—were equally unsuccessful in their efforts to sell scaled-down versions of their larger machines. In the words of microcomputer consultant George Morrow, Lowe looked out on a landscape "littered with the bloody remains of large companies that tried to understand what micros were all about."

IBM ACTS

Morrow exaggerated, of course. None of these companies failed because of a dalliance with small computers. Top management at IBM remained very interested in the market, and Lowe was invited to head a task force at corporate headquarters in Armonk, New York, to examine whether IBM should write

The Course of a Revolution

Milestones in the transformation of the personal computer from a game machine into a powerful tool for businesses and professionals appear in the time line that begins at right. The change was brought about by a cascade of developments in both software and hardware. Spreadsheet programs introduced computing to small business owners. Recognition of this huge market spurred competitors, such as IBM and the Compaq Computer Corporation. New chip designs increased processing speed and made memory cheaper and more abundant. In a decade, personal-computer memory swelled from four thousand bytes to several million bytes, power enough to perform tasks that once required a mainframe.

software for microcomputers made by others. After two weeks of deliberations, Lowe was certain that the software idea was a poor one. Before a meeting of IBM's top decision-making body, the Corporate Management Committee, he argued that Big Blue should design and build its own machine. The debate became so heated that a recess had to be called partway through the three-hour session for the tension to subside. As the meeting ended, a participant recalled, chairman Frank Cary protested that IBM "took 400 people and three years" to bring any product to market. Most of the time and energy was well spent coordinating the evolution of new computers with existing lines so that IBM did not compete against itself. Nonetheless, a thirty-six-month development period was unacceptably long in the rapidly developing personal-computer field.

Lowe said, "I think we can do it in a year."

"You're on," said Cary, and gave Lowe two weeks to formulate a plan.

Lowe returned to Boca Raton with this challenge—almost a dare—and immediately assembled a twelve-man task force of systems designers and programmers, as well as production and finance experts. They came to be called the Dirty Dozen—a none-too-apt reference to a popular adventure film about

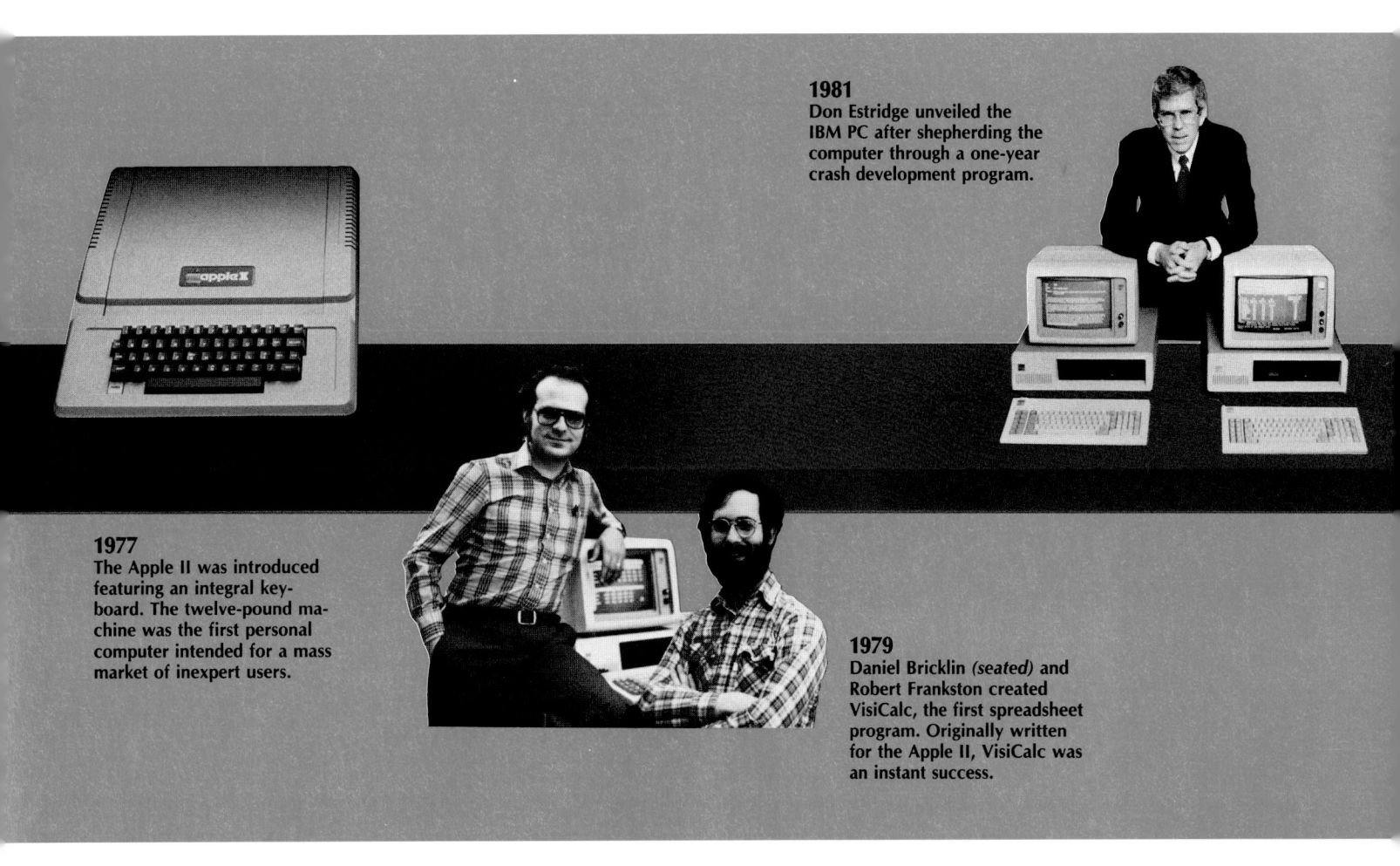

1981
Don Estridge unveiled the IBM PC after shepherding the computer through a one-year crash development program.

1977
The Apple II was introduced featuring an integral keyboard. The twelve-pound machine was the first personal computer intended for a mass market of inexpert users.

1979
Daniel Bricklin (seated) and Robert Frankston created VisiCalc, the first spreadsheet program. Originally written for the Apple II, VisiCalc was an instant success.

a ragtag band of military misfits turned commandos. In a whirlwind fortnight of brainstorming and dogged work, the team would build a working prototype. But more significantly, they would develop strategies for manufacturing and selling the machine that would have much of IBM up in arms.

The design for the new computer evolved rapidly. Like the best of its contemporaries, it would have a keyboard and a monitor. Disk drives would store programs and data. Selecting a microprocessor to power the computer needed careful attention. All such chips in 1980-vintage personal computers handled data in bytes (strings of eight ones and zeros), a feature that explains why they were known as eight-bit machines. But Lowe's task force felt that such a processor was too slow and handled too small a memory—a mere 64K. The designers preferred a sixteen-bit chip, which doubled processing speed by chewing two bytes at a time and could address at least ten times as much memory.

Two years earlier, Intel, the pioneering chipmaking firm, had unveiled such a microprocessor—the 8086—and Lowe's Entry Level Systems team had used it in the last of the 5100 series. However, other computer builders had shied away from the 8086 because other chips essential to a computer (they governed access

1982
Mitch Kapor introduced Lotus 1-2-3 for the IBM PC. This spreadsheet program, which improved upon VisiCalc in several ways, enabled the computer to turn numbers into charts and graphs.

1984
IBM released the PC/AT. Based on the Intel 80286 chip, the AT had three times the speed of Big Blue's PC.

1984
Apple Computer unveiled the Macintosh—and with it, operating-system software that greatly simplified use of the machine.

to printers, modems, and disk drives) dealt in single bytes, not double ones. Seeing that years might pass before these essential intermediaries would be redesigned to operate as sixteen-bit devices, Intel promptly modified its new chip. The result, in 1979, was the 8088. To the outside world of support chips, the 8088 presented itself as an eight-bit microprocessor. But internally, it processed information in sixteen-bit chunks, permitting faster processing and access to more memory than an eight-bit chip *(pages 20-21)*. Within days of taking up the microprocessor question, the hardware faction of the Dirty Dozen had settled on the 8088 as the heart of their new machine.

A POLICY OF OPEN ARCHITECTURE
As the prototype took shape under the skillful ministrations of Bill Sydnes and his assistant, Lewis Eggebrecht, Lowe and others evolved manufacturing and marketing policies. Except for the microprocessor, which had already been chosen, every component for the computer would be purchased from the lowest bidder. So that programming by outside software companies might begin long before the computer rolled off the assembly line, Lowe's team resolved

1988
Steve Jobs launched the computer he called NeXT. With 2,000 times the memory of the Apple II, it would become, he predicted, a "partner in thought."

1986
Compaq's DeskPro 386 was the first desktop computer to incorporate the Intel 80386 microprocessor, which was at least twice as powerful as the 80286 chip.

to disclose details of the machine's design as soon as they were finalized.

This so-called open-architecture approach was almost unheard of in the world of large computers, where companies customarily concealed the innards of their machines to thwart competition from independent suppliers of software and of hardware such as printers and disk drives. Personal-computer builders, eager for others to write software for their machines, were less secretive than mainframe and minicomputer manufacturers, but even they withheld information about some parts of their machines. Lowe planned to peel away every proprietary veil. By exposing everything, he hoped to convince outside suppliers, especially programmers, that IBM intended to loosen the reins and that writing software for its microcomputer would be profitable. "The key strategy," recalled Lowe, "was to get more applications for your product than for the other guy's." Lastly, Lowe wanted to bypass IBM's formidable computer sales force, 8,400 strong at the time, and merchandise the personal computer through independent retailers, just as Apple, Commodore, Tandy, and many others peddled their machines.

In the second week of August, Lowe, Sydnes, and Eggebrecht flew to Armonk. Lowe carried with him a pad of flip charts outlining plans for producing and selling the computer; Sydnes and Eggebrecht came along to demonstrate the prototype. It had been assembled from parts supplied by outsiders, as would be the case with the real thing if the project were given the go-ahead. It only faintly resembled the product that would eventually emerge, but it provided most of the features that would appear in the new computer: modular construction consisting of plug-in components, which among other advantages would allow the owner to upgrade it easily; a separate keyboard; a monitor sitting atop the box containing the electronics; and disk drives for data and program storage.

In an anteroom outside the conference room in which Lowe would present his plan, Sydnes and Eggebrecht put the prototype through its paces, displaying two brief sequences of animated computer graphics. Lowe and the Corporate Management Committee then closeted themselves in the conference room, where Lowe pitched the task force's plans for manufacturing and selling the desktop computer. Well-liked and trusted by the committee, he was given approval to gear up a crash program targeting shipment of the first computers just twelve months from that day. Upgraded to a Product Development Group, the task force became Project Chess. The computer was code-named Acorn. IBM made no public announcement, but word spread through the company that a bunch of "wild ducks" in Florida were hard at work on something exciting.

MARCHING IN MANY DIRECTIONS AT ONCE
The task of implementing the plans of William Lowe (he would soon be transferred to Rochester, Minnesota) and the Dirty Dozen fell to Philip Donald Estridge. Widely regarded as the perfect man for the job, Don Estridge was a genial person and a magnetic leader with eleven years' experience at Boca Raton. Almost alone among IBMers, Estridge owned an Apple II and spent hours at home fiddling with it. The maverick nature of Project Chess appealed to him.

Entry Level Systems engineers changed none of the design decisions made by the Dirty Dozen. Even so, it would be nip and tuck getting the machines built and onto dealers' shelves in the year allotted. A complex device, the Acorn consisted of scores of parts that all had to work flawlessly with one another. The team needed to contract with suppliers of these parts, set up and test assembly lines, print operating instructions, and design packaging. An advertising campaign needed concocting, and retailing agreements had to be hammered out.

Allowing for the inevitable complications and schedule cliffhangers that materialized, most aspects of the operation went smoothly. Lowe's open architecture had received an enthusiastic endorsement from the management committee in Armonk. A small Redmond, Washington, software company named Microsoft signed on to provide an operating system for the computer, as well as a version of the programming language BASIC. Intel agreed to supply the multitudes of microprocessors IBM would need. Estridge put Dan Wilkie, head of manufacturing and operations, in charge of acquiring components. Wilkie had the reputation of getting a job done—period. "I am a mail carrier," he says, unstoppable by the corporate equivalents of rain, sleet, and dark of night.

When word filtered through IBM that Wilkie was soliciting bids from suppliers outside the company for production-lot quantities of keyboards, disk drives, circuit boards, memory chips, and other computer parts, a clamor arose. IBM divisions that made such devices were accustomed to furnishing all that were needed for every line and model of computer that the company produced. For their products, these internal suppliers charged whatever it cost to make them—plus a reasonable profit. Unforeseen expenses were routinely passed along dollar for dollar. In effect, IBM was in the grip of an internal monopoly that was in part responsible for the high cost of the company's computers—from mainframes right down to the 5100 series for small businesses.

As the weeks passed, Wilkie received telephone calls from virtually every components division of the company, each one presuming that business as usual would ultimately prevail. Most were taken aback when Wilkie responded that he would welcome their bids, but that the low price, whoever offered it, would win. Even more astonishing was Wilkie's insistence on a fixed-price contract. That is, Project Chess would pay not one cent more for a component than the contracted amount. If production costs mounted unexpectedly, the supplier would have to swallow them. Cost overruns were to stop at the factory gate. "Oh, did that cause turmoil in the company," Wilkie remembered.

An IBM plant in Charlotte, North Carolina, was the first to win a bid; they would build the main circuit board, the one containing the microprocessor and allied chips. The first bid was 20 percent high. Thirteen tries later, a contract emerged. Along the way, tempers flared. A Charlotte executive, visiting Boca Raton just like any other supplier, fumed to Wilkie: "Look, we're not some little outside vendor you can play around with. We are inside. Our badges say 'IBM.'" Wilkie prevailed mostly because buying parts from IBM would have made the new computer too expensive compared to competing personal computers and because Estridge backed him up at the highest levels of the IBM hierarchy.

Everything else that went into the new computer—except for keyboards, which were to be built by an IBM plant in Kentucky—came from outside IBM. A small but reliable company named Tandon Corporation won the contract to supply disk drives. Zenith Electronics Corporation of Glenview, Illinois, agreed to furnish the power supplies, the component that converts high-voltage alternating current from a wall socket into the equivalent of a five-volt battery. Other circuit boards would come from a Silicon Valley upstart named SCI Systems.

Monitors would be supplied from Taiwan, and the printers would be made by Epson, a Japanese firm.

Retailing strategy for the Acorn caused almost as much furor as did parts acquisition. IBM—and no one else—sold and serviced IBM computers. Yet H. L. Sparks, to whom Estridge gave the job of marketing the Acorn, realized that to succeed, the new machine would have to be sold like other personal computers—in retail stores. And just as well. With a price expected to fall between $2,000 and $4,000, the Acorn would be unattractive to computer salespeople, who were accustomed to dealing with large businesses and whose compensation consisted of commissions. A salesperson would have to sell the machines on a grand scale to earn the commission that could be derived from the sale of a single large computer. Even IBM's Office Products Division (OPD) was cool to the Acorn; its sales staff was accustomed to selling typewriters and calculators. Richard Young, head of OPD at the time, reluctantly agreed to put some of the machines in his IBM Product Centers, the company's new foray into retailing. Friction arose when Young also resisted letting any outsiders sell the Acorn. In the end, Sparks prevailed because Estridge had the support of IBM's chief, Frank Cary.

At this time, there were several regional computer-store chains, but only one could satisfy Sparks's need for nationwide coverage—ComputerLand. Under the guidance of chairman William Millard, a man whose background in personal computers stretched to the days of computer kits to be assembled by electronics buffs, ComputerLand had expanded aggressively and in 1980 boasted 160 franchises in the United States and Canada, with total sales of about $125 million. IBM needed to learn from ComputerLand's vastly superior background in retail marketing. According to president Ed Faber, "we acted as consultants to IBM on how to get into the retail business. They asked us everything, including our ideas on what to name the product, what it should look like, and what its relative position should be in the market."

Sears, Roebuck and Company shared in ComputerLand's good fortune. Sears had been a longtime customer for IBM's mainframes. One of IBM's senior executives sat on the Sears board of directors, which was considering new business opportunities. Upon hearing of plans for the new personal computer, the directors settled on a network of new retail stores, Sears Business Centers. A few words in the right ears led to meetings in which the IBM marketers sat in on planning sessions for the new enterprise. Through its deals with Sears and ComputerLand, IBM established a formidable retail network.

A REMARKABLE PERFORMANCE
Estridge's team reached its goal on time and under budget. By July 1981, Acorns were rolling off IBM assembly lines, complete with the proud IBM trademark and the unassuming name Personal Computer, or PC. The unveiling was set for

Enjoying the life of a successful entrepreneur, millionaire Gary Kildall, author of the popular CP/M operating system for microcomputers, creates software on the porch of the Victorian house that served as headquarters for his company, Digital Research. In 1980, when IBM tried to buy CP/M for its PC, Kildall declined to sign the computer giant's lopsided confidentiality agreement, which protected Big Blue's trade secrets but not those of others signing it. Although Kildall missed that lucrative deal, he went on to provide other programs for IBM products.

William Gates III, youthful head of the software firm MicroSoft, grew rich in Kildall's place. Having already supplied software for the Apple II and the Commodore PET, Gates gladly signed IBM's secrecy agreement, winning a contract to supply the PC's operating system. In short order, Big Blue demanded an armload of security precautions, starting with locks for the file cabinets.

August 12, 1981, in New York City. However, two days before the event, during a final check of a few new PCs in Boca Raton, the Acorn team discovered that touching the machines resulted in an electric shock. The remedy—to insert an insulating piece of thin cardboard called fish paper between the power supply and a nearby circuit board—was simple in principle but difficult in practice. Nearly 2,000 PCs had been shipped to ComputerLand and to Sears headquarters in Chicago, where they were to be demonstrated to top executives the next morning. The shock was hardly life-threatening, but it posed an acute risk of embarrassment. The flaw had to be fixed.

At midnight, an emergency brigade composed of thirty Acorn team members boarded an IBM jet and headed for Chicago. Limousines whisked them to the Sears Tower in the dead of night, where the fish-paper insulation was hastily added to the PCs. After notifying Boca Raton of their success, the team sped westward to deal with the rest of the computers.

By the time Estridge began IBM's high-profile introduction of the PC the next day, all the machines had been fixed, including the ones on display in New York. Equipped with sixteen kilobytes of memory, the simplest model had a keyboard derived from IBM's electric typewriters and a connection for a cassette tape player. Without a monitor, the computer was priced at $1,265. A more useful model costing just over $4,300 had a 48K memory, two floppy-disk drives that could each accommodate 160K of data or programs, a monochrome monitor, and a printer. Increasing memory to the maximum—256K—added $2,000 to the price of the computer. Presented along with the machine were seven applications programs, including a game called Adventure, a word-processing package, and the much-esteemed VisiCalc electronic spreadsheet program.

Initial reaction to IBM's new product bordered on euphoria. "I can't believe," enthused one computer retailer, "that IBM got everything so right." The media response was almost as giddy. "By almost every estimate," Newsweek observed, "the personal computer world will never be the same." Even Apple dealers seemed elated. Said one: "IBM is putting its stamp of approval on the microcomputer—and that means that the microcomputer is here to stay."

17

IBM's chief competitors maintained a studied composure. Said Tandy president John Roach: "I don't think it's that significant." Mike Markkula, the man in charge at Apple, echoed Roach's view but acknowledged the PC with a full-page advertisement in the Wall Street Journal headlined "Welcome, IBM. Seriously." The ad proclaimed that Apple looked forward "to responsible competition in the massive effort to distribute this American technology to the world." Asked how Apple would respond to the PC, Markkula said: "We're the guys in the driver's seat. It's IBM who is reacting and responding to Apple."

A TIDAL WAVE OF PENT-UP DEMAND
In the IBM camp, the PC was regarded as just another new product—and one with only modest prospects. "When we began," Lowe recalled several years later, "we didn't understand the size of the opportunity. We expected to install fewer than 250,000 machines in the life of the product." In reality, the computer would be a bonanza. During the two years following the PC's introduction, fortunes would be made across the spectrum of hardware, software, and services.

PC shipments climbed from fewer than 20,000 in 1981 to more than 500,000 in 1983. By then, IBM was leading the pack with 26 percent of the personal-computer market, and Apple's Markkula had long ago listed his three biggest rivals as "IBM, IBM, and IBM." Few, including Lowe and Markkula, had recognized how ripe the business market was. Throughout the United States, enterprises of every size, eagerly waiting to computerize, had held back for fear of buying the wrong machine. Suddenly there was a product with "IBM" on its sheet-metal case and, with undisguised relief, they snapped it up. Even though IBM was producing nearly 50,000 PCs a month, assembly lines could not meet the demand. As a result, other computer makers prospered. Some customers who could not find an IBM computer to buy purchased an Apple II or Tandy's TRS-80. Apple's revenues rose to $1 billion a year, and Tandy's sales soared.

IBM's PC also created opportunities for agile, enterprising companies to earn fortunes by producing add-on equipment for the computer. The first—and, at the outset, one of the most successful—of these so-called aftermarket companies was Tecmar, Inc., founded by a physician and engineer named Martin Alpert. (The name of the company was a play on the phrase "Marty's technology.") When the IBM PC was announced in 1981, Dr. Alpert had just set up shop in Cleveland to manufacture electronic laboratory equipment. He had a hunch that the new PC would succeed and that he could win big if he supplied peripherals faster than IBM could introduce their own. Tecmar engineers bought the first two PCs ever sold and tore them apart to see how peripherals had to be made. Six grueling weeks later, at COMDEX, the industry's major trade show, Tecmar introduced twenty add-ons for the PC. Ultimately, the company's products would range from dust covers to memory-expansion boards and disk drives. Alpert's strategy paid off handsomely as Tecmar's revenues quickly climbed into the millions.

The software industry welcomed IBM's PC as a potential solution to the difficulties of creating programs for the great variety of small computers. Michael Shrayer, for example, author of an early word-processing package called Electric Pencil, had written seventy-eight different versions of the program. With the arrival of a best-selling machine, software developers could afford to ignore the many small makes of computers. Focusing their efforts, they created a flood of new software for the IBM PC that made the popular machine even more desirable to potential buyers. By 1983, a thousand programs were available for it and, just as Apple sales had once been boosted by the arrival of VisiCalc, the PC enjoyed a big lift in 1983 from a new and improved spreadsheet program named 1-2-3, produced by Lotus Development Corporation of Cambridge, Massachusetts.

Lotus and Tecmar were just two specimens of the more than 300 companies that would be founded to serve the IBM aftermarket, providing peripherals, software, training, and repair service for the PC. "No one in his fondest dream, on the craziest night," said Estridge, "would have guessed the amount of activity going on around our machine."

THE HOLY GRAIL OF COMPATIBILITY
The rapid rise of the IBM PC encouraged other computer manufacturers—venerable names in the field and upstarts alike—to stake claim to a share of Big Blue's success. Within a couple of years after the PC's debut, perhaps 150 imitators had emerged, all trying to set themselves apart by outdoing IBM in one way or another. Some offered more memory; others included special hardware features—such as superior monitors or large-capacity storage disks—in the price of their machines. A few simply sold computers for less money than IBM.

Most of these machines were touted as being "compatible" with the PC. But

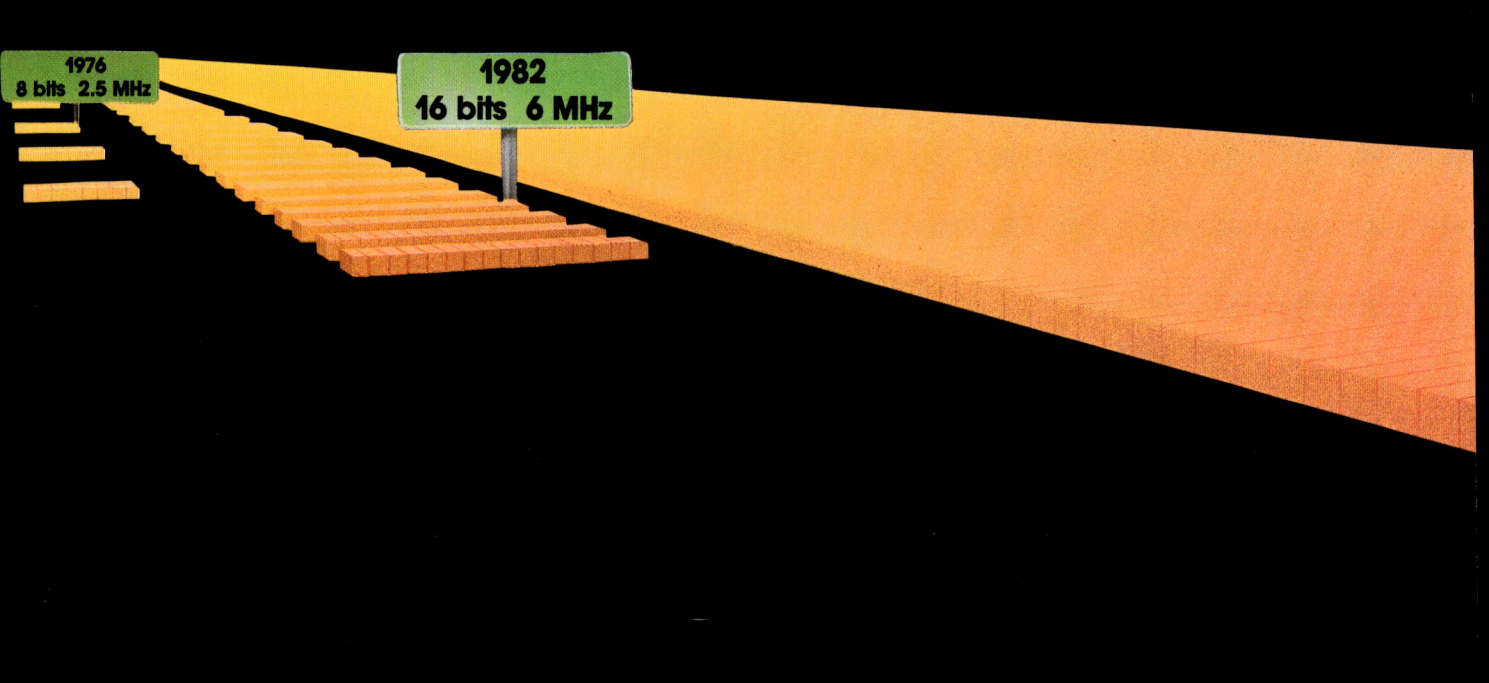

The Measures of Microcomputer Power

Ever since personal computers first became popular in the late 1970s, the microprocessors at their heart have accumulated more and more power. By leaps and bounds, these core chips have evolved from the computer equivalent of a lawnmower motor into racy, high-performance engines capable of feats once believed to be achievable only by mainframes and minicomputers.

Microprocessors are commonly rated according to three factors: clock speed, expressed in millions of cycles per second (megahertz, or MHz); word length or size, stated as a number of bits; and memory capacity, the amount of random-access memory (RAM) that the chip can control.

Although word size, clock speed, and memory capacity of microprocessors have all risen together, there is little connection between them. Long words promote computer efficiency by permitting the machine to process data in larger parcels. Thus, a thirty-two-bit microprocessor has the potential to work four times faster than its eight-bit ancestor—even if clock speed remains unchanged. In the early days of microprocessors, thirty-two-bit chips were too expensive to produce, so eight-bit chips became the rule, even though mainframes of the era typically processed sixty-four-bit words.

High clock speed in a microprocessor results from physical properties of the chip that are entirely independent of word size; these include the length of its internal circuits, the qual-

1985
32 bits   16 MHz

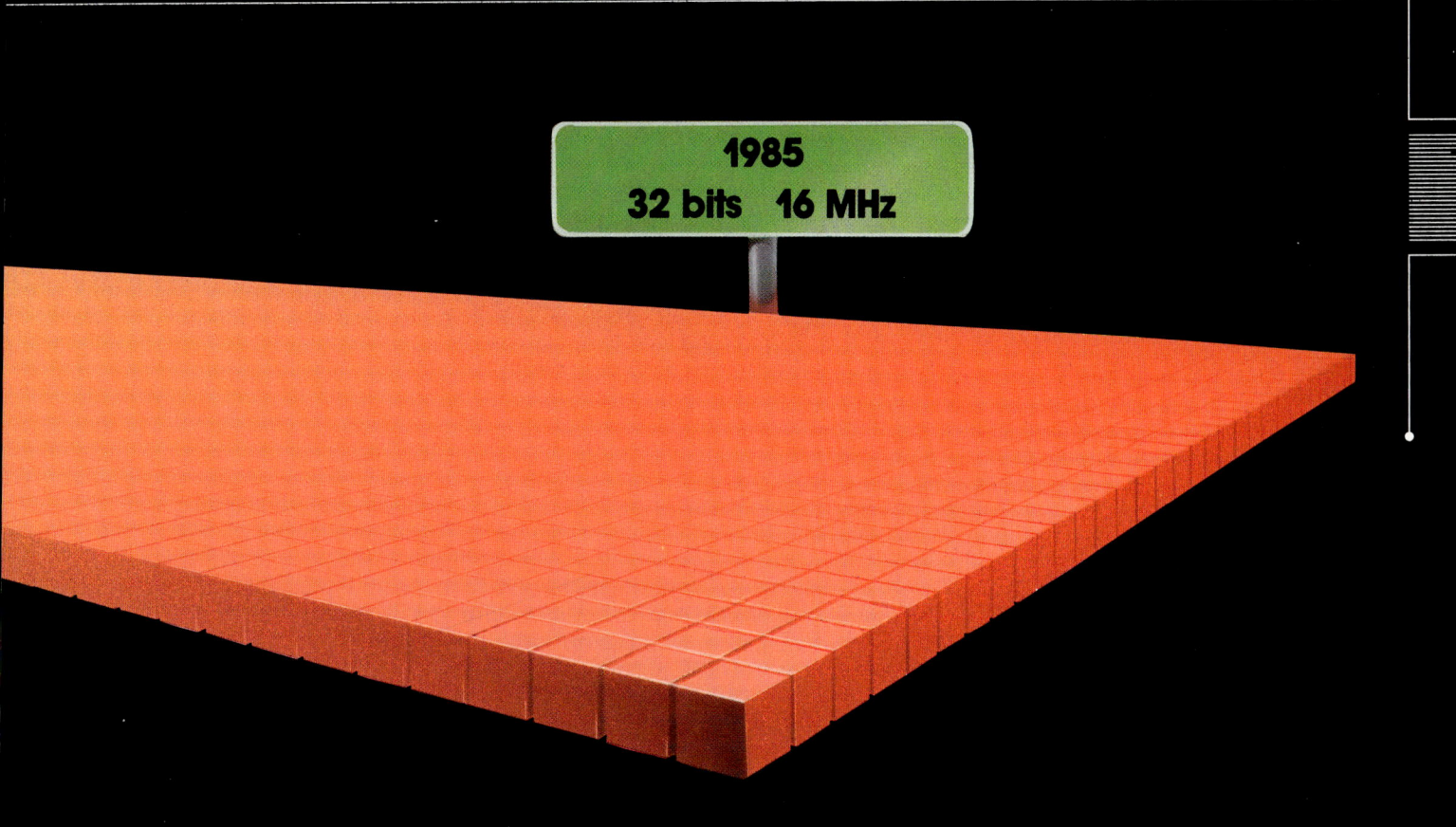

ity of its transistors, even its capacity for dissipating heat. Consequently, it is no more than coincidence that clock speeds have risen in step with word length, and there is no particular clock-speed limit associated with a given word size. For example, eight-bit chips have been built that operate at 20 MHz, nearly four times faster than the originals. Thirty-two-bit microprocessors, introduced with a clock speed of 16 MHz, were soon streaking along at 25 MHz, with expectations that clock speed might rise as high as 40 MHz.

Though clearly unrelated to clock speed, memory capacity, usually expressed in eight-bit parcels of data called bytes, may seem at first glance to be a function of word size. Each location in RAM must be identified with a unique binary code known as an address. An eight-bit address, for example, permits an inventory of only 256 memory cells (two multiplied by itself eight times). With a sixteen-bit memory address, a microprocessor can handle 65,536 such locations.

To maximize memory capacity, however, chip builders customarily design microprocessors to use memory addresses longer than the chip's word size. Eight-bit chips commonly employ a sixteen-bit address, although a few, like most sixteen-bit microprocessors, have been designed for a memory address of twenty-five bits. With an address that long, memory capacity exceeds 33 million bytes of RAM.

Each bit of a memory address requires its own path to and from the microprocessor through a connector called a pin. For a time, few microprocessors were built with more than forty such pins, and no more than twenty-five of them remained unused after basic microprocessor functions were accommodated. In order to increase memory capacity beyond 33 million bytes, chipmakers evolved designs having more than 100 pins, plenty for the thirty-two-bit memory address now common among the most advanced microprocessors. With thirty-two ones and zeros in the address, a microprocessor can deal with more than four billion bytes of memory, more than could fit in an average-size shower stall.

As remarkable as a thirty-two-bit chip may be, when installed in a computer it is often a Hercules in chains. In some machines, the operating system limits the amount of memory despite a long address. A high clock speed may mean little if, as is common, the computer's memory chips respond so slowly that the microprocessor must pause a count or two for data or program instructions to arrive.

Nor may the benefits of greater word length be realized. Software written for an eight-bit personal computer runs on a thirty-two-bit machine only because the more powerful microprocessor was designed to be compatible with existing programs. But such software runs no faster on a sixteen-bit or thirty-two-bit computer than on an eight-bit machine of identical clock speed.

at the time, one popular definition of compatibility was inherited from the world of mainframes, where the word signified a comparable machine that could run similar software. A non-IBM computer that flawlessly handled software written expressly for the PC became the rara avis of the personal computer scene.

In part, this software incompatibility was a matter of choice, since many hardware makers were trying to set themselves apart from IBM by offering superior technology. Such companies as Hewlett-Packard, Digital Equipment, Texas Instruments, and Japan's NEC were willing to forgo true software harmony for hardware that sparked rave reviews in computer journals. But for many smaller companies, software compatibility was becoming a matter of life or death.

Although IBM had assembled its PC mostly from off-the-shelf components, the company had safeguarded one vital link in the software-hardware chain—the Basic Input-Output System, or BIOS. This computer program, usually etched permanently onto a chip, controls the way a computer interacts with its monitor, its disk drives, and all other peripheral devices. In keeping with the notion of an open architecture, IBM had published the code for its BIOS but had also copyrighted the program. As a result, rival companies could produce machines that ran IBM software only if they created from scratch versions of the BIOS that worked like IBM's but did not infringe on the copyright. Doing so involved a substantial engineering effort that few could afford.

First to accomplish the task was Compaq Computer Corporation, which became one of IBM's most successful imitators. Compaq was founded in 1982 by Rod Canion, Bill Murto, and Jim Harris, three Texas Instruments engineers who had collaborated on TI's fully compatible, high-capacity storage disk for IBM's larger computers. Eager to strike out on their own, the three men were looking for some kind of business opportunity. One morning on a visit to a computer store, Canion, Harris, and an industrial designer named Ted Papajohn saw VisiCalc displayed on the monitor of an IBM PC. Over lunch in the House of Pies restaurant across the street, they mused on how they might become rich by producing a portable computer that could run IBM software.

There was no disputing the commercial possibilities of such a machine. A year earlier, journalist Adam Osborne had commissioned the design of a self-contained computer with built-in monitor and disk drives. Introduced a few months before the IBM PC, the computer weighed twenty-four pounds and cost

$1,795, a price that included software valued at $1,500 if purchased separately. Called the Osborne I, it was sometimes ridiculed for its clunky appearance, but 11,000 sold in its first eight months on the market. Osborne's computer, the three TI engineers knew, was utterly incompatible with the PC; it used an operating system called CP/M. Once predominant in small computers, CP/M had been eclipsed by IBM's personal-computer operating system from Microsoft. Canion and company wagered, moreover, that IBM would be slow to bring out a portable to complement the deskbound PC. The window of opportunity was open wide.

Funded by high-rolling venture capitalists, the trio spent $1 million over a period of nine months for a team of fifteen programmers to write a fully IBM-compatible BIOS. To protect against the possibility of a copyright-infringement lawsuit, Compaq used a strategy known as reverse engineering. Employing a two-team process, one group studied IBM's BIOS and wrote detailed descriptions of its role in the computer. The second group, composed of programmers ignorant of the IBM code, worked from the descriptions to write the new BIOS.

Apart from the input/output system, the performance of IBM PC was simple to duplicate, so Canion and his colleagues were able to concentrate on designing a stylishly rugged machine. The Compaq Portable Computer was ready for market in January 1983, and immediately it found a receptive audience. With fewer IBM PCs available than customers eager to buy them, dealers snapped up the Compaq. Offering high profit margins—roughly 38 percent, as opposed to IBM's 32 percent—Compaq quickly signed up nearly a thousand dealers, then enjoyed first-year sales of $111 million, setting a record in the history of U.S. business. None of this would have been possible without the new BIOS, which permitted the Compaq portable to run, without modification, virtually any software written for the PC. In one stroke, Compaq had redefined compatibility.

MAKING WAY FOR THE CLONES
Other companies, recognizing the desirability of a fully compatible BIOS, were not as fastidious as Compaq in acquiring one; they simply copied the IBM program. In February 1984, Big Blue sued two imitators, Eagle Computer and Corona Data Systems, for copyright violation and won the litigations. The courts required the offending companies to cease shipping computers that included the infringing BIOS. Corona was able to recover from this setback; the company had

already begun developing a legal BIOS and was soon back in the market. But for Eagle Computer, the judgment was a catastrophe. After seeing investors purchase 2.5 million shares of stock within five minutes of going public in mid-1983 and after posting a $500,000 profit for the final quarter of that year, Eagle lost nearly $10 million in the first quarter of 1984. Eventually, the company solved the BIOS problem, but not in time. After months of reorganizing, refinancing, and reducing staff—Eagle Computer bowed out of the market.

Impediments to creating a legal BIOS and the risks of plundering IBM's program created an opportunity that Phoenix Software Associates Ltd., a small Massachusetts programming house, was quick to exploit. Even as IBM was celebrating its victory over Corona Data Systems and Eagle Computer, Phoenix had begun to offer would-be makers of IBM-compatible computers—clones, in the parlance of the microcomputer bazaar—BIOS software guaranteed compatible with IBM's. Although Phoenix stopped short of assuring against copyright lawsuits, the risk was minimal. The company wrote its BIOS using a two-team approach much like Compaq's. For a one-time license fee of $100,000, Phoenix permitted a clonemaker unlimited use of the program in its computers. Phoenix President Neil Colvin recalled that, as the project got started, his firm "spent more on legal fees than on development." But the expense paid off. Although Phoenix BIOS code has defined the computers of nearly 200 manufacturers, the company has never been accused of copyright violation.

A HOST OF COMPATIBLE RIVALS

With the path to software compatibility paved by the Phoenix BIOS, the majority of IBM's imitators gave up any pretense of technical superiority. A new crop of upstarts jostled their way into the market by undercutting the prices that IBM—and even Compaq—charged for computers. Michael Shane, for example, a purveyor of wigs and Faded Glory blue jeans, had founded Leading Edge Products in 1979. He introduced Elephant Memory Systems, his own brand of floppy disks ("An Elephant never forgets"), and made a fortune. He next sold low-cost printers under the Banana label ("Buy a Banana and save a bunch"). In 1983, Shane turned to the clone business. To assure his company a source of low-cost labor, he teamed up first with the Japanese firm Mitsubishi and later with a South Korean manufacturer named Daewoo Telecom. The result was a family of clones that sold for roughly two-thirds the price of comparable IBM PCs. Shane's computers proved highly reliable and won a top recommendation from the influential *Consumer Reports*. Annual sales quickly topped 150,000 units.

Another winning clonemaker was Michael Dell, founder of Dell Computer Corporation. Dell was a freshman majoring in biology at the University of Texas when he discovered that he could make a lot of money by enhancing basic IBM PCs with special features, such as added memory or hard disks, and selling the machines to local businesses. During spring vacation, after his sales had already hit $50,000 a month, he revealed to his parents his secret occupation and his intention to drop out of school. They were reluctant to give him permission because they hoped that he would become a doctor. But in May, revenues exceeding $180,000 clinched Dell's decision. Within a year, he moved from customizing IBM's machines to manufacturing his own compatibles, sold under the brand name PCs Limited. He adopted the then-unusual strategy of bypassing

Compaq chief executive Rod Canion leans left to counter the weight of the twenty-eight-pound portable computer that carried his company to annual sales of a billion dollars in the record time of five years. To lay out the IBM-compatible machine, Compaq hired only seasoned engineers who felt no need to prove themselves by reworking IBM's design.

computer retailers entirely and selling directly to customers through mail and telephone orders. With middlemen excluded, Dell posted revenues of $33 million in 1986, just two years after starting the business.

Besides Dell and Leading Edge, dozens of other companies piled up massive revenues. Even computer stores hitched their wagons to the trend. Both BusinessLand and ComputerLand, two of IBM's largest retailers, began selling clones under their own house labels. Meanwhile, the original clonemaker, Compaq, continued to steamroll along. Its first-year sales nearly tripled to $329 million in 1984 and would surpass $500 million the following year. The appeal of the clones was understandable. Priced lower than comparable IBM machines—and delivering equal or better performance—they were plainly a prudent use of assets. For a company on a tight budget, buying clones could mean the difference between having personal computers and doing without.

In August 1984, IBM gave the clonemakers a new target to shoot at. Following its custom of regularly introducing new models, the company brought out the PC-AT, for Advanced Technology. Commonly known as the AT, the computer was based on Intel Corporation's successor to the PC's 8088 microprocessor, the 80286. This chip endowed the AT with as much as three times the speed of IBM's first personal computer. In one model, a hard disk for storing data and programs was built into the machine. With a capacity of twenty megabytes, the disk could find information and send it into the computer's memory bank strikingly faster than the PC's floppy disks.

Demand for such speed had sprung up in companies that had very large databases to sort or that had developed complicated spreadsheets as planning and accounting aids. The AT sold briskly, but some critics objected that it could handle no more memory than the PC, even though the 80286 microprocessor was capable of managing sixteen times as much. The fault lay with the operating system, which limited both the PC and the AT to 640K of memory, an ample supply three years earlier but now being rapidly filled up with programs and data. More frustrating than the AT's limited memory was the hard disk, which proved unreliable in some machines. For no apparent reason, it would suddenly stop working, leaving users stranded without access to their software and data. Many months passed before the problem was solved (with IBM stubbornly asserting all the while that nothing was amiss).

DRAGGING THE PC BACK INTO THE FOLD
Many observers predicted that IBM would soon have to share this technological high ground with the clonemakers, and they were right. Within eight months, Phoenix Software had mimicked the new computer's BIOS, inspiring a boisterous new round of imitators from the competition. With so much at stake, corporate management had begun to bring the freewheeling Entry Level Systems unit, by now restructured as the Entry Systems Division, and its PC operations under tighter control. The first step, in January 1985, was to reassign the role of supervising relations with retailers to the National Distribution Division in Montvale, New Jersey. The move brought Entry Systems more in line with the customary division of responsibilities at IBM.

The Incredible Shrinking Portable

Taking a tool to the job is often handier than bringing the work to the tool, an axiom that led to the invention of the portable personal computer. In less than a decade, this type of machine has evolved from a device with the bulk of a sewing machine into a svelte featherweight known as a laptop computer.

The road to the laptop has been paved with new technology. Flat, lightweight, liquid-crystal screens replaced conventional cathode-ray tubes, which of necessity must be built at least as deep as they are wide. Disk drives for pocket-size, 3.5-inch floppies occupy less than one-fifth the volume of the drives for 5.25-inch disks supplied with the original Compaq portable. Memory made of chips that can hold a million bits of data occupies about one-sixteenth the space claimed by 64K chips. Compact, long-lasting batteries and power-saving designs that turn off components when they are not needed have freed laptop computers from power cords plugged into electric sockets.

Today, some laptop portables weigh as little as five pounds. Boasting memories in the megabyte range, hard-disk storage, and computing speed equal to that of their deskbound cousins, these machines have brought the power and convenience of the personal computer to an ever-broadening range of endeavors, from tracking whales near Alaska to auto racing.

The Indy-car-racing team of Randy and Debbie Lewis makes extensive use of laptop computers, from keeping a spare-parts inventory to analyzing engine performance during a race. At trackside (above), Debbie records the passage of each car in the field with a single keystroke on her specially programmed laptop computer, which instantly calculates and displays the speed and position of every driver.

Product development and manufacturing are generally carried out by independent divisions, but sales and marketing are almost always centrally controlled.

Two months later, headquarters announced that Don Estridge would be transferred to Armonk and that Lowe would return to Boca Raton to take Estridge's place as president of the Entry Systems Division. As the man in charge in Florida, Estridge had been credited with the runaway success of the PC and blamed for problems like the AT's balky disk drive and, more seriously, for a flop called the PCjr. Introduced in late 1983 and intended for use at home, this computer had an unpopular keyboard with keys that looked like pieces of candy-coated gum. It cost nearly as much as a regular PC. All in all, however, Estridge's tenure in Boca Raton had enhanced his reputation within IBM, and he was promoted to a corporate staff job. (Tragically, Don Estridge and his wife were killed in a commercial airplane crash before he could take up his new duties.) Finally, 200 key members of the Entry Systems Division staff, with William Lowe in charge, were moved to Montvale, drawing the management of the entire personal-computer operation toward the geographical corporate center.

A SMALLER PIECE OF THE PIE
During these upheavals, the number of personal computers being sold each year continued to grow, and the Entry Systems Division went on reporting sizable profits. But there were clouds on the horizon. IBM's share of the market was in sharp decline. In 1984, Big Blue manufactured 63 percent of the IBM-compatible personal computers sold that year. During the next two years, this figure declined dramatically—to 53 percent in 1985 and 40 percent in 1986. That year, IBM profits plunged 27 percent, a drop partly attributable to fewer of the personal-computer sales the company depended on for about 15 percent of its business.

These alarming developments spurred a reevaluation of IBM's approach to the personal computer business—and a lineup of completely redesigned machines. In April 1987, Lowe's Entry Systems Division announced a new family of IBM desktop computers—Personal System/2. The PS/2 line, which consisted of four machines at the outset, was a mixed bag of technology, comprising both familiar and strikingly fresh ideas. Microprocessors ranged from the prosaic 8086—the chip rejected for the first IBM PC—to the 80386, Intel's latest marvel of chip design, capable of processing four million instructions per second. In between stood computers based on a speeded-up version of the AT's 80286 chip. All four PS/2 models ran the same software as IBM's earlier microcomputers and boasted highly miniaturized circuitry, faster processing speeds, and with OS/2, a new operating system promised by IBM and Microsoft, the capacity to manage more memory than any of the machines in the now seemingly obsolete PC line. A host of peripheral hardware, ranging from a laser printer to a 200-megabyte optical storage device, were available for the PS/2s on the day that they were introduced.

The new computers continued IBM's open-architecture policy—up to a point. The company furnished extensive technical documentation to any and all interested parties, including outside hardware and software developers. Although Big Blue did not publish the PS/2 BIOS, such companies as Phoenix were no more constrained than before from mimicking it. However, IBM had taken extensive measures to preclude a repetition of the rampant cloning that had undercut prices for the company's earlier computers.

The first line of defense was extensive use of custom-designed chips that would be difficult and costly for rivals to duplicate. An even greater barrier to competition was a data-bus design dubbed Micro Channel Architecture (MCA), which permitted information to move in sixteen- or thirty-two-bit chunks between the microprocessor and circuit boards containing memory, disk controllers, and video electronics. Introduced on all but the smallest of the new machines, it was touted as an important personal-computer advance. Unfortunately for would-be emulators, it required very sophisticated and expensive manufacturing techniques. IBM hoped that the up-front cost of duplicating the design would be beyond the reach of smaller competitors. IBM also filed for patents on the architecture, permitting the company to sue others thought to be copying MCA and to exact a licensing fee for building MCA into computers, just as Phoenix charged its BIOS customers. This levy, IBM expected, would make unprofitable the bargain-basement prices that had become the rule for clones.

Media and market reactions to the Personal System/2 were less than euphoric. Since 1981, when the IBM PC had easily won over the press and the public, a true mass market had emerged for the first time in the history of the computer industry. A host of customers with a wide variety of needs were now served by many well-established suppliers who had proved themselves capable of delivering top-flight machines. When the proprietary philosophy behind the PS/2 line became obvious, buyers were slow to embrace the new products. Having grown accustomed to the richness of the microcomputer bazaar, they were reluctant to tie themselves to a single manufacturer. Initially, the vast majority of PS/2 computers sold were the least expensive models, which were little more than souped-up PCs. Many months passed before sales of the more advanced models rose to respectable levels. By that time, the venerable IBM PC had been retired. Strong until the end (the computer posted its best-ever first-quarter sales in the spring of 1987), the machine had been discontinued by the end of that year.

IBM's attempt to return personal computers to the era of closed architecture not only slowed sales of the PS/2 line but resulted in the rise of the so-called Gang of Nine. Formed in 1988 by Compaq Computers and eight other manufacturers of computers and other equipment compatible with Big Blue's popular AT model, the Gang of Nine proposed to counter IBM's move by improving on the AT data bus instead of abandoning it. They widened it from sixteen bits to thirty-two bits and gave it other features that would make it competitive with MCA. Perhaps most important, the new bus, known as the Extended Industry Standard Architecture (EISA), would run all the software and peripheral equipment that businesses had invested in. For example, a company could attach a few new, powerful computers to its existing office network without replacing network components or its older computers.

Battle has thus been joined over issues that pierce to the core of the computer bazaar, and the outcome may very well decide whether the open marketplace survives. IBM has immense clout. The company succeeded, for example, in persuading BusinessLand, one of the largest nationwide computer retailers in America, to favor IBM's PS/2 computers over its competitor's machines, prompting Compaq to sever relations with the chain. On the side of EISA seem to be multitudes of personal-computer owners who would never have benefited from the machines had not IBM decided for an open architecture in its original PC.

Secrets of Word Processing

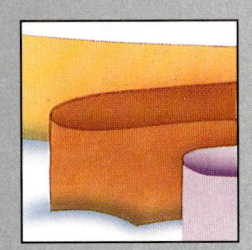

Word processing, the single most popular use of personal computers, is a kind of electronic prestidigitation. A modern word-processing program can summon forth large bodies of text, change the form and content of documents in a trice, and consign words to permanence or oblivion at the touch of a print or delete key.

Behind this easy magic lie years of effort by computer scientists. As hardware designers expanded the main memory of personal computers throughout the 1980s, software engineers capitalized on the added capacity by endowing programs with the ability to move, copy, delete, search through, reformat, display, and print out the words in a text. By decade's end, the two groups' parallel efforts had dovetailed in a bonanza of word-processing programs, some so advanced as to check spelling, flag infelicities in style and grammar, and suggest synonyms from an electronic thesaurus.

Such powers were undreamed-of when IBM coined the term "word processing" in 1964 to herald a new typewriter that could record words (and, to a limited extent, revise them) on magnetic tape. The computer giant predicted that the market for the devices might eventually total 5,000 systems. That guess proved wildly off the mark, of course. By 1983, many word-processing companies were selling 20,000 or more hardware and software systems per year. Today, total sales of word-processing programs for personal computers exceed three million units a year in the United States, generating approximately $750 million in revenues for the software companies that produce them.

Described on the pages that follow are the principal features available in a hypothetical word-processing program. Although the implementation of such features varies from program to program, they all share a simple secret: Each dazzling effect is based on the adroit management of a personal computer's memory.

Secrets of Word Processing

A Behind-the-Screen View of Memory Manipulation

A word-processing program is a tour de force of deception. The key to its smooth responsiveness is the partitioning of a computer's main memory into specialized chambers that remain invisible to the user.

A surprisingly large number of memory elements clamor for inclusion: As shown at right, these include the operating system, which resides in the machine's random-access memory, or RAM; the word-processing program itself; the program's working memory, a specialized area of RAM that holds blocks of text undergoing such operations as "move" and "copy"; the document memory, where the actual text data is stored; the video memory, whose contents dictate what will be displayed on the screen; and the printer buffer, a way station furnished by the operating system for words en route to "hard copy," or printed-on-paper, form. Because these various elements inhabit memory in a contiguous, or side-by-side, fashion, they are shown on these pages as spliced lengths of a continuous "memory ribbon."

Every machine from mainframe to laptop possesses a finite amount of random-access memory, so a multitude of schemes have been devised for parceling it out. The most common is dynamic allocation. When instructed to create a new document, the word-processing program requests a chunk of memory—typically 300 to 500 kilobytes—from the operating system. In response, the operating system tells the program at which memory address, or location, it should begin lodging data. Since large documents tend to exceed a PC's main memory, only a single, active portion of the document normally resides there. The rest is relegated to storage on a disk, whence any segment may be ushered into main memory at the program's request.

Upon reaching the operating system, the scan code representing each keystroke is translated into a byte—a string of eight binary digits, or bits, that stands for a number, a letter, a symbol, or a control code such as a carriage return. The word-processing program, shown as the ribbon's orange segment, requests bytes from the operating system, which releases them one at a time. The program then channels the bytes it has received to two discrete memory areas, illustrated at right: document memory (purple) for storage, and video memory (pink) for display. The ribbon's gray area represents document memory that is available but so far unused.

The document—in this example, a food company's new-product announcement—begins its passage through the word-processing program as a few initial keystrokes, represented by the seven lighted keys at right. The keyboard converts each keystroke into electronic pulses called scan codes and flashes them to the computer's electronic overseer, or operating system, shown as the blue segment of the continuous memory ribbon above.

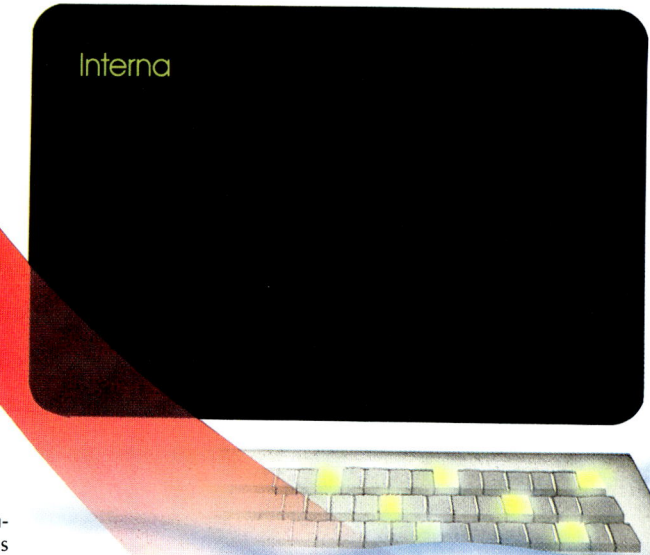

Working Memory

Document Memory

Unused Document Memory

Video Memory

As characters take up residence in the document area of memory, they are also forwarded to video memory for display on the screen. Some video memories require two bytes of information for each character: The first consists of the data bits representing the character itself, while the second—called the attribute byte—defines how the character will appear on the monitor. The range of such display styles, or modes, includes normal, boldface, underlined, and inverse video.

Printer Buffer

Printer

When the document is completed and ready for printing, the word-processing program reads, or retrieves, the text from document memory (and, if it is long, from disk storage) and sends it character by character through the operating system to another specialized area of memory known as the printer buffer *(above)*. The buffer serves two functions: It holds the bytes representing the document until the printer is ready to interpret and print them out, and it allows the computer to respond to additional operator commands without suspending the printer's operation.

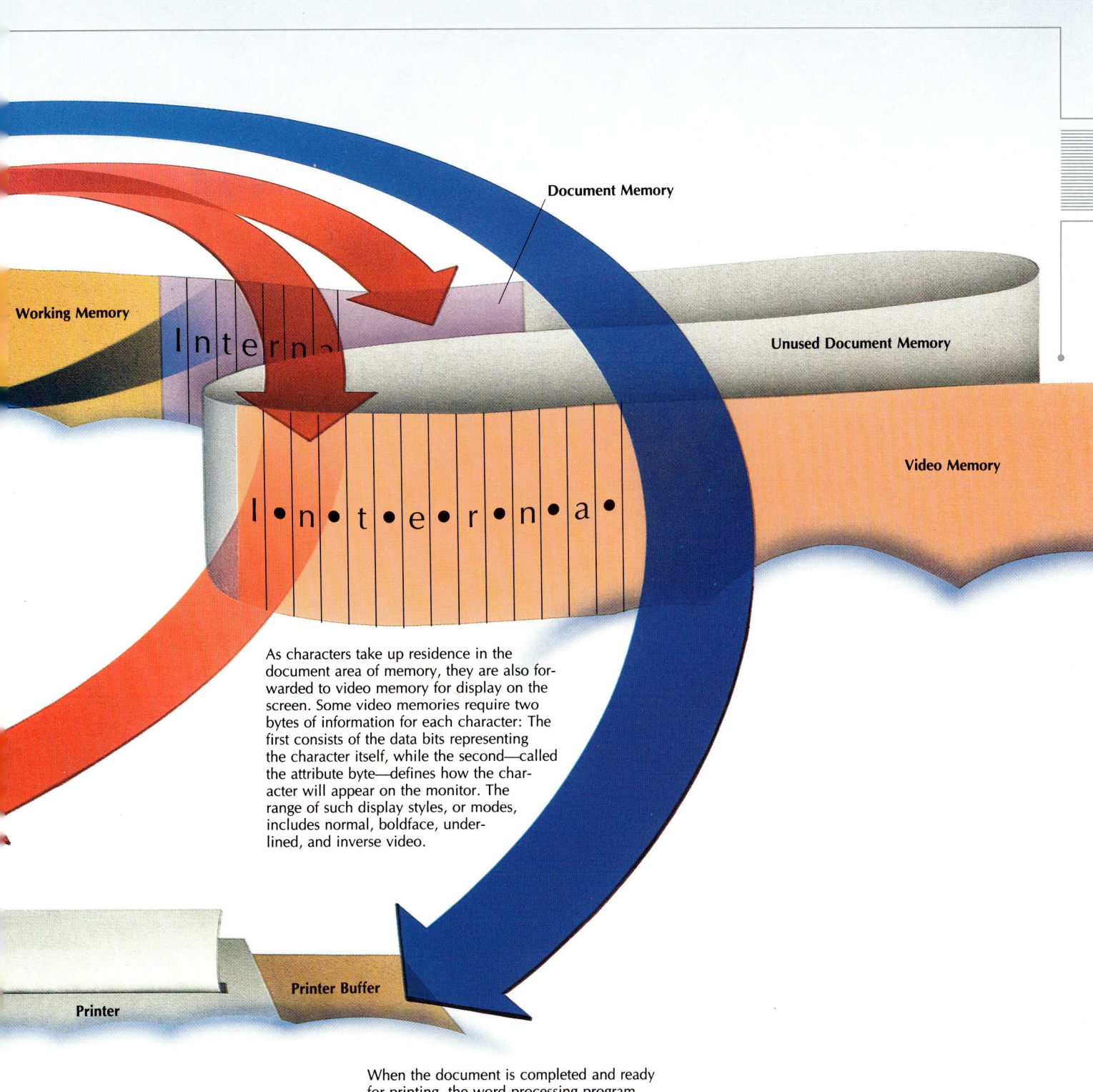

Secrets of Word Processing

Tactics for Putting Letters on Display

Just as stagehands work in speed and quiet, a specialized group of memory-management functions present text to the user without revealing the bustle behind the scenes. The means of concealment vary, yet most screen-display techniques utilize either character-based video memory *(below)* or graphics-based video memory *(opposite)*.

The character-based approach—so called because it displays standardized characters similar to those that are produced by a typewriter—is the older of the two, yet its speed and simplicity lend it continuing appeal. The graphics-based approach, by contrast, offers a much richer array of display modes than its rival's classic four—normal, underlined, boldface, and inverse video. Such increased flexibility is offset, however, by the slower speed and higher cost of graphics-based screen displays.

Whatever the style of presentation, the role of stage manager is played by the computer's operating system. The operating system reviews all data bound for display, determining whether each byte represents an alphanumeric character or a control code—that is, a software command spelling out such minutiae as page format or typeface. The distinction is crucial, because while characters appear on the screen, control codes do not.

In character-based video memory, the operating system converts the control codes that govern typeface into a single attribute byte for every displayable character. The characters and their attributes are then written to video memory, a small data store containing no more than a screen's worth of data at a time. Finally, the video memory channels the characters and their paired attributes to the CRT controller, a preprogrammed chip that causes the appropriate pattern of pixels, or picture elements, to light up on the screen.

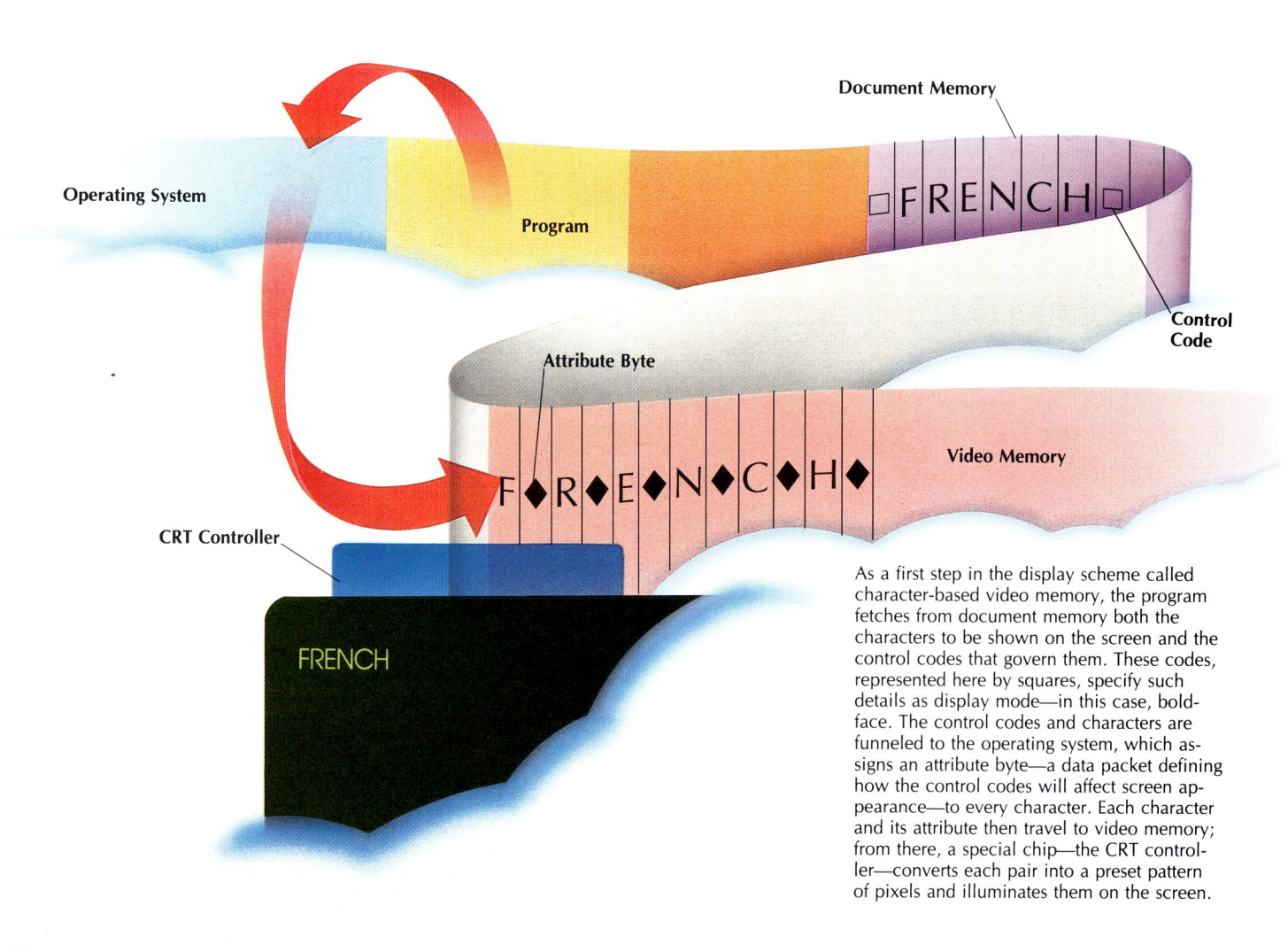

As a first step in the display scheme called character-based video memory, the program fetches from document memory both the characters to be shown on the screen and the control codes that govern them. These codes, represented here by squares, specify such details as display mode—in this case, boldface. The control codes and characters are funneled to the operating system, which assigns an attribute byte—a data packet defining how the control codes will affect screen appearance—to every character. Each character and its attribute then travel to video memory; from there, a special chip—the CRT controller—converts each pair into a preset pattern of pixels and illuminates them on the screen.

A Bit-by-Bit Approach

As word-processing programs assume starring roles in desktop publishing systems *(pages 50-57)*, a more flexible display scheme known as graphics-based video memory has begun to receive the plaudits of personal computerists. This alternative approach allows a wide choice of fonts, or typefaces, ranging from the traditional styles made popular in the eighteenth century to such modern styles as the headline above.

The expanded repertoire stems from the higher degree of control exerted by the operating system in a graphics-based display. The operating system contains font tables detailing precisely which pixels must be illuminated on the screen in order to form a given character in a particular typeface. It sends this information to video memory bit by bit, with each bit representing a single pixel. Because the video memory is arranged as a matrix of individual bits, the bit patterns it receives serve as detailed templates, called pixel maps, that the CRT controller can then use to light the proper pixels on the screen.

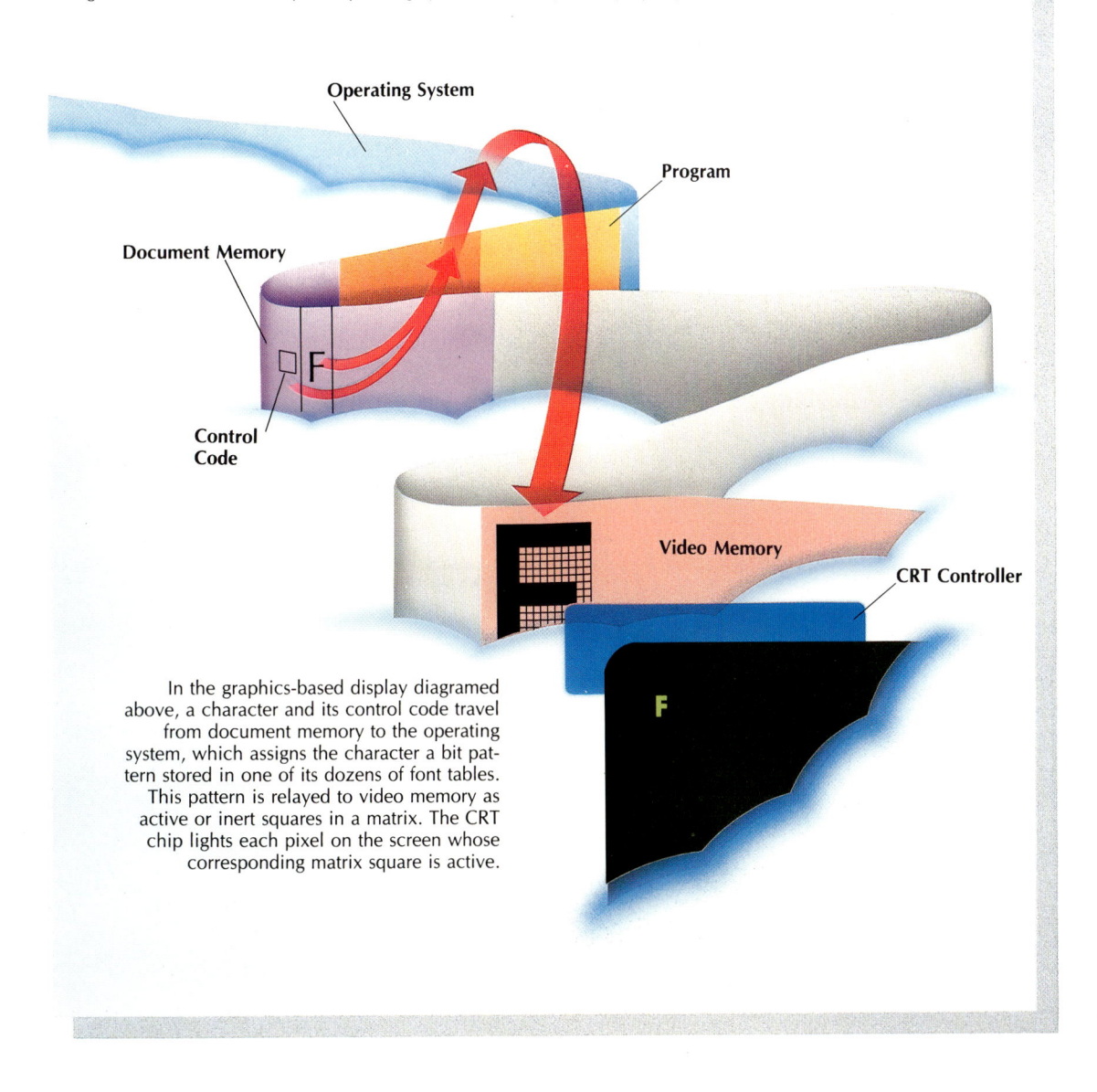

In the graphics-based display diagramed above, a character and its control code travel from document memory to the operating system, which assigns the character a bit pattern stored in one of its dozens of font tables. This pattern is relayed to video memory as active or inert squares in a matrix. The CRT chip lights each pixel on the screen whose corresponding matrix square is active.

Secrets of Word Processing

Pointing the Way to the Proper Address

There was a time when moving a word, a sentence, or a paragraph from one spot in a document to another required such crude implements as pencils, scissors, and tape. Today's word-processing programs, by contrast, perform this linguistic surgery with a precision tool called a pointer.

Like many other elements of modern word-processing programs, the pointer is a memory-management device. As such, it can be likened to an address book that chronicles changing locations from a fixed position: The pointer—a string of bytes occupying a constant address in working memory—details the current abode in document memory of data elements whose location tends to vary widely and often. Two typical examples of such variable addresses are the end point of a text in progress, and the point in document memory that is being marked by the cursor on the screen.

In addition to serving individually as a locator, a pointer may work in concert with several others to copy data from one part of a document to another. For such an operation, three separate pointers are each provided with a unique address—say, 64, 71, and 228 (right). The first two addresses denote a text block's present locale in memory, while the third designates the block's target destination. When the user invokes the "copy" function, the processor fetches the data bracketed by the first two addresses and reproduces it at the third.

An electronic bookmark. In its simplest role, the software device known as a pointer keeps track of the user's place in a document. The pointer is a fixed address in working memory that contains the variable address of an item in document memory—in this case, the cursor's position in the text. Even though the pointer's location in working memory never varies, the memory address that it contains, or points to, increases by one (or more, if control codes are being inserted) with every new character that is added to the document.

In the two small diagrams at right, the numbers above the memory ribbon represent the pointer's address in working memory (dark orange) and each character's address in document memory (purple). The arrows indicate cursor movement and the corresponding change in the pointer's value. In the upper diagram, the pointer holds the document-memory address of 14, indicating that the user has entered only seven characters since beginning the document at memory address 7. (Because the operating system and the program occupy the lower ranges of memory, actual document-memory addresses would be much higher.) The lower diagram shows that each depression of the backspace key—here, to correct a typo at memory locations 10 and 11—decreases the memory address stored in the pointer by 1.

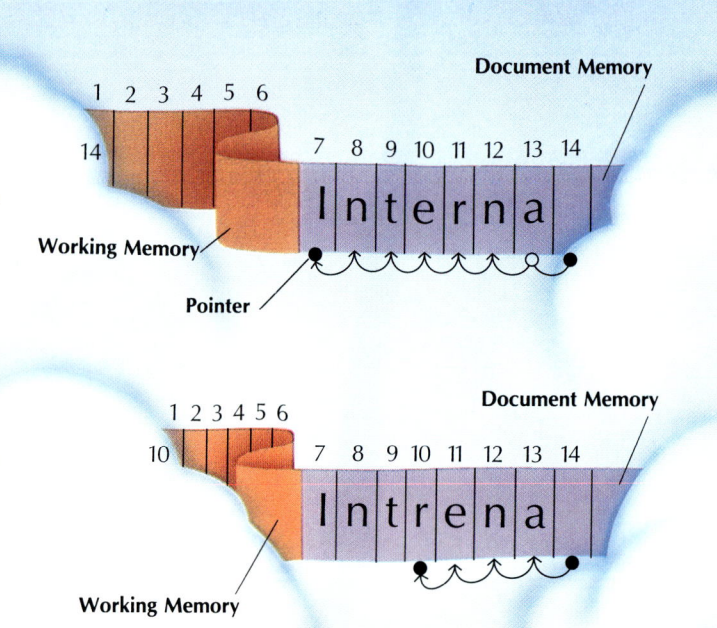

34

Document Memory

Working Memory

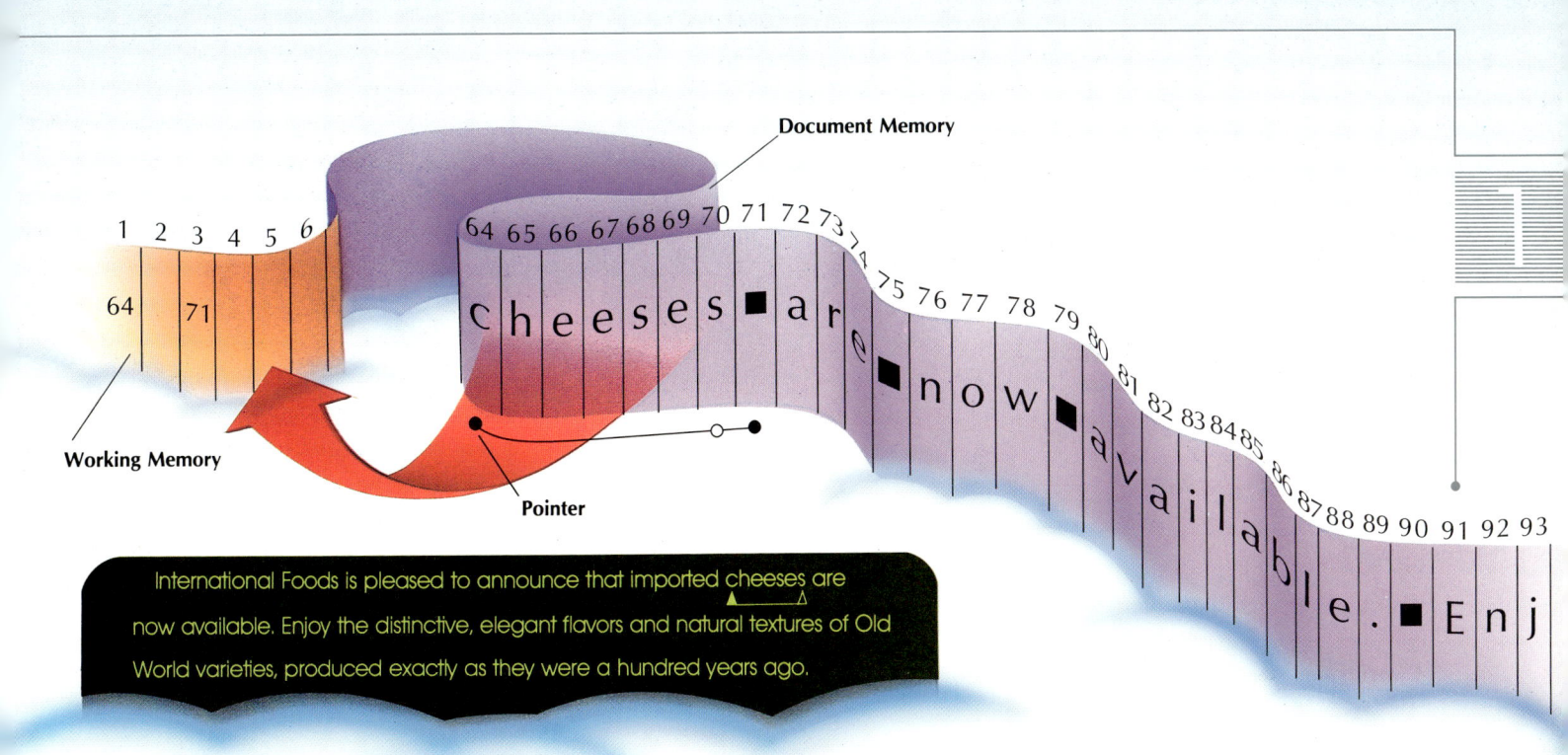

Pointer

International Foods is pleased to announce that imported cheeses are now available. Enjoy the distinctive, elegant flavors and natural textures of Old World varieties, produced exactly as they were a hundred years ago.

To copy a section of text from one locale to another, the user must first inform the program which portion of the document is to be replicated. As the cursor highlights the target phrase on the screen, the program brackets the phrase in document memory by storing its beginning and ending addresses —above, they are 64 and 71—in two separate pointers in working memory.

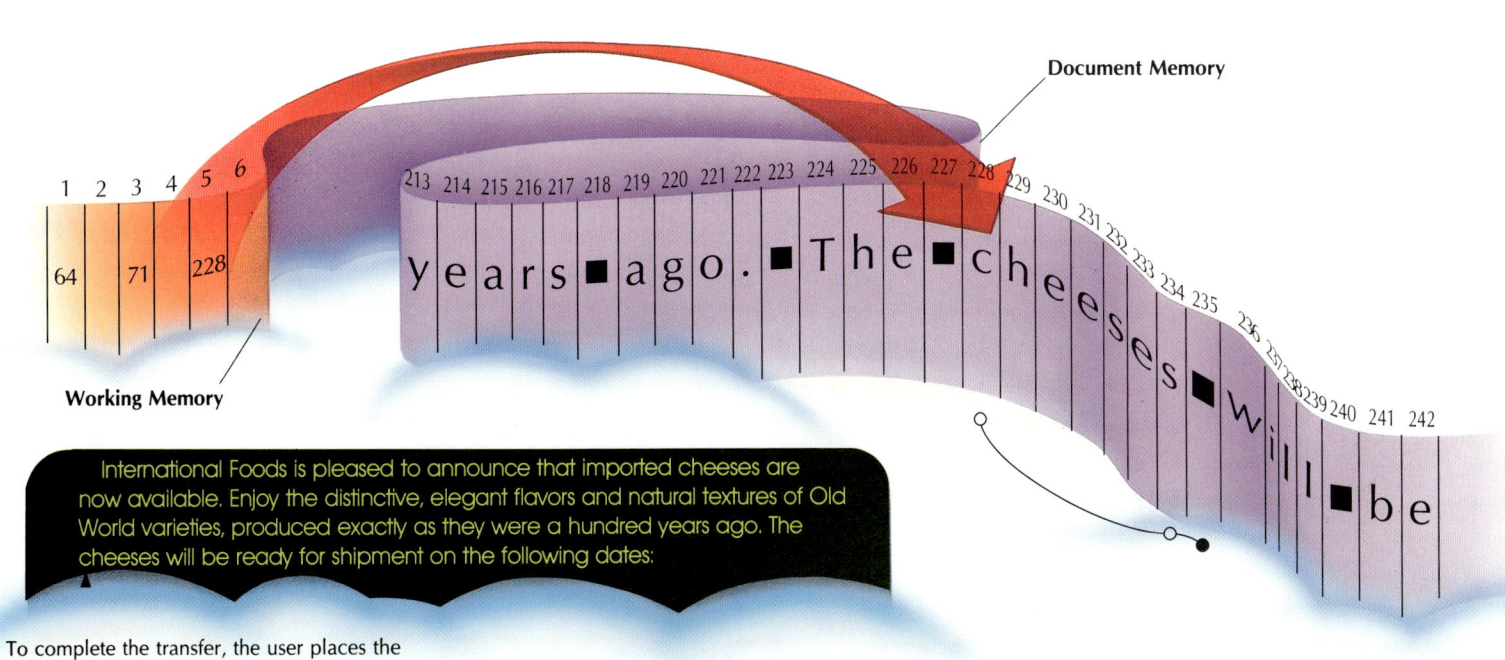

Document Memory

Working Memory

International Foods is pleased to announce that imported cheeses are now available. Enjoy the distinctive, elegant flavors and natural textures of Old World varieties, produced exactly as they were a hundred years ago. The cheeses will be ready for shipment on the following dates:

To complete the transfer, the user places the cursor at the new location selected for the highlighted chunk of text. He or she then presses the function key responsible for "copy" operations, which supplies the new destination address—in this case, 228—to yet a third pointer. With the three critical memory addresses now accessible to it in the three pointers, the program can clone the contents of memory locations 64 through 71 at their specified locale, address 228.

35

Secrets of Word Processing

Functions That Enhance Format

The formatting features of a word-processing program are dedicated to improving the document's appearance on the page. By inviting refinements in such cosmetic details as the margins, tab stops, line spacing, and typeface of a document, these features enable the user to display and print text in its most readable format. Although the majority of programs contain built-in, or default, values specifying a generic format, the default values can be overridden, or customized, as the user sees fit. Programs that display a document on the screen in precisely the same way it will appear when printed out possess a desirable trait known as WYSIWYG—"What You See Is What You Get."

Document Memory

Enjoy the distinctive, elegant flavors and natural textures of Old World varieties

80

International Foods is pleased to announce that imported cheeses are now available. Enjoy the distinctive, elegant flavors and natural textures of Old Wo

Enjoy the distinctive flavors and natural textures of Old World varieties

Document Memory

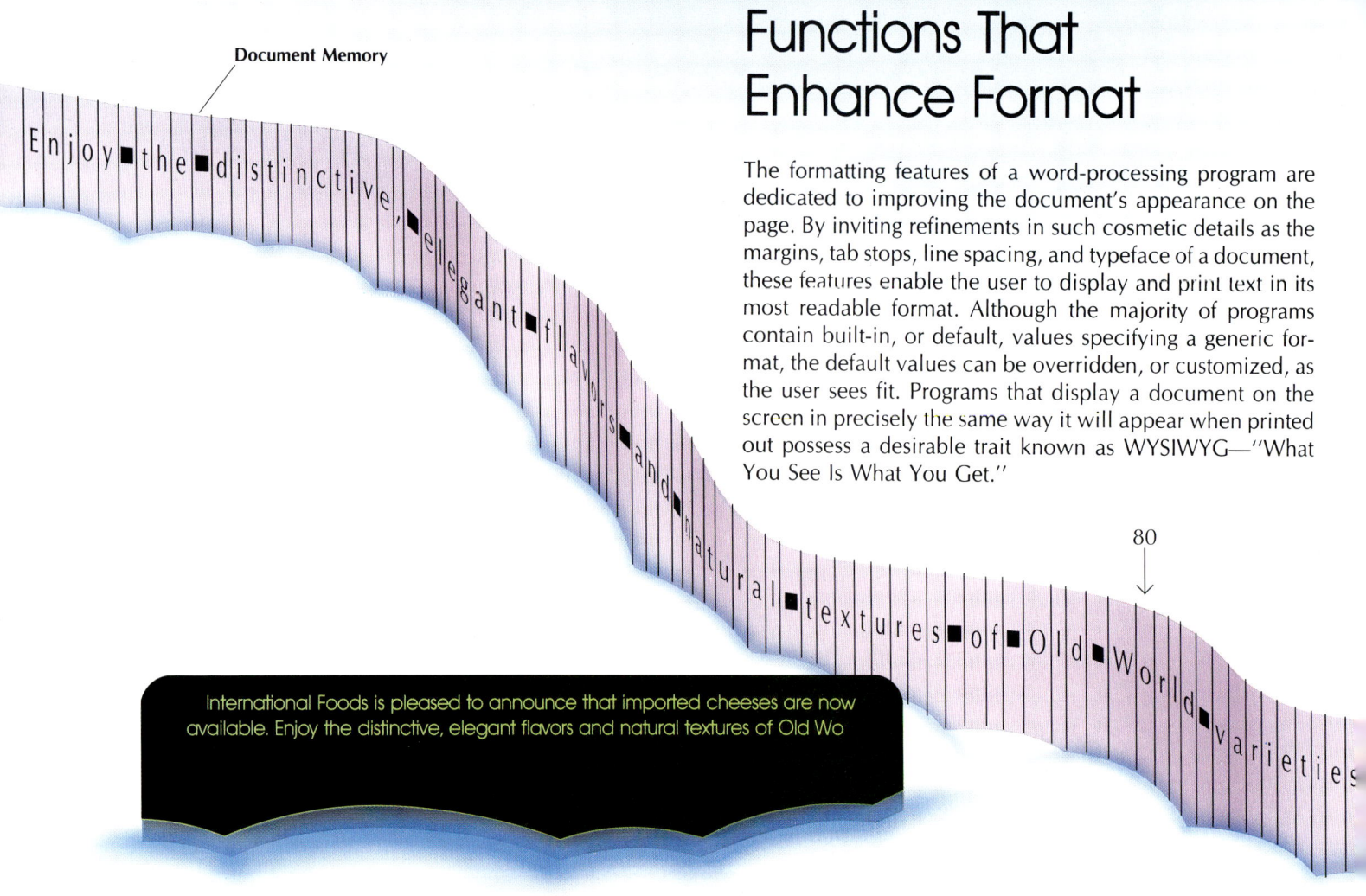

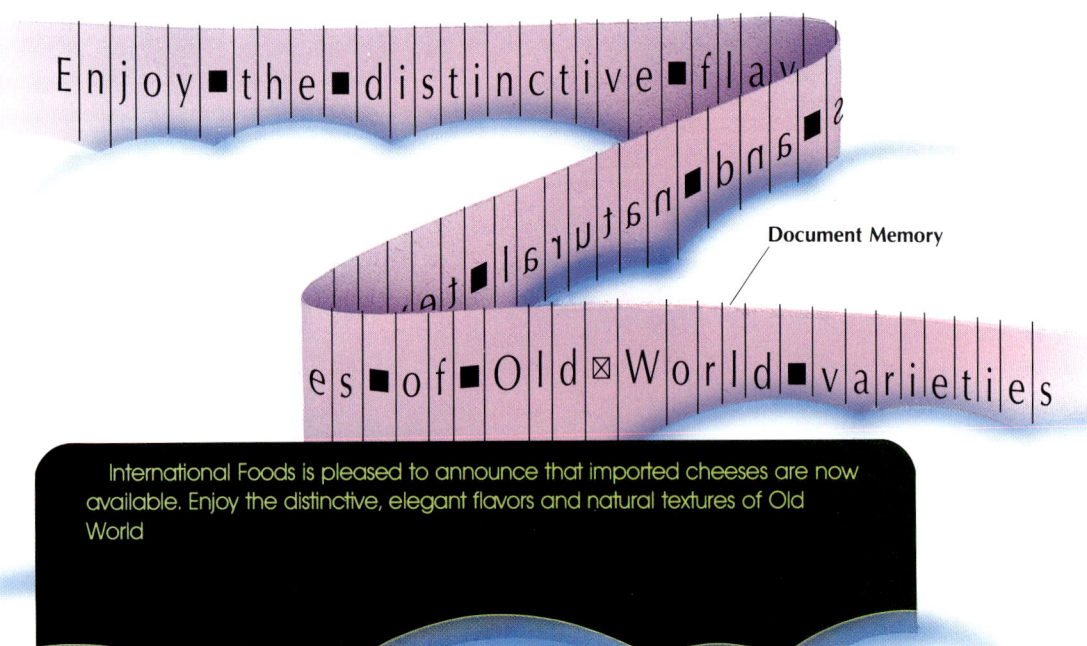

International Foods is pleased to announce that imported cheeses are now available. Enjoy the distinctive, elegant flavors and natural textures of Old World

The formatting feature called word wrap causes the program to execute an automatic carriage return every time the user types in a word that extends beyond the document's right margin. As shown on the top screen in the sequence at left, the right margin has been set at 80 characters, and the user is entering a word that will exceed the maximum line length. When the user types the 81st character, an "r," a screen-formatting routine inserts a "soft" carriage return—a control code indicating the site of a word wrap—after the last full word on the line; it then bumps the offending word to the start of the next line *(bottom screen)*.

A more sophisticated program—one with the power to H&J, or hyphenate and justify—attempts to break the word at the correct syllabic division. This requires the program to invoke a subroutine, or series of instructions, setting out general rules of hyphenation; alternatively, the program may consult a stored hyphenation dictionary similar to those used by spelling checkers for spelling *(pages 38-39)*.

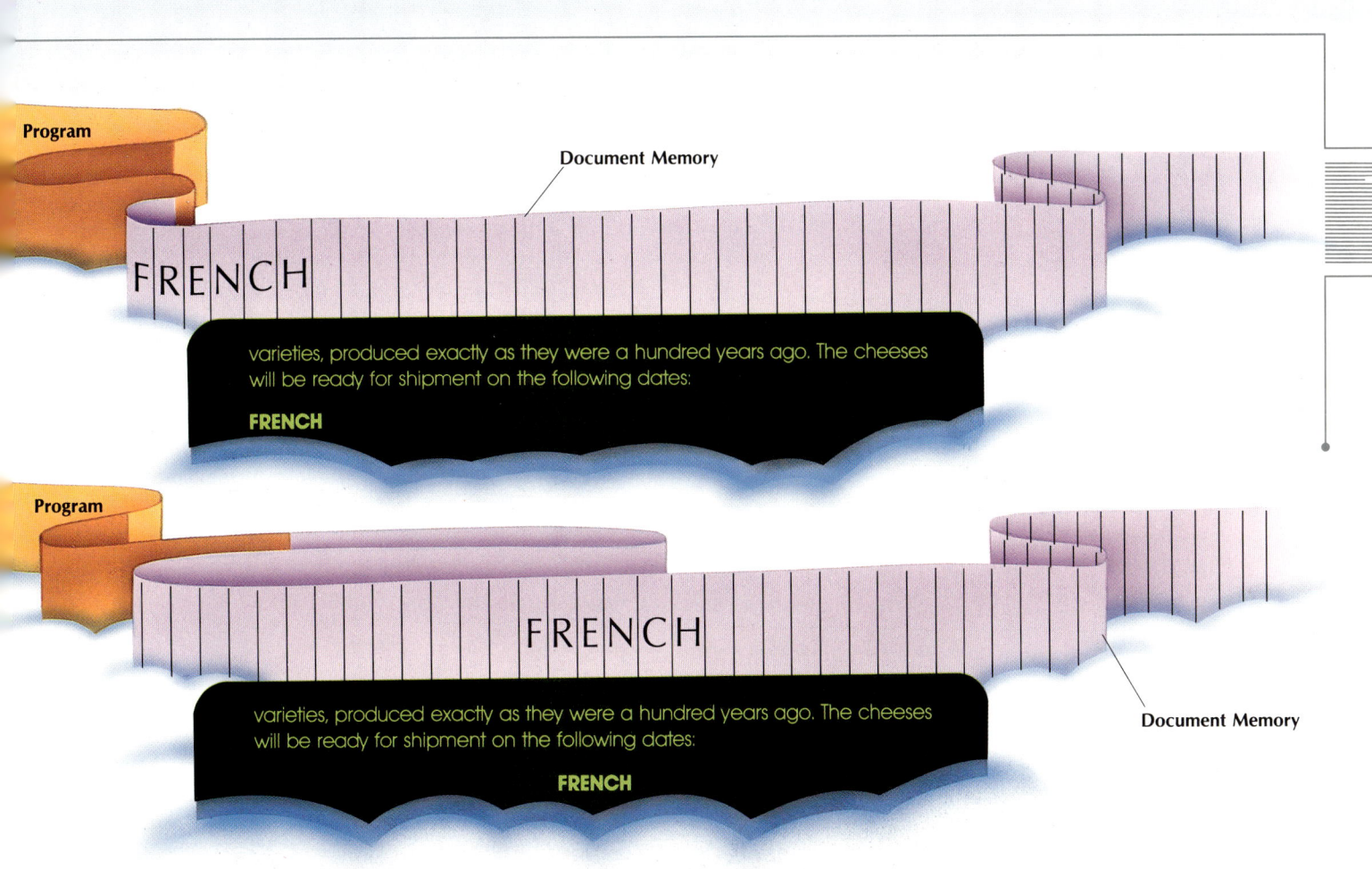

A simple algorithm enables the word-processing program to center type elements—above, the boldface heading "FRENCH"—in the middle of a text column on a printed page. The algorithm subtracts the number of characters in the target word from the maximum number of characters in the line, then divides the result by two; this figure reveals how many spaces must be inserted before the word in order to center it. In the example illustrated above, the algorithm computes that 6 from 80 is 74, and 74 divided by two is 37; it then centers the word by placing 37 spaces between it and the left-hand margin.

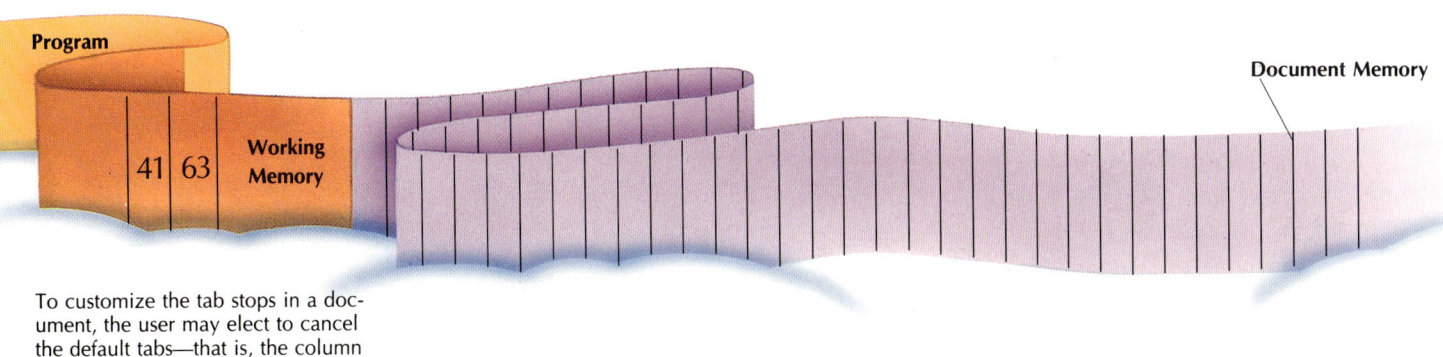

To customize the tab stops in a document, the user may elect to cancel the default tabs—that is, the column positions supplied automatically by the program. New tab-stop values—above, 41 and 63—can then be stored in working memory. The tab algorithm is similar to that for centering: The cursor's present position is subtracted from the position of the next tab stop, and the program interprets the result as the number of spaces by which it must move the cursor.

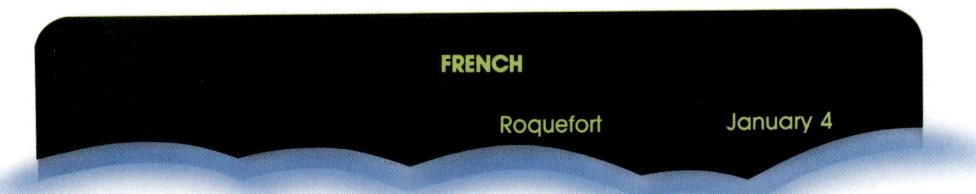

37

Secrets of Word Processing

Tracking Down Words and Spelling Them Right

For anyone seeking kernels of information amid the chaff of a lengthy document, a word processor's "search" function offers a powerful winnowing device. Researchers value the capability because it can help them locate every occurrence of a term in works that have been published in electronic form; writers and editors, for their part, prize the routine as an antidote to monologophobia—Theodore Bernstein's neologism for the fear of using the same word more than once in three lines. Searches may be conducted backward or forward in a document, with the cursor stopping to signal each appearance of the target word or the program totting up its total frequency.

The refinement of text-searching techniques has ushered in an even more sophisticated feature, the spelling checker.

Document Memory

■the■order■form■and■return■it■promptly.

To determine whether (or how often) a given word or phrase appears in a document, the user specifies the object of the search—at right, the word "promptly"—by typing the word on the program's command line or in a pop-up window *(pages 40-41)*. At the proper keyboard command, the program's search routine races through the stored text, comparing sequences of letters in document memory with the character string it has been asked to match.

Because words are compared character by character, infinitesimal delays result as the program pauses to examine such look-alikes as "produced"; upon discovering that the fourth letter of "produced" differs from that of "promptly," however, the searching routine moves on to the next potential match. The process continues until the program locates the sought-after word—in this case, it is one of the last in the document—and the cursor marks its position in the text. Should the search prove fruitless, the cursor simply remains in its original spot.

se:promptly
▲
International Foods is pleased to announce that imported cheeses are now available. Enjoy the distinctive, elegant flavors and natural textures of Old World varieties, produced exactly as they were a hundred years ago. The cheeses will be ready for shipment on the following dates:

FRENCH
Roquefort	January 4
Port-Salut	January 6
Bucheron	January 9
Livarot	January 9

ITALIAN
Gorgonzola	January 15
Taleggio	January 15
Pecorino Romano	January 16

SWISS
Emmenthaler	January 19
Raclette	January 19
Sapsago	January 19

Don't miss out on these delicious cheeses, made with all-natural ingredients and aged to perfection. Please fill out the order form and return it promptly.
▲

Research into the idea of electronic proofreading began in 1957, yet it was not until 1971—when Ralph Gorin of Stanford University wrote a program to check the spelling of words stored in a DEC-10 mainframe—that any computer was endowed with the skill. The first program able to verify orthography in a personal computer was written by software specialist Dennis Coleman in 1980.

Since then, hardware and software improvements have helped spelling checkers grow from laboratory curiosities into workplace essentials. A word-processing program stored on a floppy disk can hold as many as 150,000 correctly spelled words, and the hard disk now available in many personal computers allows users to add thousands of words more. Breakthroughs in algorithms that compress such lists have had an equally proliferative effect. One common tactic stores only the part of a word that differs from the one listed before it; "promptly," for example, may be stored as "6ly," indicating that its first six letters duplicate those in the previous entry, "prompt." A more advanced scheme has shoehorned a spelling dictionary of 100,000 words into 114,000 bytes of storage space—small enough for the spellcheck routine to reside in the program's working memory rather than on disk.

Shown in action below is a generic spelling checker, which uses a pattern-matching algorithm to compare, letter by letter, the words in document memory with those in a precompiled list. Most spellcheckers also incorporate phonetic algorithms; these suggest sound-alike alternatives to misspelled words, helping the program correct as well as detect mistakes.

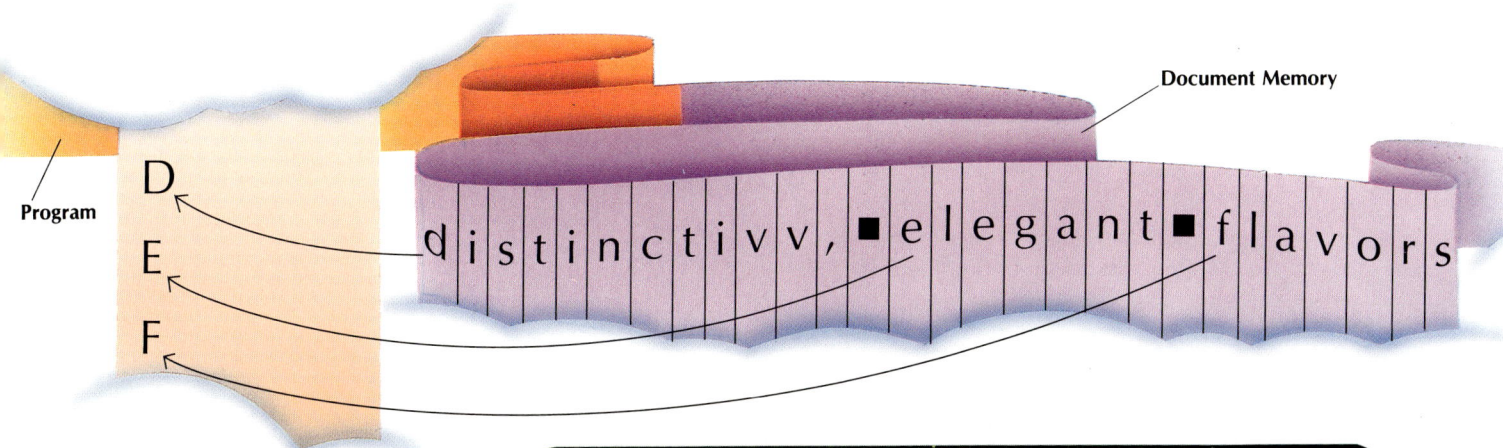

The program feature known as a spelling checker compares each word in the document to a master word list *(letters, above)* in the program's memory and flags those it cannot find. In the example at right, the spellchecker spied the typo in "distinctivv" because the faulty spelling appeared nowhere in its dictionary. As the misspelled word is highlighted on the screen, the program prompts the user to supply the correct spelling, which then takes its rightful place both in document memory and on the screen *(below)*.

International Foods is pleased to announce that imported cheeses are now available. Enjoy the distinctivv, elegant flavors and natural textures of Old World varieties, produced exactly as they were a hundred years ago.

correct word or press return for no change

International Foods is pleased to announce that imported cheeses are now available. Enjoy the distinctive, elegant flavors and natural textures of Old

Secrets of Word Processing

Willing and Able to Do Windows

To maximize the limited screen space of a typical personal-computer monitor, PC designers have come up with a technique called windowing. A window is a square or rectangular display area, smaller than a full screen and set off from it by a border, that may be superimposed on a document occupying the screen. Because windows are allowed to overlap, as many as a dozen or more may be displayed at one time. Users may also adjust the size, color, position, and format of windows, whose contents can range from basic menus and help messages, such as the summary of function keys shown at far right, to complex data-entry forms and text files.

Summoning forth windows and keeping their contents from spilling into one another is, like other word-processing features, a matter of memory management. Most PCs use a method known as memory-mapped video, in which video displays are generated in a portion of the program's working memory that can be accessed directly by the processor; this allows windows to be opened and closed at a speed that will not delay the user. To preserve the portion of a document that a window is about to surprint on the screen, the windowing software furnishes a special memory buffer that receives the displaced text. The program can then display the window without corrupting any of the data in the original document. When the user decides to store or delete the window's contents, the data in the save buffer is rewritten to its previous place in memory, and the document resumes its former appearance on the screen.

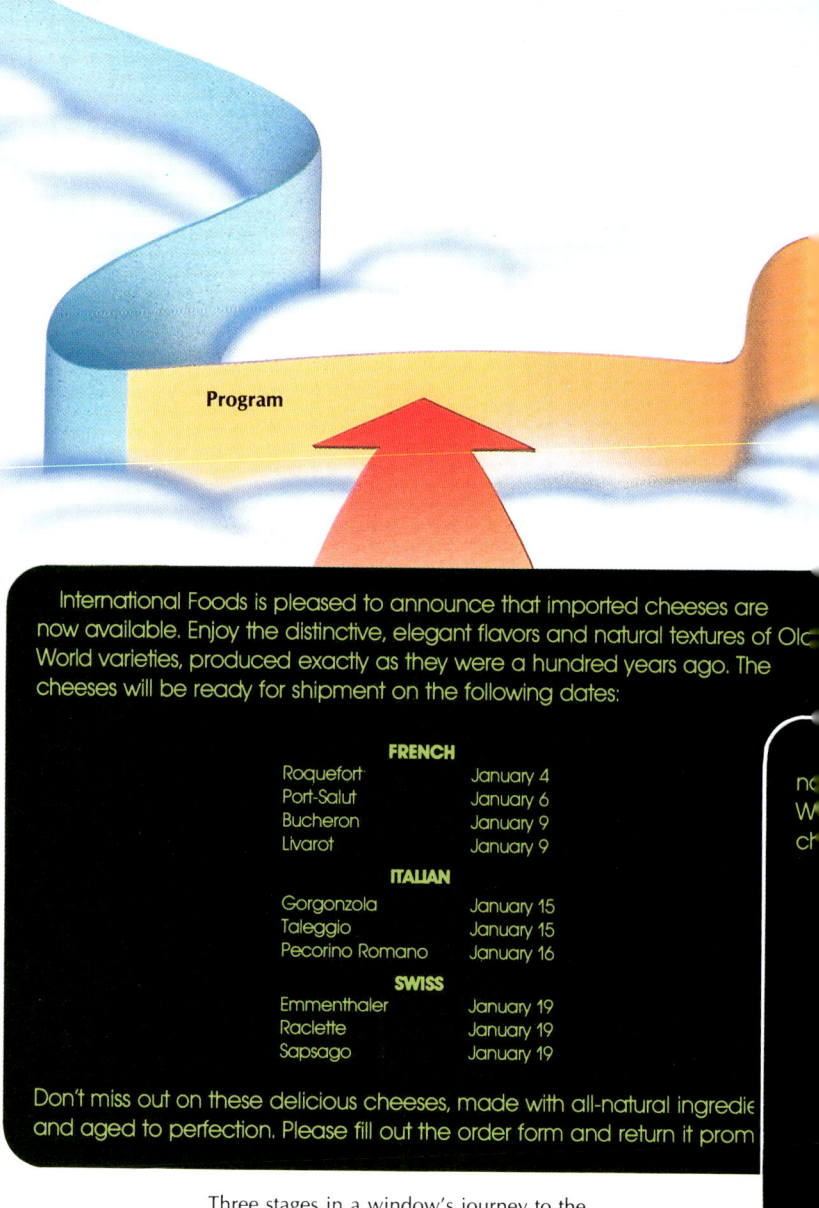

Three stages in a window's journey to the screen are shown here. One frequently displayed window reminds the user of the duties performed by each function key. Like other windows, this function-key summary may be conjured up with a single keystroke. The keyboard command is channeled *(red arrow)* to the program *(orange)*, which contains the instructions necessary for constructing the window on the screen.

40

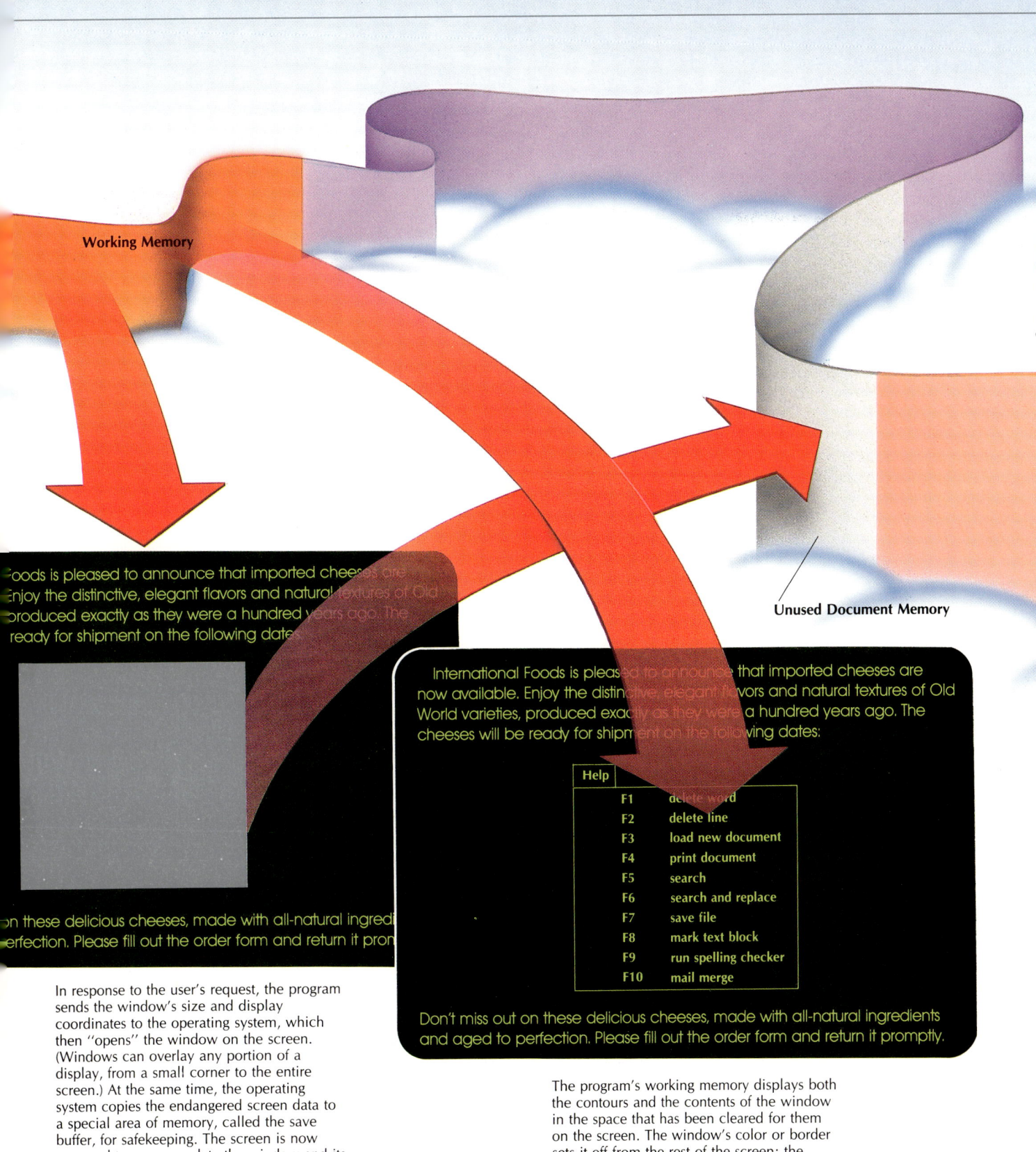

Working Memory

Unused Document Memory

oods is pleased to announce that imported cheeses are
njoy the distinctive, elegant flavors and natural textures of Old
roduced exactly as they were a hundred years ago. The
ready for shipment on the following date

International Foods is pleased to announce that imported cheeses are now available. Enjoy the distinctive, elegant flavors and natural textures of Old World varieties, produced exactly as they were a hundred years ago. The cheeses will be ready for shipment on the following dates:

Help		
	F1	delete word
	F2	delete line
	F3	load new document
	F4	print document
	F5	search
	F6	search and replace
	F7	save file
	F8	mark text block
	F9	run spelling checker
	F10	mail merge

n these delicious cheeses, made with all-natural ingredi
erfection. Please fill out the order form and return it pron

Don't miss out on these delicious cheeses, made with all-natural ingredients and aged to perfection. Please fill out the order form and return it promptly.

In response to the user's request, the program sends the window's size and display coordinates to the operating system, which then "opens" the window on the screen. (Windows can overlay any portion of a display, from a small corner to the entire screen.) At the same time, the operating system copies the endangered screen data to a special area of memory, called the save buffer, for safekeeping. The screen is now prepared to accommodate the window and its contents; because the process occurs in microseconds, the blank area shown above would not normally appear to the user's view.

The program's working memory displays both the contours and the contents of the window in the space that has been cleared for them on the screen. The window's color or border sets it off from the rest of the screen; the individual pixels that make up the window and its border are in turn switched on and off by the operating system.

Secrets of Word Processing

Merging Text to Customize Mail

Of the many features offered by modern word processors, one in particular is making the personal computer more personable. Called "mail merge," it allows a PC to combine a single document held in memory with hundreds, thousands, or even millions of names and addresses stored in a database. The result is a corresponding number of personalized communiqués.

Each name and its address constitute a record, the basic storage unit of a database. Every record in turn comprises a number of smaller data elements, or fields. In the sequence at right, a record contains six fields: first name, last name, street address, city, state, and zip code. In addition to inserting these fields in the heading and salutation, the sender may weave one or two of them into the body of the text itself.

At a command invoking the mail-merge function, the program sends a copy of the text held in its document memory to available memory. It then fetches a record from the database, billets it in available memory, and assigns each field in turn to the proper spot in the text in document memory. When all fields have been merged, the text is printed out. Its place in document memory is taken by a copy of the master text in available memory, and the process can begin anew.

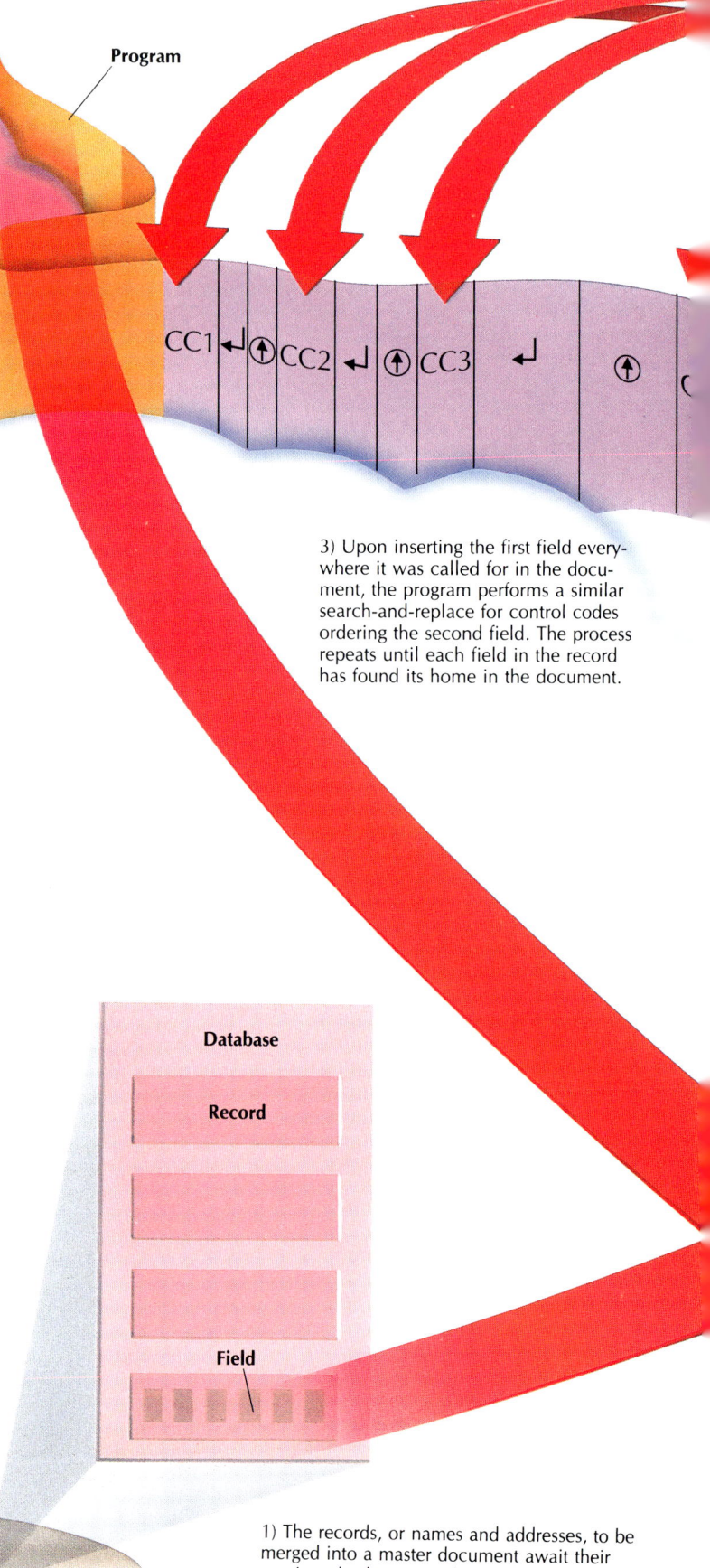

3) Upon inserting the first field everywhere it was called for in the document, the program performs a similar search-and-replace for control codes ordering the second field. The process repeats until each field in the record has found its home in the document.

1) The records, or names and addresses, to be merged into a master document await their cue in a database stored on a disk *(left)*. Each record contains six segments, called fields, detailing such particulars as first and last name, street address, city, state, and zip code.

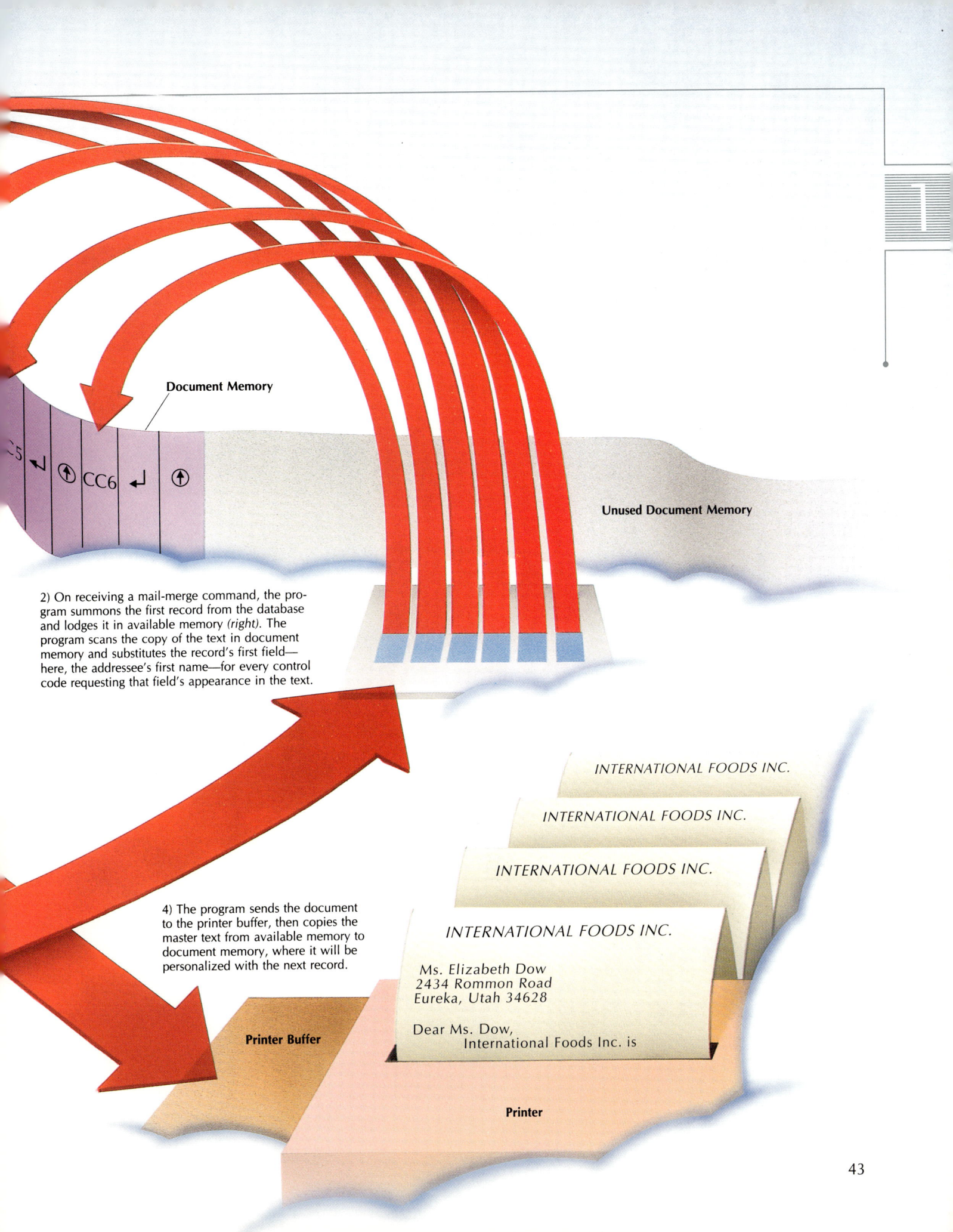

Document Memory

Unused Document Memory

2) On receiving a mail-merge command, the program summons the first record from the database and lodges it in available memory *(right)*. The program scans the copy of the text in document memory and substitutes the record's first field—here, the addressee's first name—for every control code requesting that field's appearance in the text.

4) The program sends the document to the printer buffer, then copies the master text from available memory to document memory, where it will be personalized with the next record.

Printer Buffer

INTERNATIONAL FOODS INC.
INTERNATIONAL FOODS INC.
INTERNATIONAL FOODS INC.
INTERNATIONAL FOODS INC.

Ms. Elizabeth Dow
2434 Rommon Road
Eureka, Utah 34628

Dear Ms. Dow,
  International Foods Inc. is

Printer

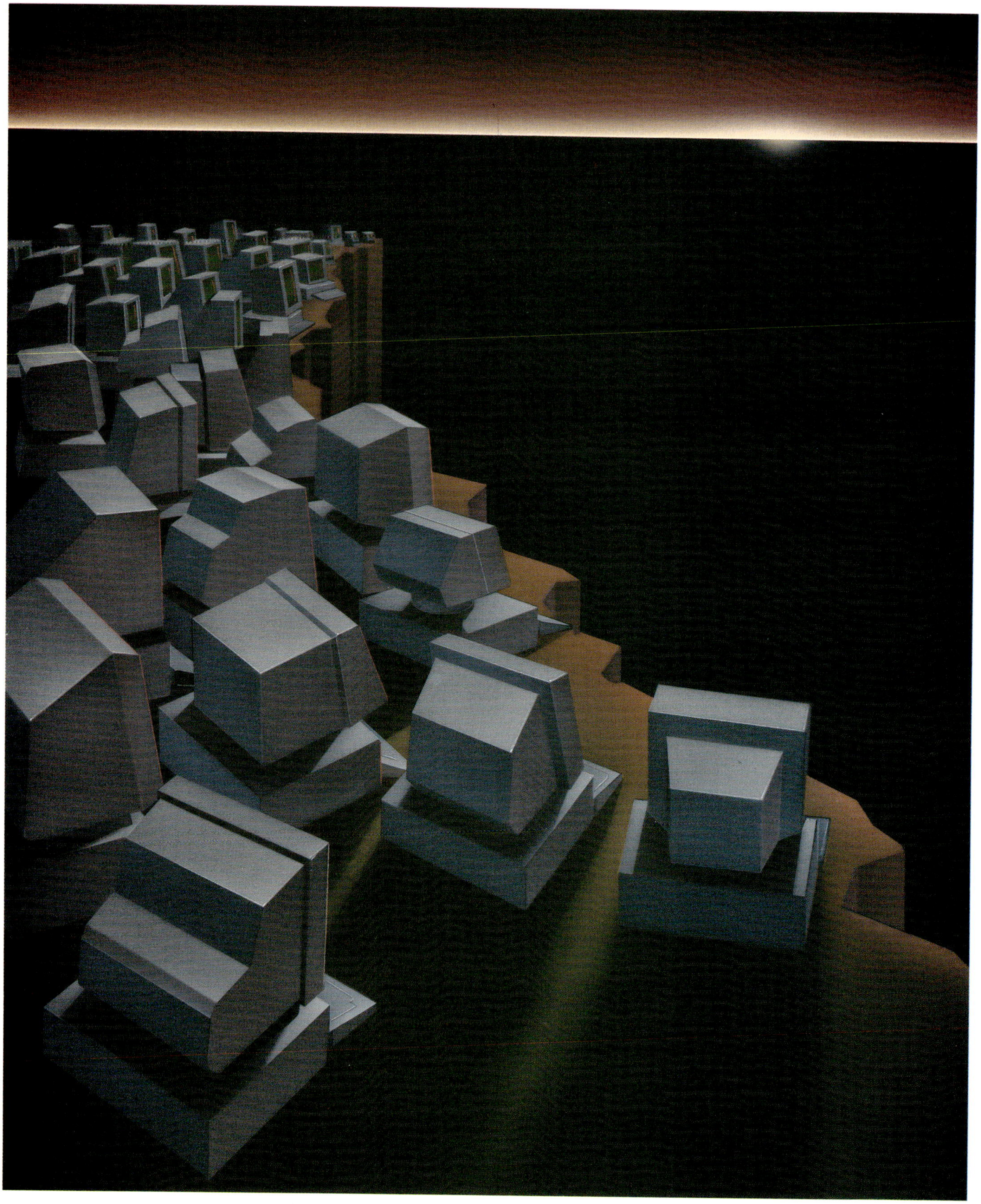

The Apple Alternative

One computer company enjoyed phenomenal success throughout the 1980s, even though it never bought a BIOS from Phoenix Technology, never cloned a PC or an AT, and never fell in step with the industry trend toward an alphabet soup of IBM standards. Confronted with MS DOS, PS/2, and MCA, Apple Computer has singlemindedly gone its own way. The company that Steven Jobs and Steven Wozniak founded at the end of the preceding decade thought of itself—not IBM—as the center of the PC universe. Apple had been going great guns in the business for four years before IBM arrived, and it was not about to suddenly turn into a follower. Even when IBM seized control of the most lucrative segment of the market—sales to businesses—and forced most competitors to adapt or perish, Apple stubbornly refused to be led. Due as much as anything to this obstinacy, the California hardware maker has played a unique role in shaping the character of personal computers.

Apple's maverick nature reflected Steve Jobs's deep-seated conviction that few people outside his company fully understood the potential of the new machines. Back in the days when personal computers were barely known outside the readership of specialty magazines such as *Popular Electronics,* Jobs saw the machines as a potential mass-market product. When desktop computers were still rare, he believed that he could sell them to anyone. Even more important, he was firmly convinced that all sorts of people would find Apple's products useful. In Jobs's view, there was little room for doubt that personal computers would soon change the world.

The key to Apple's success in the pre-IBM PC era was having a machine that was at once affordable and appealing to a broad range of customers. For this, Jobs could thank his partner, Steve Wozniak, who seemed to have an intuitive feel for the right machine. No modern marketing savant, Woz based most design considerations purely on his personal taste. He was fascinated, for example, by computer games, so he gave the Apple II color in its video display—the better for blasting asteroids or chasing centipedes through mazes. But the color graphics, despite the frivolous origin of the idea, also proved to be a major boon when parents sought out the Apple II as a vehicle for children's educational software. In addition to his instinct for amiable hardware, Woz had a knack for holding down costs. An inveterate tinkerer with things electronic, he was unaccustomed to having funds for expensive components. By force of habit, he engineered the Apple II to include the smallest possible number of chips. As a result, the computer could be priced low enough for people of his own modest means.

Jobs's part in making the Apple II suitable for mass consumption was more subtle. His most substantial contribution was to insist that the intimidating circuitry of Wozniak's creation be disguised in a harmless-looking plastic case. He saw to it that the Apple II looked like an everyday household appliance.

When sales of the Apple II went through the roof in the months and years following its 1977 introduction, the warm reception heightened Jobs's confidence in Apple Computer's ordained role as a leader. However, sustaining Apple's self-anointed status as a vanguard of sweeping technological change would prove to be anything but simple. Like all new businesses, Apple would make its share of mistakes and would learn that it could not always stay a step ahead of the competition. Nevertheless, Apple has been remarkably successful in providing an alternative to the IBM approach to personal computers. In part, Apple has done this by remaining true to Jobs's original idea—that computers should be for everyone, and not just for businesses. At times, this commitment has seemed more a liability than an advantage. Over the long term, however, Jobs's vision has been the source of the company's most significant contributions and its greatest commercial successes.

BUILDING HARDWARE SUCCESS ON SOFTWARE
Throughout its short history, Apple has been able to gamble on innovative ideas rather than play the game safe. The company had this luxury because it was able to establish, early on, a firm economic base of loyal Apple II owners. The Cupertino firm was particularly strong in sales to homes and schools, but it also found customers in small businesses and larger companies among so-called early adopters. These were independent souls who were willing to experiment with different ways of doing the everyday tasks of business—oftentimes, even before the alternative methods had been perfected or proved effective.

In part, the hardware maker won its broad-based constituency by playing the software game well. Advertising campaigns trumpeted the fact that the Apple II did the work of all sorts of people—farmers, poets, stamp collectors, mathematicians, and school children, as well as secretaries, accountants, and financial analysts. Board Chairman Mike Markkula and Michael Scott (the man Markkula tabbed to run the day-to-day affairs of the company) saw to it that software for all of these forms of work and play was produced in abundance.

Rather than try to grind out the programs at Apple, they introduced a number of key products that paved the way for software developers outside the company. The most important contribution was a floppy-disk drive called Disk II, which Apple made available in June 1978. The new storage unit was an external device linked to the computer by a cable. At the time, it was one of only two on the market (Tandy Radio Shack had the other) and they gave the two companies a decided advantage in the eyes of most software producers. Apple also arranged

In 1985, Apple's two Steves—Jobs and Wozniak—are photographed with two computers that led to fame and fortune. The Apple I, displayed in a makeshift box, was originally sold without a case, keyboard, or power supply. The Apple IIc, by contrast, was ready to use right out of the carton and gave its owners access to an extraordinary variety of software. By the time this picture was taken, more than two million Apple IIs had been sold.

to make available a version of the programming language Pascal, which was well liked by software professionals. Eventually, other languages were offered as well. Because Apple put such tools in place, many popular programs—including games and learning packages for homes and schools, and VisiCalc and Personal Filing System for the early adopters—were developed first for the Apple II.

In the personal computer business, having the best software makes hardware sales snowball. Customers buy the computer because of the great things that software makes it do. Then, as hardware sales pile up, software developers are more inclined to provide additional programs, which in turn draw additional computer customers.

Markkula and Scott were able to set such a cycle in motion for the Apple II, and they carefully nurtured it. They were particularly successful at locking in a special relationship for Apple with buyers from the schools. Beginning in 1979, they awarded hundreds of thousands of dollars in grants to school systems and educational associations for the development of software teaching aids. Apple established a particularly fruitful relationship with the Minnesota Educational Computing Consortium in St. Paul, which had a substantial collection of educational programs up and running on a statewide time-sharing system and adapted them for the Apple II. This gave Apple a big advantage over other suppliers of low-cost computers for education. To attract schools that were reluctant to buy computers, Apple launched a program called Kids Can't Wait, which made available to every school in California one free Apple II. The strategy behind the donations was that one computer in a school would lead to others. And with all those Apple IIs in classrooms, who would write educational software for any other machine? The plan paid dividends for years.

The result of Apple's meticulous efforts in promoting third-party software was an astonishing outpouring of programs. No fewer than 15,000 software packages were developed for the Apple II in its various configurations between 1977 and 1982. An increasing number of these products were business applications, but they ran the gamut from music composition to flight simulators, from tax preparation to tarot-card reading. To keep its hardware product in step with the rising expectations of buyers, Apple introduced four enhanced versions of its basic computer between 1979 and 1986. In the course of this evolution within the product line, the base memory of the Apple II rose from 4K to 256K.

AN APPLE TRUE BELIEVER
A by-product of Apple's special franchise within the smaller, more highly personalized segments of the computer market was the rise of a group of hard-core supporters for the company's technology. Some customers did more than simply buy Apple products—they embraced Steve Jobs's vision of computers as a boon to humankind. A number of these true believers, among them programmer Andy Hertzfeld, came to work for Apple and made important contributions to the company's fortunes.

Hertzfeld was a second-year graduate student in computer science at the University of California at Berkeley when he attended the 1977 West Coast Computer Faire and saw the unveiling of the Apple II. His reaction was immediate and unreserved: "That's the one I want." It took him nearly a year to put together the cash to buy his own Apple II, but the purchase changed his life.

Delving into the most obscure inner workings of the machine, he refined his skills in programming the Apple II and swapped information with other programmers in the San Francisco Bay area. The more he discovered, the more he admired the machine. For a time, he even thought of Steve Wozniak as his personal hero.

After months of selflessly sharing his programs with the members of his local Apple II user group, Hertzfeld turned professional. His first commercial software package was a complicated piece that overcame a rather glaring deficiency in the Apple II—its inability to display anything but uppercase characters. The program netted him a quick $40,000 and attracted the attention of Steven Jobs. When Hertzfeld completed his master's degree in the summer of 1979, he was hired by Apple and quickly discovered that he knew more about the functionings of the Apple II than most of the engineers on the company payroll. Hertzfeld would stay with the company for five productive years. He would play a central role in creating software for a later groundbreaking machine, the Macintosh.

A WORLD OF ITS OWN

Apple Computer presented unusual opportunities to self-motivated people such as Andy Hertzfeld, because it was everything that a traditional corporation was not—unstructured, informal, unbound by convention. There was little or no distinction between managers and workers; most dressed alike in T-shirts, blue jeans, and running shoes, and they blew off steam together in regular Friday afternoon beer busts. Buildings on the Apple "campus"—a term preferred to the more corporate-sounding "headquarters"—were given whimsical names. One was called the Land of Oz and had conference rooms marked Dorothy and Toto. To celebrate creativity, other rooms were given names like Picasso and Matisse.

Most of the inhabitants of this free-form environment were genuinely unawed by the August 1981 arrival of the IBM PC. In addition to the flippant welcoming newspaper ads, there was general disdain for the IBM product among the company engineers and programmers. The overriding confidence at Apple was rooted in the spectacular successes of the preceding four years. Eight months earlier, the privately owned company—which up to that point had given stock or options on shares only to its employees and to investors who had supplied start-up capital—had gone public in one of the most keenly anticipated stock offerings in Wall Street history. Enthusiasm was understandable. In purely financial terms, Apple had registered growth unparalleled in American industry. The company had sold more than 300,000 computers and had achieved yearly sales totaling nearly a third of a billion dollars. The initial stock sale raised approximately $100 million and made instant millionaires of dozens of Apple employees—many of them still in their twenties. Porsches and other expensive cars sprouted overnight in company parking lots. One car owner displayed his gratitude with the vanity license plate "THX APPL."

Inevitably, not everyone was happy with all that had transpired. The stock offering, in particular, caused some dissension in the ranks. Caught up in fifteen-hour workdays, some employees had

Some of the men and women who brought the Macintosh computer to life show off their creation at the time of its introduction in 1984. Among the most prominent appearing here is Andy Hertzfeld *(far left)*. As principal author of the Mac's operating system, he was identified on his business card as the team's Software Artist. Burrell Smith *(second from right)*, standing with an arm over the shoulder of ace programmer Bill Atkinson, was the computer's chief architect. Smith's card presented him as the Hardware Wizard.

failed to exercise their stock options in the months before the firm went public. Others feverishly bought up shares from their fellow employees. As one programmer recalled: "The people who cared about having the most stock had the most stock. When you wake up after the party and some guys are worth $5 million and others are still just earning their $30,000-a-year salaries, you certainly notice." Rapid expansion also led to overhiring, which ultimately resulted in the layoff of forty engineers—and a predictably negative effect on morale.

Such incidents aside, the prevailing mood at Apple by the summer of 1981 was unreservedly optimistic. The upbeat outlook was based on the continuing popularity of the Apple II and on great expectations for a stable of new computers under development: Sara, Lisa, and Macintosh.

THE SHORT, UNHAPPY LIFE OF THE APPLE III
Of the three projects, the computer named Sara had the most limited objectives. Begun in 1979, it was planned as a hedge against a possible downturn in the company's profits before the Lisa or Macintosh were ready to ship. Recalled
continued on page 58

HELLAS

GREECE

A Language for Printed Pages

No sooner had personal computers appeared in the 1970s than futurists began to speculate that the machines would replace the printed word and picture. So far, the effects have been quite different. Computers have instead wrought a quiet revolution called desktop publishing. With a personal computer, a scanner to digitize pictures, and a laser printer *(below)*, individuals can produce thousands of copies, in black and white or color, of almost anything—letterheads, instruction manuals, magazines, books, or whatever else inspiration suggests. There is no need for the specially skilled craftsmen of the traditional publishing industry, such as press operators, photoengravers, and paste-up workers, or for their complex equipment.

Sophisticated desktop publishing is made possible by programs called page-description languages (PDLs). Among the newest and most powerful of these high-level languages is Adobe System's PostScript, described here and on the following pages. A PDL serves as an intermediary between printers and many desktop publishing programs—such as Ventura or Pagemaker—running in a variety of computers. These applications packages translate the information for a page into a PDL for transmission to the printer. There, a memory chip called an interpreter converts the PDL code into so-called low-level instructions that tell the printer how to render letters, graphics, and pictures as the pattern of tiny dots that constitute a computer-printed page. Such translations are necessary to establish communications between different makes of computers and printers.

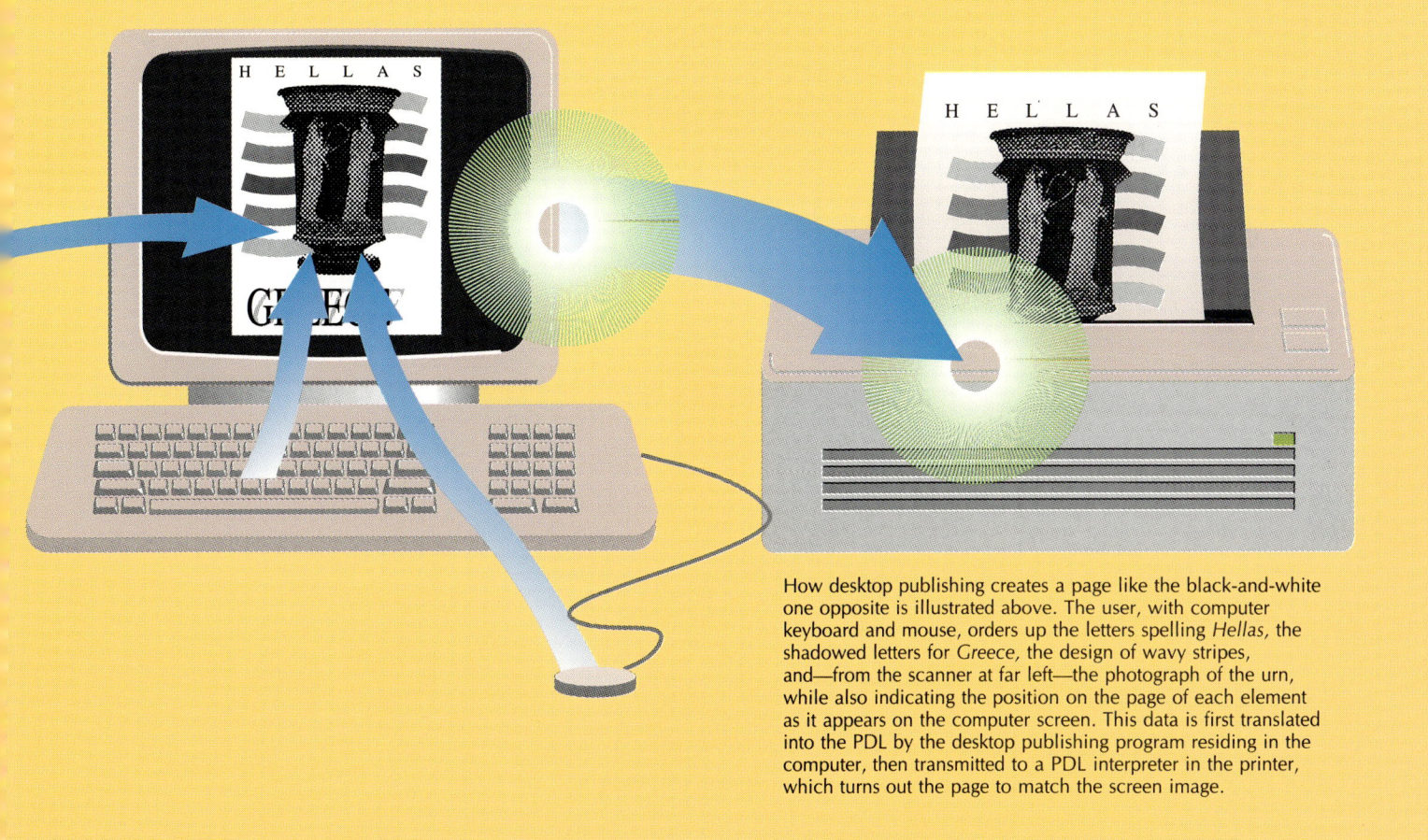

How desktop publishing creates a page like the black-and-white one opposite is illustrated above. The user, with computer keyboard and mouse, orders up the letters spelling *Hellas*, the shadowed letters for *Greece*, the design of wavy stripes, and—from the scanner at far left—the photograph of the urn, while also indicating the position on the page of each element as it appears on the computer screen. This data is first translated into the PDL by the desktop publishing program residing in the computer, then transmitted to a PDL interpreter in the printer, which turns out the page to match the screen image.

A Language for Printed Pages

Painting Letters and Graphic Designs

A page-description language builds up all the images on a page—letters and graphics as well as pictures—by "painting" them as an artist would, either in color or in black, white, and shades of gray. This permits effects that are difficult to achieve in old-fashioned printing: Words can be overlapped, stretched, squeezed, twisted, or turned so that they run in circles or spirals.

Much of the work of guiding the PDL's artist's brush is done automatically. The user provides only the basic information

```
36 616 translate
0 0 moveto
180 -50 360 100 540 50 curveto
50 setlinewidth
.8 setgray
stroke
```

To create a page, the user types text, data, and instructions for the applications package into the computer through the keyboard. Some graphics descriptions (like those for the wavy stripes in the illustrations at right) are typed. Other graphics are not described but are hand-drawn by moving a mouse in the desired pattern on a desk or table. Lines corresponding to the mouse's path then appear on the computer screen and, like the typed descriptions, are translated into PDL operators and transmitted to the printer.

To create the top stripe shown here, the PDL operators *(bold type above)* first specify its starting point in the grid—36 right, 616 up—then, to simplify computing, the grid's 0,0 origin is shifted to those coordinates by combining "translate" and "moveto" commands. In the next instruction, translated coordinates specify three grid points through which the stripe must pass, as ordered by the "curveto" operator. The "50 setlinewidth" command establishes the width of the stripe at 50 units, and ".8 setgray" selects the shade of the stripe—80 percent white and 20 percent black. The final operator, "stroke," commands the computer to paint the line specified. Except for grid coordinates and gray-scale shades, instructions for the remaining stripes are identical.

to the computer applications package: location of an element on a grid, style of a letter or design, and such traits as size, color, or shade.

This data is translated by the applications package into one or more of the PDL's 250 English-word commands, called operators, for transmission to the printer. For example, supplied with a center point, a radius, and a number of degrees between 1 and 360, the operator "arc" creates all or part of a circle in the printer's memory. The operator "stroke" actually draws the line on the screen, "fill" colors in the arc or circle, and "showpage" starts the printer.

If the designated shape is a letter or character, it is simply called up by the name of its typeface. This command brings from memory the instructions for generating a particular font, or collection of letters and characters, in the typeface desired; standard styles are stored in ROM chips, and others can be added by purchasing them on disks that feed the necessary programs to RAM.

```
/Galliard-Bold findfont
48 scalefont setfont
41 771 moveto
(Hellas)show
```

```
/Galliard-Bold findfont
[157.7 0 44 sin 44 cos div
157.7 mul 157.7 0 0] makefont setfont
.7 setgray
93 146 moveto
(Greece)show
```

To create the word *Hellas*, the PDL uses instructions that readily translate into English: The type font is Galliard-Bold—find it; adjust the size of this font to 48 points (⅔ inch high); set this font using the preceding instructions; coordinate location is 41 right, 771 up; move the lower left corner of the first letter there; the word to print is *Hellas*—print it. With no instructions for rotating the letters or changing their shapes, the program assumes the text is straight up and down and not stretched or compressed. Similarly, the absence of "setgray" instructions for shade tells the PDL that the letters are to be printed solid black.

To create the shadowed word *Greece* requires two separate sets of operators, one for the word, one for the shadow, a pale 70 percent white. So that the solid black word can be painted over it, the shadow is drawn first. Its PDL commands start with the typeface, but then they provide bracketed data for scale and trigonometric angle; the bracketed numbers and the operator "makefont" indicate that the stored font, Galliard-Bold, must be altered to create the slanted letters. The other instructions follow the standard pattern. The solid black, unaltered letters are specified by operators (not included in the list above) similar to those used for *Hellas*.

A Language for Printed Pages

Reproducing Pictures with Pixels

A PDL handles pictures in a special way because basic image data comes not from a keyboard or mouse but from a scanner, which measures light reflected from each of many tiny areas of the picture. Black-and-white scanners ordinarily used in desktop publishing read 90,000 of these pixels, or picture elements, per square inch and assign binary numbers to the shade of gray in each; a typical scanner distinguishes between 16 and 256 shades of gray.

When the scanner signals reach the computer, the image

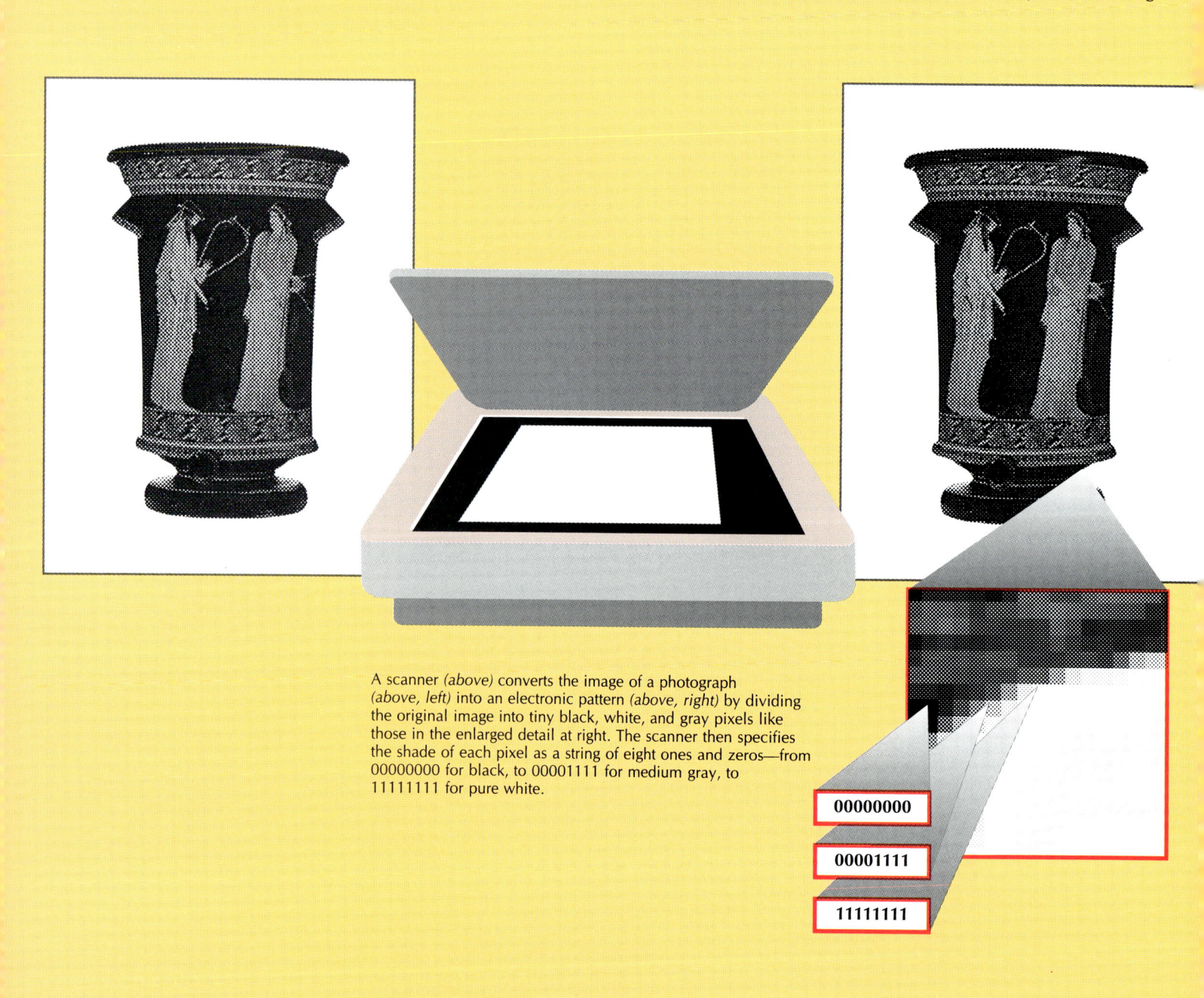

A scanner *(above)* converts the image of a photograph *(above, left)* into an electronic pattern *(above, right)* by dividing the original image into tiny black, white, and gray pixels like those in the enlarged detail at right. The scanner then specifies the shade of each pixel as a string of eight ones and zeros—from 00000000 for black, to 00001111 for medium gray, to 11111111 for pure white.

00000000

00001111

11111111

still has coordinates assigned by the scanner. To be incorporated into the page, the image must be placed in the printer's coordinate system, but the computer does not do this. Instead it sends the digital pixel data to the printer's PDL interpreter, along with user-supplied instructions.

The applications package tells the printer interpreter to prepare for arriving scanner data. It specifies gray shades per pixel, gives the height and width of the original image, and specifies how big it should appear on the printed page. It also instructs the PDL to transform the image from the scanner's coordinate system into the printer's coordinate system. The interpreter in the printer then executes the transformation.

Although this system enables the PDL to link any combination of many types of computers, scanners, and printers, it involves the transmission of a large amount of digital data. Reproducing this particular image in 256 shades of gray requires a stream of ones and zeros that would fill more than 550 typewritten pages.

The computer screen displays the completed page design with text, graphics, and picture combined as they will appear when printed. Instructions for achieving this result are sent on to the printer interpreter.

A Language for Printed Pages

Printing the Page Dot by Dot

A computer speaking high-level language to a printer is like a college professor talking to a cave dweller. Printers understand only bit mapping, which conveys messages in grunts of "on" or "off"; each grunt causes an opaque dot to be applied or not applied. A PDL therefore needs a translator, in the interpreter in the printer's PDL ROM, to get a page description across to the printer.

The interpreter changes the PDL information about text and graphics into a form that is compatible with printer char-

In the data flowing from the computer into the printer's PDL interpreter *(green)*, the word *Greece* and the operator "show" are the tail end of a group of commands specifying text. Coming from the computer in high-level PDL, they instruct the interpreter to print *Greece* at the correct position and at a resolution appropriate to the printer. The operator "image" tells the interpreter that the succeeding digital data describes picture pixels from the scanner, yet to be converted to the printer's coordinate system. As the data comes in, the interpreter specifies every single dot to be applied. It writes the description of every page element sequentially into printer memory dot by dot.

01010011 IMAGE (GREECE)SHOW

The light gray shadow of the letter *G* is made up of many small cells like the one magnified at right, each with its 256-square grid containing only a few black dots. Combined in the shape of the shadow, the mixture of black and white creates the illusion of a smooth gray letter. The sharpness of the result depends on the size of the dots and cells the printer produces. Laser printers commonly used for desktop publishing can make 300 dots per inch to construct images with cells only 1/33 of a square inch, coarser than pictures in a newspaper. Much finer detail is possible with more capable printers having as many as 2,540 dots per inch. These devices, instead of printing directly on paper, make films for standard offset presses like the one that produced this book.

acteristics, and expresses the information in the printer's co-ordinate system. Picture data received from the scanner is sized and positioned on the page by the interpreter, then converted from the original gray scale to a different one called a digital halftone.

Now the printer works in its simpleminded way, either applying a dot to a particular spot or not applying one. It cannot make a gray dot, only black. For a variety of shades, it divides the page into microscopically small squares called cells. It creates black areas by filling cells there with dots, intermediate shades by grouping in each cell an amount of dots proportionate to its shade, and white areas by applying no dots at all.

The printer produces all text, graphics, and pictures the same way, made up of shaded cells. The larger the cell—the more dots it can hold—the greater the range of shades but the coarser the image; conversely, smaller cells with fewer dots increase detail but restrict shading.

The completed page, shown below emerging from the printer, is produced all at once but is built up in printer memory in four stages indicated at left. As each element—stripes, *Hellas*, shadowed *Greece*, urn—is sent through the PDL, it paints over elements entered before it, so the image of the urn obscures stripes behind it. The last overlap makes the page ready to print.

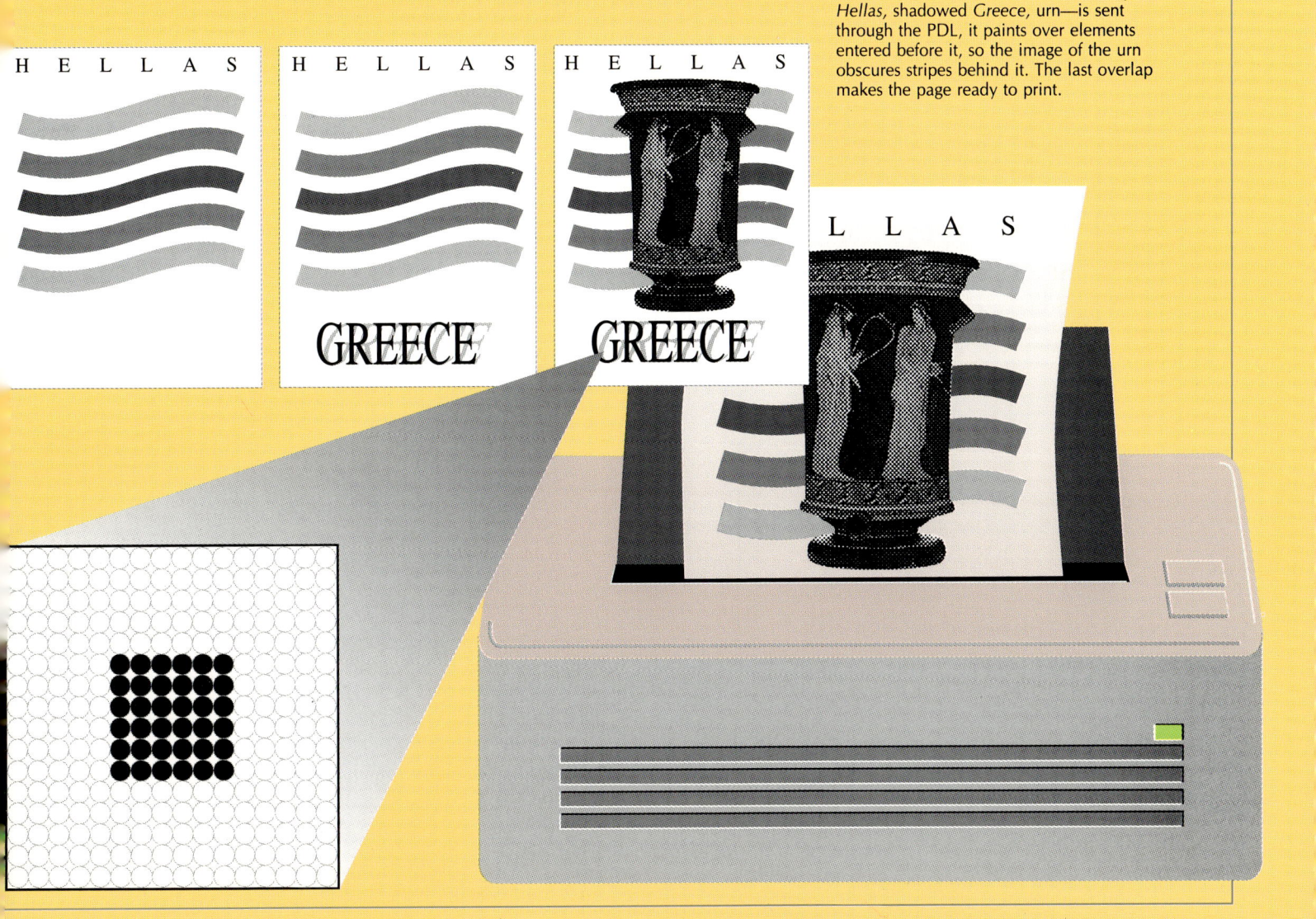

Wendell Sanders, hardware-design chief for the Sara: "We kept wondering when the bubble was going to burst on the Apple II." This uncertainty prompted a substantial outlay of funds to ready a stopgap product. From a technical standpoint, the Sara was much less ambitious than either the Lisa or the Macintosh, and it was slated for delivery long before the other machines.

Named for Sanders's daughter, the Sara was designed to improve on the Apple II in several important ways. It would be given bigger memory—128K, expandable to 256K—and come with a disk drive built into the case of the computer. Sara would overcome one serious limitation in the Apple II, its overly narrow forty-character lines. The new machine's higher-resolution screen would display eighty characters per line, enough for professional-looking business correspondence. The new computer would also have the capacity to display both uppercase and lowercase characters—no surprise, since Andy Hertzfeld took a hand in its operating system.

The Apple strategic planners set for the Sara a recklessly ambitious schedule—from conception to assembly line in just ten months. Working day and night, the design team met this deadline. They unveiled their machine, renamed the Apple III, in September 1980, at the National Computer Conference in Anaheim, California. Apple provided typical fanfare for the occasion, renting Disneyland for a night and ferrying 20,000 guests to and from the park in a fleet of red double-decker buses. But the product did not merit the celebration. New owners discovered to their dismay that not all Apple II programs ran very well on the Apple III, even though the two machines had been billed as compatible. Less serious but nevertheless embarrassing for Apple, a faulty chip caused the computer's built-in clock to fail after only three hours. Dissatisfaction among customers soon turned to rage when, all too often, the machine broke down entirely and the screen lit up with the message "SYSTEM FAILURE."

Furthermore, the Apple III was poorly engineered. Circuit boards did not fit properly, chips slipped from sockets, and ill-placed screws cut into wires. Assembly-line workers took to tapping on the machines with rubber mallets, hoping that all the parts would settle into place. With customers howling and the trade press savaging the machine, Apple called a halt to production and embarked on a major redesign. The computer reappeared as the Apple III+ in December 1983, but it never recovered from its shaky debut. Planners at Apple had originally hoped to sell 50,000 units in the six months following the original product launch. But sales never even approached that level. In all, the company sold just 65,000 Apple IIIs before retiring the model for good in April 1984.

AN OUTSIDE SOURCE OF INSPIRATION
Sobered by the evolving Apple III debacle, the development teams at work on the Macintosh and the Lisa were determined not to make the same mistakes. Both the Mac and the Lisa were viewed by Markkula and Scott as carrying Apple's hopes for expanding its presence in the lucrative business market. The two development efforts differed in their price objectives and in the level of investment that they represented for Apple. The price of the Mac was intended all along to be rock-bottom low. Project leader Jef Raskin had balked at attempting a $500 machine, but he was determined to keep the Mac under $1,000. Raskin's team was a mere splinter group. It comprised only five researchers during its first

Bill Atkinson, inventor of the distinctive pull-down menus for the Lisa and Macintosh computers, joined Apple during its second year in business. For a time the company's only full-time applications programmer, Atkinson wrote the tour-de-force drawing program MacPaint and an innovative system for data management called HyperCard. At various times, both packages were offered free of charge to Mac buyers.

months of operation. The Lisa, by contrast, was never envisioned as a low-price computer. Although its projected cost swung at various times between a minimum of $2,000 and a maximum of $10,000, the product planners intended all along to demand whatever the office market would bear. Development of the Lisa was a major financial undertaking, involving approximately 200 engineers, technicians, programmers, and support personnel. Steve Jobs would personally spearhead the effort, which was named for his infant daughter.

In a roundabout fashion, these two very different teams came to find their inspiration in the same source—the Xerox Corporation's Palo Alto Research Center (PARC). Situated not far from Cupertino in the hills south of Stanford University, Xerox PARC was a kind of technological think tank with a vague mandate to create "the office of the future." Xerox had spent lavishly on the facility and kept it stocked with an outstanding research staff. Scientists specializing in such areas as microchips, programming languages, computers, and laser printers were given virtually free rein in their investigations. Over the years since the center opened in 1969, the PARC staff had created a remarkably open atmosphere for the commerce of ideas. They drew on influences outside the facility that ranged from the theories of child psychologists to the concepts of the Norwegian inventors of the approach to software called object-oriented programming, and they freely shared their own findings with almost any organization curious enough to ask.

Xerox PARC researchers who were engaged in computer development benefited from a cooperative relationship with the nearby Stanford Research Institute, another highly regarded center for the study of computers. One of the guiding lights at SRI was Douglas Engelbart, who had long been involved in an effort to develop easy, natural ways for people to interact with computers. Engelbart's most intriguing contribution to this area of research—referred to as the "user interface"—was called a mouse, patented in 1964. Moving the mouse moved a pointer on the screen, allowing computer operators to issue instructions by selecting commands from lists, or menus, rather than by typing them. Comparable arrangements are possible without the mouse, if the pointer, or cursor, is controlled by the keyboard. But Engelbart was searching for a more natural way of pointing. He encouraged Xerox PARC to follow up on his work in making computers easier to use.

The first PARC computer, the Alto, drew upon advances in both hardware and software. Built in 1973, the machine used Engelbart's mouse to great advantage by allying it with a process called bit mapping in which the operating system controls each dot, or pixel (picture element), on the screen according to a map in the computer's memory. This gives the computer far more precision in its visual display than is possible in less-sophisticated systems, which rely on special chips called character generators to define shapes. A major breakthrough was the Alto's ability to display multiple documents or images, each in a box called a window that the operator could move around like papers on a desk.

PARC's machine also benefited from its reliance on a visually oriented programming language known as Smalltalk, designed in part by researcher Alan Kay. Using Smalltalk, programmers were able to carry out a certain portion of their work by selecting from menus with the mouse. As a result, the language was relatively easy to learn. The approach was carried over into the routine operation of the Alto and was refined by the addition of icons, which are pictures of everyday objects representing procedures on the computer. An outline of a mailbox, for example, signified Alto's message-passing features for communicating with other computers.

The graphical interface of the Alto made it notably easy to master, but Xerox Corporation was slow in bringing the technology to market. Not until 1981 did the company release the Star 8010, which included many Alto features. Priced at $16,000, however, the Star was simply too expensive to create much of a stir.

BORROWING FROM XEROX
Apple's Raskin had first become acquainted with the Xerox research as a visiting scholar at the Stanford Artificial Intelligence Laboratory during the early 1970s. Since then, he had continued to exchange ideas with friends at PARC. Raskin was particularly impressed with the Alto's bit-mapped screens, its graphics approach to text, and its ease of use. When he came to work for Apple in 1978, as the company's thirty-first employee, he drafted a plan for a new computer that would incorporate the Alto innovations. He called the machine Macintosh in honor of his favorite apple, subtly changing the spelling from McIntosh to avoid future litigation over trademarks. Raskin won some converts for his proposal and lobbied Steve Jobs to consider the Alto approach. Eventually, Raskin was given the go-ahead by Markkula and Scott to put together a small research group to flesh out the Macintosh concept.

Perhaps because Jobs had so much confidence in Apple's capacity for innovation, he resisted the importunings of Raskin and others to take a look at the Xerox PARC research. By December 1979, however, Jobs was still less than satisfied with either of the two prototypes that his team had developed for the Lisa. Both designs were practical but unimaginative. In search of fresh inspiration, Jobs finally accepted an invitation from Xerox—an early investor in Apple stock—to witness the computer of the future.

Like many before him, Jobs was awed by what he saw. Although the demonstration of the Alto and its Smalltalk programming language lasted less than an hour, it crystallized Jobs's vision for the Lisa and for all Apple computers. Before leaving the premises, he asked a member of his party, programmer Bill Atkinson, how long it would take to produce software like the Alto's and have it up and running on the Lisa. An optimist, Atkinson guessed the job could be done in about six months. When the group returned to Cupterino, Jobs discovered that a number of the engineers and programmers on his development team were already sold on the value of the Xerox PARC approach. Within days of Jobs's conversion, the Lisa group set to work on a bit-mapped machine that would have windows, a mouse, and a graphical interface like that of the Alto. None of these features would be simple to implement.

THE REBIRTH OF LISA AS A BIT-MAP MACHINE
To avoid starting from scratch, the Lisa team set about hiring away a substantial number of Xerox PARC engineers and programmers. Of the 200 people who would work on the computer, some twenty were former Xerox employees.

Ken Rothmueller, chief hardware architect for the Lisa, stuck with an earlier decision to use the Motorola 68000 as the central processing unit for the new computer. The 68000 bridged the gap between a chipmaking industry that was technologically ready to produce thirty-two-bit chips and a personal-computer industry that had not yet made the jump from eight-bit processors to the sixteen-bit variety. The Motorola chip had the data-transferring capabilities of a sixteen-bit chip and the internal-processing speed of a thirty-two-bit chip. It could handle twice as many operations as the Apple II's eight-bit microprocessor at roughly three times the speed. The Lisa would need every bit of that processing power to individually direct each of the 262,080 pixels on its black-and-white monitor. Even with the 68000, Rothmueller's engineers had their hands full squeezing the capacities of the Alto, which was roughly the size of a dishwasher, into a computer that could sit comfortably on top of a desk.

Although the hardware problems posed by the Lisa were substantial, they paled beside the challenges confronting the programmers. In addition to improving on the Alto's user interface and writing a battery of complicated application programs, the software team hoped to endow the Lisa with all sorts of niceties in its graphics capabilities. For one thing, they planned to leap beyond the Apple III realm of simple capital and lowercase characters. The Lisa would generate letters, numbers, and other symbols in a variety of typefaces and in many sizes. To keep these complicated features from devouring memory at an impractical rate, programmers would need to write very tight, efficient code—a demanding and time-consuming process. Ultimately, the basic routines on which Lisa's graphics software was built would take three years to compose.

The guiding force behind the Lisa software was Bill Atkinson—the voice of optimism on Steve Jobs's Xerox PARC reconnaisance mission. A tremendously talented programmer, Atkinson had joined Apple in 1978. Like many of the company's best and brightest, he had a restless, inquisitive mind. At one point, he had pursued a Ph.D. in neurochemistry, but he gave it up for his first love, computers. Early on in his involvement with the Lisa, Atkinson wrote a group of basic software instructions called graphic primitives to be installed in the computer's read-only memory. Named Quickdraw, the code allows other programs to create lines and shapes, such as arcs, circles, and squares. It is the basis for all of the Lisa's graphics. Atkinson also took a hand in crafting Apple's version of the Alto graphical interface, writing a thirty-five-page manual that spelled out in great detail how to operate the Lisa. Members of the development team regarded this document as their bible. Embracing its doctrine of simplicity with near-religious zeal, they placed great emphasis on keeping the Lisa easy to learn and use. As the machine progressed, it was routinely tested by new employees.

RIVALS WITHIN APPLE
Steve Jobs and the Lisa team never settled into a productive working relationship. Jobs's imperious style grated on his colleagues, and he was roundly criticized for slowing progress by continually revising the design. Late in 1980, he was removed from the project by company heads Markkula and Scott. Although Jobs left his mark on the Lisa in a few aesthetic details, such as the shapes of the icons displayed on the screen, the machine evolved largely without his participation.

Casting about for a new project, Jobs set his sights on Raskin's group and forced his way onto the Macintosh team. He was determined to prove to Markkula and Scott that he could push a new computer to completion. The relationship between Jobs and Raskin, who suspected the Apple founder of trying to kill the Macintosh project at its inception, had never been warm. And when the two headstrong men were forced to work at close quarters, sparks inevitably flew.

At first, Jobs confined himself to directing hardware development, but soon he began to assert himself on software issues as well. Before long, he had demoted Raskin to overseeing production of the Macintosh user's manual. Rather than accept that role, the originator of the Mac resigned from Apple altogether. Recalled one programmer: "Since Steve was a bigger kid than Raskin, he said, 'I like that toy!' and took it."

During his tenure with the Lisa team, Jobs had chafed under what he saw as creeping bureaucracy within Apple. Many of the engineers on that project had come from larger, more established firms such as Hewlett-Packard and were most comfortable working in a clearly defined management hierarchy. Jobs worried that the company he had started was becoming too big and stratified, and he hoped to recapture in his Mac group some of the old Apple spirit. While a few critics derided his efforts as a back-to-the-garage fantasy, Jobs began assembling a crew that was more attuned to his style. He kept Raskin's chief hardware engineer, Burrell Smith, whom he knew to be a hard-core Apple junkie. With no formal training in computer design, Smith had gotten his start repairing Apple IIs in the service department. He was highly respected for his self-taught engineering skills. To head up the software effort, Jobs spirited Hertzfeld away from the Apple II division, where he had returned after the Apple III debacle. By then something of a fixture at Apple, Hertzfeld was so at ease in the casual environment that he was known to show up barefoot for work. Hertzfeld and Smith, who lived and breathed their work, became the core of an energetic band of proven Apple contributors. The group included, among others, documentation specialist Chris Espinosa and software engineer Randy Wigginton.

Jobs pushed his team hard, hoping they could beat the Lisa group in bringing a product to market. Employing one of his favorite phrases, he described the Mac as an "insanely great" computer that would match or exceed the Lisa's capabilities, while selling for a fraction of the price. Despite his sense of urgency, Jobs allowed the Mac developers to find their own distinctive working style, and the environment they created bordered on anarchy. Rock music blasted day and night from six-foot-high stereo speakers, while a toy robot skittered about the halls. During breaks in grueling sixteen-hour workdays, engineers played table tennis and video games or banged on the keyboard of a concert piano, which Jobs had installed for their use. From the building's roof, Jobs flew a black flag with the skull and crossbones that symbolized the Mac team's maverick style and its willingness to plunder other Apple projects for the best people and ideas.

Flying the Jolly Roger was a Peter Pan gesture typical of Jobs, for whom work and play were one and the same. Still in his twenties, he combined an adolescent enthusiasm with an uncompromising demand for perfection. He lived by a Zen aphorism, which he posted throughout the Mac building: "The journey is the reward." Jobs's absolute self-confidence came across to many as arrogance. To a reporter's question about the role of market research in the design of the Mac, he shot back: "Did Alexander Graham Bell do any market research before he invented the telephone?" He managed his team intuitively—alternately praising, cajoling, ridiculing, and rebuking in ceaseless pursuit of every ounce of effort he could inspire. He loved to pass out medals and uncork champagne, but he was also not above throwing tantrums or humiliating people in front of their peers.

A SWEET-AND-SOUR RECEPTION
Despite the team's best efforts, the Macintosh was still a year away from its introduction when the Lisa was unveiled in January 1983. The Lisa was to be sold with a bundle of software that had cost Apple $100 million to develop, including a word processor, a database manager, and a powerful graphics program called Lisa Draw. Despite the software's complexity, experiments showed that novices could get up to speed on the Lisa in roughly one twentieth the time required for other computers. Reviews were generally filled with praise. "Lisa is a dream," said *Fortune. BYTE* called it "the most important development in computers in the last five years," a period that covered virtually the entire history of the PC.

Glowing tributes aside, the Lisa had serious faults that would handicap it in head-to-head battle with the IBM PC—by then the computer of choice for the office. The Lisa's impressive graphics strained the power of even the 68000 microprocessor, so that it executed commands more slowly than the IBM PC. The word-processing program, Lisa Write, was inferior to rival PC products. Promised hardware and software to link multiple machines into networks was not immediately available. Perhaps most damaging, potential customers were gulping at the hefty $10,000 price—nearly twice that of rival business computers—and complaining about its incompatibility with both the IBM PC and the Apple II.

Although the Lisa was a technological milestone, it proved a commercial failure. To spur sales, Apple cut the price by 20 percent, but by the end of 1983, only 11,000 units had sold. Apple finished the year with a record $983 million in revenues, but most of that figure was attributable to the continued popularity of the reliable Apple II line.

In the midst of Apple's disappointments with the Lisa—and with the Macintosh team still hard at work—the company underwent a major shift in command. Mike Markkula, who had succeeded Mike Scott as president of Apple in March 1981, made it known that he wanted to remove himself from the day-to-day operations of the company. The board members charged with hiring a replacement set their sights on easterner John Sculley, the young president of the Pepsi-Cola division of New York-based PepsiCo. Sculley was considered something of a wunderkind in marketing circles. He had earned his wings in the soft-drink industry as developer of the enormously successful "Pepsi Generation" advertising campaign during the 1970s. He wasn't much interested in selling computers, and only a persistent campaign by Steve Jobs persuaded him to leave Pepsi. As Sculley later recalled, the turning point in his decision making came when Jobs abandoned all tact and asked: "Do you want to spend the rest of your life selling sugared water or do you want a chance to change the world?"

When Sculley took over the helm in Cupertino in April 1983, he found himself immersed in an alien environment. He also discovered that at the age of forty-four, he was one of the oldest Apple employees.

FINISHING TOUCHES FOR THE MAC
To bring the Macintosh to the finish line, Steve Jobs's troops had to overcome software problems as formidable as those that had confronted the Lisa's devel-

63

opers. In an effort to hold down the cost of the Mac, its designers had given it only 128K of memory. This was precisely one-eighth the capacity of the Lisa, and yet the smaller computer was supposed to perform most of the same functions. To use the Mac's memory with maximum efficiency, Jobs recruited Bill Atkinson from the Lisa group and asked him to produce a compact machine-language version of Quickdraw. That program, a fundamental part of the Lisa software, was also to be the basis for all of the Macintosh graphics. Converting it from the original Pascal was an arduous, mind-numbing task that took Atkinson more than two years. By the time he was finished, he had shrunk Quickdraw's code nearly sevenfold—from 160,000 bytes to an astonishingly small 24,000 bytes.

Hertzfeld and his team performed many such feats in their contest with the Mac's limited memory. Some of their most formidable programming achievements reside in the code for the various software routines that, along with Quickdraw, make up the machine's user-interface "toolbox." This collection of programs is the centerpiece of an ambitious scheme on the part of the Mac designers to make all application software for the computer operate in a uniform way, and thus be easy to learn. Routines to handle all aspects of user interface—windows, the mouse, menus, specialized fonts, and many other features—are stored in read-only memory, to be called upon time and again by application programmers. The challenge was getting them to fit, since the entire body of code had to be small enough to be imprinted on a sixty-four-kilobyte ROM chip. The finished work, in fact, takes up two-thirds of that space and runs extremely fast.

As the Mac project neared completion, team members were convinced that they were participating in something historic. For posterity, Jobs arranged to have the signatures of forty-seven key contributors molded inside the computer's plastic case. Sculley and the Apple board of directors caught "Mac fever" and agreed to launch the new product with an unprecedented $15 million advertising and promotion blitz. They spent more than $1.5 million of the sum on a single television commercial that was aired one time only, during the 1984 Super Bowl. The provocative ad played on George Orwell's vision of a totalitarian world as portrayed in his novel *1984*. It showed a mass of zombielike men with shaved heads and baggy, colorless uniforms dumbly watching a giant TV screen filled with the face of a Big Brother figure. The scene culminates with the arrival of an athletic young woman who hurls a sledgehammer into the screen, breaking the spell of Big Brother. A voice-over announces: "On January 24th, Apple Computer will introduce Macintosh. 1984 won't be like *1984*."

Savvy viewers of this not-so-subtle allegory recognized Big Brother as a slap at Big Blue. Apple was taking direct aim at IBM, which a few months before had captured the lead in personal computer sales, bumping Apple to second place. A follow-up commercial played on a favorite Apple theme that "simplicity is the ultimate sophistication." The commercial showed a stack of bulky instruction manuals tumbling from above and crashing down next to an IBM PC. The camera then cuts to a single slim booklet floating down next to a Macintosh, and a voice intones: "Now *you* decide which one is more sophisticated."

By and large, the Macintosh lived up to the hoopla surrounding its arrival. In both its overall configuration and in many small details, critics found the machine a marvel of outward simplicity that masked the complexity of its software and the extraordinary care that had gone into its engineering. The Mac had fewer chips than either the IBM PC or the Apple II, making it easier to manufacture and less prone to component failure. So simple was the initiation of commands by mouse that the keyboard lacked cursor and function keys.

Most people found the Mac stylish and sleek. Its ten-by-ten-inch "footprint"—the area it occupied on a surface—was significantly smaller than that of most PCs; and, weighing less than twenty-three pounds, the machine was portable if protected by an optional carrying case. Buyers of the Macintosh received two software packages—a word processor called MacWrite and a drawing program called MacPaint. The base price of $2,495, while nearly double the figure originally targeted, was still comparable to the cost of an IBM PC, when the value of the software was considered. Also included in the price of the Mac was the operating system, which was an extra-cost item in the IBM world.

BYTE hailed the Macintosh as "a breakthrough in adapting computers to work with people instead of vice versa," while *Consumer Reports* touted it as "far and away the easiest computer to learn and use that we have yet seen." Much of the praise was for the resemblance of the Mac's interface to a desktop. Most jobs were accomplished in ways that made sense to anyone who had worked in an office. For example, files to be erased were moved by mouse, in icon form, to a "trash can" and discarded. Notes could be held on a "clipboard" for later use.

THE ROLLER-COASTER RIDE OF APPLE'S FORTUNES
Apple sold more than 100,000 Macintoshes in the six months following the machine's introduction, exceeding the company's most optimistic projections. *Business Week* put Sculley and Jobs on its cover. The "dynamic duo," as they were dubbed, could seemingly do no wrong. Looking ahead, they decided to make the most of the Mac bonanza by building inventory for the traditionally

big Christmas market. Fueled by a $100 million investment in parts and materials, Apple's factories went into overdrive, churning out 110,000 Macs per month.

The outlook remained upbeat as Apple entered 1985. Within weeks of the new year, however, Sculley began seeing signs that all was not right with the Macintosh, the Apple, or the personal computer industry in general. Sales figures for both the Macintosh and the Apple II were coming in well below expectations. The anticipated Christmas boom had failed to materialize—in part because IBM had granted deep discounts for its short-lived PCjr home computer. Apple dealers were choked with excess inventory, and instead of selling the projected 80,000 Macs every month, they were barely moving 20,000 units. In a further blow to morale, cofounder Steve Wozniak quit, amid grumblings that the company had lost its sense of direction.

It soon became apparent that the entire industry was in the beginnings of a major shakeout resulting from sagging demand and cutthroat competition. The slump was particularly bad in the so-called consumer market. Thousands of computers purchased for use at home were now gathering dust in closets as their owners discovered that the machines were more trouble than they were worth for charting credit card balances or maintaining Christmas-card lists. As the number of personal computer manufacturers dropped from more than 200 to 150, Apple shut down four of its six factories for a week and canceled production of the Lisa altogether. When Apple posted its first-ever quarterly loss—a whopping $17.2 million—its stock plummeted by a third, prompting rumors of a possible takeover by AT&T or Xerox.

Apple would recover from these problems, but not before the company had undergone a wrenching period of change—one that would witness, among other things, the departure of Steve Jobs. At the height of the Mac euphoria in 1984, Sculley had boasted that "Apple has one leader, Steve and me." Sculley had awarded Jobs more responsibility than he had held at Apple since the company had left the garage. In addition to his largely titular role as chairman of the board, he was now the firm's executive vice president and general manager of the Macintosh division. He had 1,000 people working for him and was responsible for all the complex operations involved in manufacturing, marketing, and distributing the Mac. Many felt that Jobs's lack of management experience was hurting the performance of the Macintosh group, and that his arrogant personality was splitting the company into two feuding camps—Mac and Apple II.

As Apple's problems reached crisis proportions, Sculley took action on several fronts. His most drastic step was to cut Apple's work force by 20 percent, firing

1,200 people and permanently closing three of the firm's six factories. To end the growing acrimony between the Macintosh and Apple II factions, he reluctantly determined to remove the major source of divisiveness. With the backing of the board of directors, he stripped his friend Jobs of his positions as executive vice president and Mac general manager. Jobs remained chairman of the board, but he had been effectively isolated within his own company. He stayed on for another four months before resigning and selling his Apple stock. Within days of his departure, Jobs announced the formation of a new company called NeXT.

GETTING THE MACINTOSH BACK ON TRACK
Slashing payroll and neutralizing Jobs were tactical actions important to Apple's recovery. However, Sculley believed that to assure the company's long-term viability he would have to shift the overall marketing approach away from Apple's traditionally broad-based clientele and focus much more heavily on businesses. With its moderately priced Apple II and Macintosh, Apple occupied a middle ground between the low-end consumer market, where it competed with such companies as Commodore, and the high-end business market ruled by IBM. The business arena dwarfed the other market segments and offered much greater potential for growth. Apple executive Alfred Mandel described Sculley's new marketing objective as the "Fortune 500,000—those half-million smaller companies that are a major part of America's business scene."

Apple had already tried selling a concept called the Macintosh Office—networks of Macs that could also be linked to other computers, including IBM machines. The company had been slow, however, in developing the necessary software. Sculley ordered those efforts redoubled. He began to court two key constituencies, the independent dealers who sold Apple products and the software companies that developed the programs that ran on them. To strengthen the loyalty of Apple dealers, Sculley expanded their opportunities to market Apple products to larger businesses, a territory previously reserved for Apple's direct-sales force.

Independent producers of business software figured to be a tougher nut to crack. They would only make the investment in developing complicated business packages, such as spreadsheets and word processors, if they believed that a large market would exist for the products. Sculley took to the road and personally visited key people in the industry, such as Microsoft chairman Bill Gates and Lotus founder Mitch Kapor. He managed to convince a number of them that by 1986, Apple would be selling 50,000 Mac computers a month.

When Apple met and exceeded this goal, the confidence of the software makers was restored. Several major programming houses spurred development of business software for the Mac. Microsoft introduced a powerful spreadsheet package called Excel, which became one of the biggest sellers in its category. An even more eye-catching addition to the Mac software library was a package called PageMaker from Aldus Corporation, which charted new ground for office computer use. The success of PageMaker, which turned the Macintosh into a one-person graphic-design and print shop, benefited from a fortuitous coincidence. About the same time that the Aldus Corporation introduced the software, Apple brought to market a high-quality printer called the LaserWriter. Together, the Mac, the software, and the hot new printer made it possible to produce newsletters and magazines with a highly professional look. Suddenly the Macintosh could play a business role that no other computer could easily duplicate.

LOOKING TO THE FUTURE
Signs of Apple's resurgence appeared as early as the fall of 1985. Steve Wozniak accepted Sculley's invitation to return to his old company as a goodwill ambassador, talking up Apple products to user groups around the world. As a show of his renewed confidence, Woz announced a large purchase of Apple stock. At a company Halloween party, Sculley showed up in white long underwear and face paint and told his fellow revelers that he was Apple's spirit brought back to life. The next year, the company posted record sales of $2 billion. In 1987, revenues jumped to $3 billion, a figure that included $2.3 billion in computer sales, with the balance in software and peripherals. Apple's totals were still far short of the $7 billion recorded for the IBM PC, but they were comfortably ahead of those of other manufacturers such as Compaq, Tandy, and Zenith.

Modifications to the Macintosh since 1984 have moved it steadily closer to the mainstream of competing business computers. The 1986 Mac Plus, for example, added a numeric keypad for customers whose primary concern was efficiency in working with spreadsheets. Completing the transformation was the Mac II, introduced in 1987. This latter-day Macintosh abandoned the distinctive upright contours of its predecessors in favor of a more conventional box with room for expansion slots, which did not exist in the original. Expansion slots opened up the Mac to customization with products from third-party hardware manufacturers. The machine could be fitted with cards that increased its memory, for example, or connected it to a wide variety of peripherals. Mac II also marked Apple's jump into the next great race for personal computers—a rush to acquire some of the powers of much larger minis and mainframes. By abandoning the 68000 microprocessor in favor of a combination of more powerful chips (the 68020 and the 68881), Apple achieved a fourfold boost in performance over the Mac Plus.

The one distinctive feature that has remained through every incarnation of the Macintosh has been its trademark graphical interface. If Apple has been forced to narrow its focus in targeting business customers, it has not lost the advantage it gained in the days when it courted a broader market. There are all sorts of people in the business world too.

Wizards of Number-Crunching

Though well known in the office for its word-processing prowess, the personal computer came into its own as an indispensable business tool with the development of spreadsheet programs, software packages that put the personal computer's resources to work on the world of numbers rather than letters. Most cover a wide range of applications, from inventory management and budgeting to all kinds of sophisticated financial and statistical analyses—particularly situations that involve repetitious mathematical calculations or large volumes of numerical data.

Spreadsheet programs provide the numerical equivalent of the word-processing program's blank page—a vast grid of cells for organizing information into rows and columns, much like the bookkeeper's ledger or the statistician's record book. These programs' special skill is being at the same time both record keeper and calculator, able to churn reams of figures through programmed computations and automatically display the results. They also are adept at creating an impression of boundless operating room, primarily through ingenious manipulation of the limited memory resources available in most personal computers.

Originally developed for mainframes, early spreadsheet programs adapted for personal computers had difficulty finding enough space in memory for an adequate number of rows and columns and were often too restricting to be of great value. Lotus 1-2-3 led the way in overcoming these problems and quickly became the industry standard, but programmers are continually devising effective new strategies for getting to the bottom line.

The following pages illustrate some of the basic features of spreadsheet programs, offering at the same time a simplified glimpse at some of the programming tricks behind a spreadsheet's seemingly effortless manipulation of numbers.

Wizards of Number-Crunching

Starting from a Clean Slate

One of the most appealing features of spreadsheet programs is the freedom they permit in the construction of individual spreadsheets. The basic rules are simple and unrestricting: Numerical values are entered into cells arranged in rows and columns, as are formulas for performing calculations with these values; the formulas are expressed in terms of cell locations rather than actual values, so that established routines can be used again and again to process new data. Within this framework, virtually any kind of organization is permissible. It is up to the spreadsheet creator to arrange information

A framework on-screen. The illustration below represents the typical display that appears on-screen when a spreadsheet program is first loaded into the computer. The spreadsheet's top and left borders label columns with letters and rows with numbers. Each intersection of row and column is an individual cell for holding a distinct item of information. Here, cell A1 has been selected; it is highlighted within the spreadsheet and also designated on the command line above the top border. A numerical value, descriptive label, or mathematical formula for a specific cell is typed in at the command line, and the data or result appears in the spreadsheet at the push of a button.

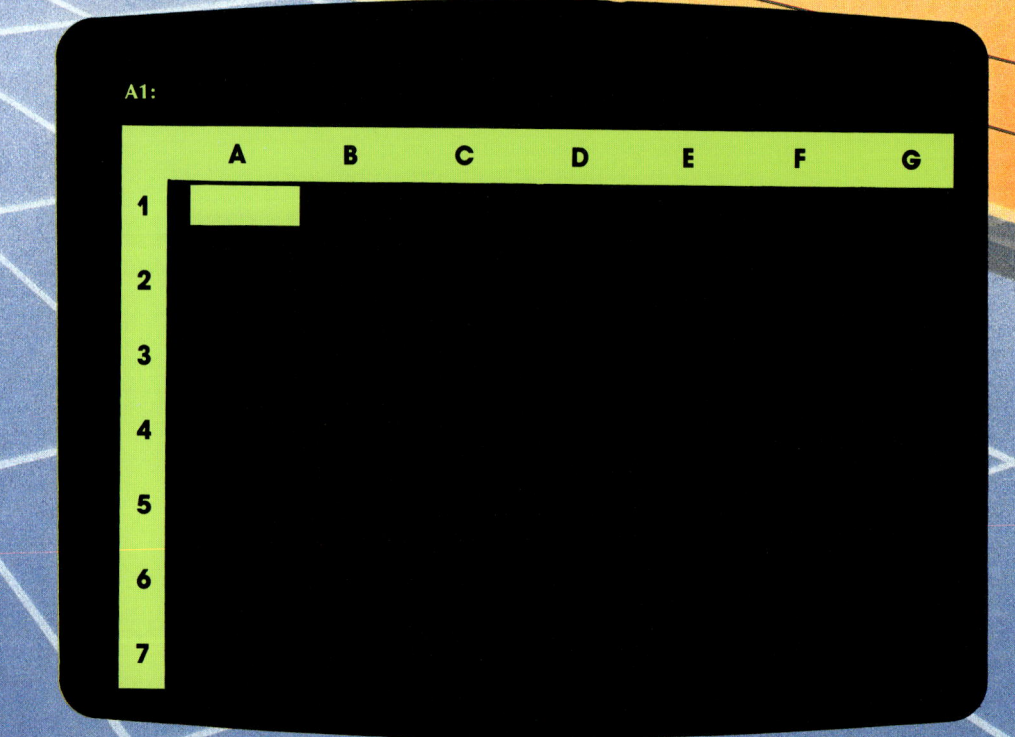

logically and construct mathematical expressions that will manipulate the data as intended.

Programs provide a variety of tools to help keep things straight and facilitate the building process. In addition to values or formulas, cells can also contain strings of characters for labeling rows, columns, or blocks of figures. Commands available through a menu make it easy to move or copy data, to define groups of cells for action, and to create formulas by invoking standard functions, such as addition or averaging, without having to spell out each mathematical step. The spreadsheet's appearance can even be altered to display values as currency, say, or to accommodate large numbers.

The ability to perform these and other tasks resides in the program coding, which takes up one of several reserved blocks in the computer's memory, as diagrammed below. The actual contents of a spreadsheet—all its values, formulas, and labels—must fit within the larger but nonetheless limited space that remains.

The memory foundation. A personal computer's internal memory, as represented schematically above, must accommodate several different functional purposes during the running of a spreadsheet program. The operating system—the indispensable coding that enables the computer to run programs—takes the first slice of memory, followed by the instructions of the spreadsheet program itself. Storage space must also be allocated for video memory, to handle the display of data on a monitor, and for scratch memory, where intermediate results in calculations are temporarily stored. The remaining memory reserves are available for the contents of any spreadsheet developed by the user.

The mechanics of scrolling. Moving around on a spreadsheet often involves scrolling, in which cells appear to roll smoothly offscreen, either up or down, or to the left or right, while new cells emerge from the opposite side. As illustrated below and opposite, the process within the computer's memory actually requires a carefully orchestrated series of steps. Below at left are displayed the contents of video memory for the first nine columns and six rows of a spreadsheet, with each cell containing its row-and-column address. When a command is issued to move three columns to the right, the program begins by erasing the three leftmost columns from video memory (below).

Wizards of Number-Crunching

Getting around in a Spreadsheet

To be at all serviceable to even the small-scale user, spreadsheets must, of course, be many times more capacious than the relatively few rows and columns that can appear on the screen at one time. In fact, columns typically number in the hundreds and rows in the thousands, so that large quantities of data can be recorded and manipulated together on one work sheet. Moving from one place to another over such a vast field requires only a few simple keystrokes. Using the appropriate command with the name of a cell currently off-screen, for example, instantly changes the display; directional keys make the spreadsheet appear to scroll across or up and down the screen to new locations. Titles for columns, entered across the top of the screen, and for rows, typed down the left side, may be "frozen" so they do not disappear from view.

Behind the scenes, some clever manipulation of memory built into the programming gets the job done. Although the spreadsheet seems to be a giant two-dimensional array of cell locations, it exists within the computer's memory as one long sequence of memory addresses, along with directions on where rows and columns begin and end. Whenever a particular move is requested, whether to jump to a new location or to scroll, the program feeds the information through an algorithm, or set of problem-solving procedures, that determines which cell addresses to send on to video memory so that the correct two-dimensional arrangement of cells ends up on the screen.

Completing the move. With the three columns to the left emptied of data, the program instructs video memory to rewrite its entire contents starting in the leftmost column, so that the three rightmost columns are emptied *(below, left)*. Having identified by a simple algorithm that the next three columns in the spreadsheet are labeled J, K, and L, the program copies the addresses of their first six rows into the three blank columns of video memory *(below, right)*. The addresses are used not only to adjust the row and column designations in the spreadsheet's on-screen borders but also to call up from the main spreadsheet memory and display any data stored for these locations.

D1	E1	F1	G1	H1	I1
D2	E2	F2	G2	H2	I2
D3	E3	F3	G3	H3	I3
D4	E4	F4	G4	H4	I4
D5	E5	F5	G5	H5	I5
D6	E6	F6	G6	H6	I6

D1	E1	F1	G1	H1	I1	J1	K1	L1
D2	E2	F2	G2	H2	I2	J2	K2	L2
D3	E3	F3	G3	H3	I3	J3	K3	L3
D4	E4	F4	G4	H4	I4	J4	K4	L4
D5	E5	F5	G5	H5	I5	J5	K5	L5
D6	E6	F6	G6	H6	I6	J6	K6	L6

Wizards of Number-Crunching

A Scheme That Conserves Memory

The size of an electronic spreadsheet is, in a sense, an illusion. Although most programs appear to provide hundreds of thousands or even millions of cells, each capable of holding hundreds of bits of information, the internal working memory of most personal computers falls far short of accommodating that much data. In practice, however, the majority of a spreadsheet's cells contain no data at all. Whole rows and columns are left blank to create spaces between categories of items and to give the work sheet a clean and uncluttered look. Another feature accounts for other cells remaining empty; long descriptive labels that do not fit into the column width displayed on the screen are allowed to extend into the space for adjacent blank cells, though the label is still stored in one cell.

Spreadsheet programs take advantage of such anticipated blanks to save space in memory. The approach is, in essence, quite simple. Whenever data is initially entered in a cell, a block of memory large enough for the cell's maximum number of characters is set aside; the next cell to be filled then receives the next reserved block, regardless of that cell's location in the spreadsheet, and no memory space is wasted on any intervening blank cells. Because cells are stored in the sequence in which they are filled and not in their row-and-column order, a separate index is needed to keep track of which saved blocks belong with which cells *(right)*.

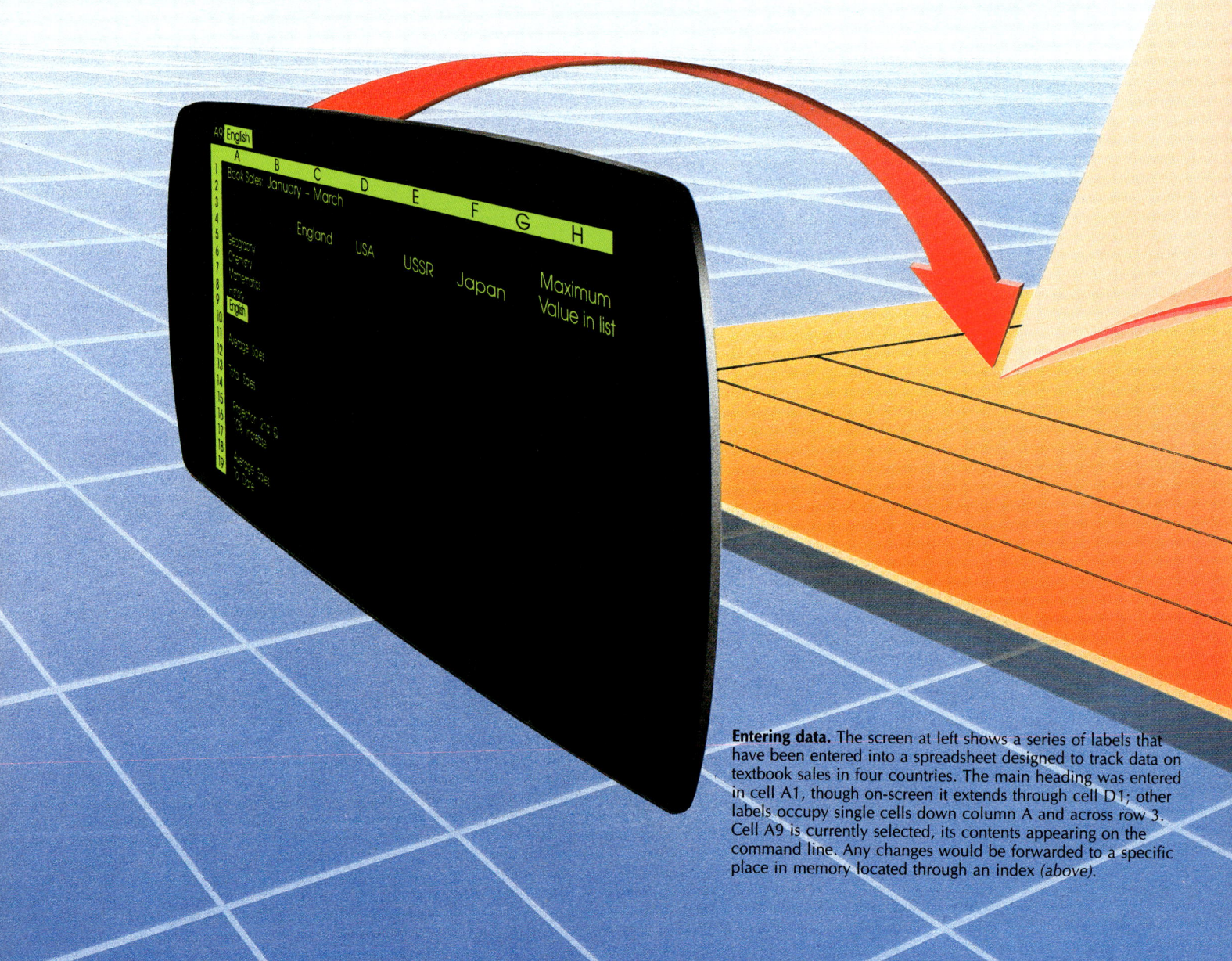

Entering data. The screen at left shows a series of labels that have been entered into a spreadsheet designed to track data on textbook sales in four countries. The main heading was entered in cell A1, though on-screen it extends through cell D1; other labels occupy single cells down column A and across row 3. Cell A9 is currently selected, its contents appearing on the command line. Any changes would be forwarded to a specific place in memory located through an index *(above)*.

74

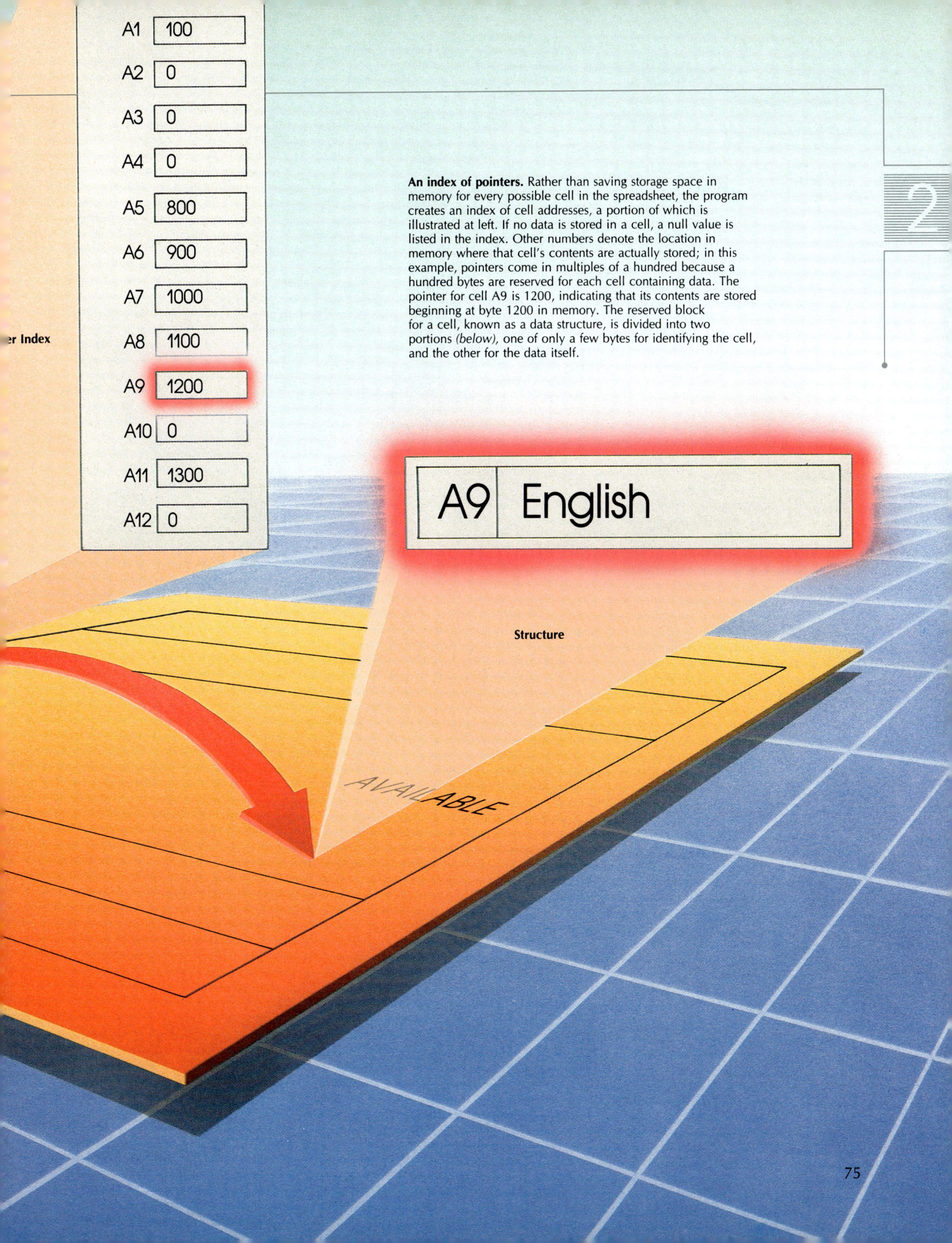

A1	100
A2	0
A3	0
A4	0
A5	800
A6	900
A7	1000
A8	1100
A9	1200
A10	0
A11	1300
A12	0

Index

An index of pointers. Rather than saving storage space in memory for every possible cell in the spreadsheet, the program creates an index of cell addresses, a portion of which is illustrated at left. If no data is stored in a cell, a null value is listed in the index. Other numbers denote the location in memory where that cell's contents are actually stored; in this example, pointers come in multiples of a hundred because a hundred bytes are reserved for each cell containing data. The pointer for cell A9 is 1200, indicating that its contents are stored beginning at byte 1200 in memory. The reserved block for a cell, known as a data structure, is divided into two portions *(below)*, one of only a few bytes for identifying the cell, and the other for the data itself.

| A9 | English |

Structure

AVAILABLE

Wizards of Number-Crunching

Tailoring a Spreadsheet's Looks

Designed for versatility, spreadsheet programs are readily able to adapt their appearance to suit many different types of numerical analysis, with minimal effort from the person entering data at the keyboard. Scientific applications, for example, may call for calculations to be carried out to many decimal places or for exponential notation to be used to express extremely large numbers. Financial work sheets re-

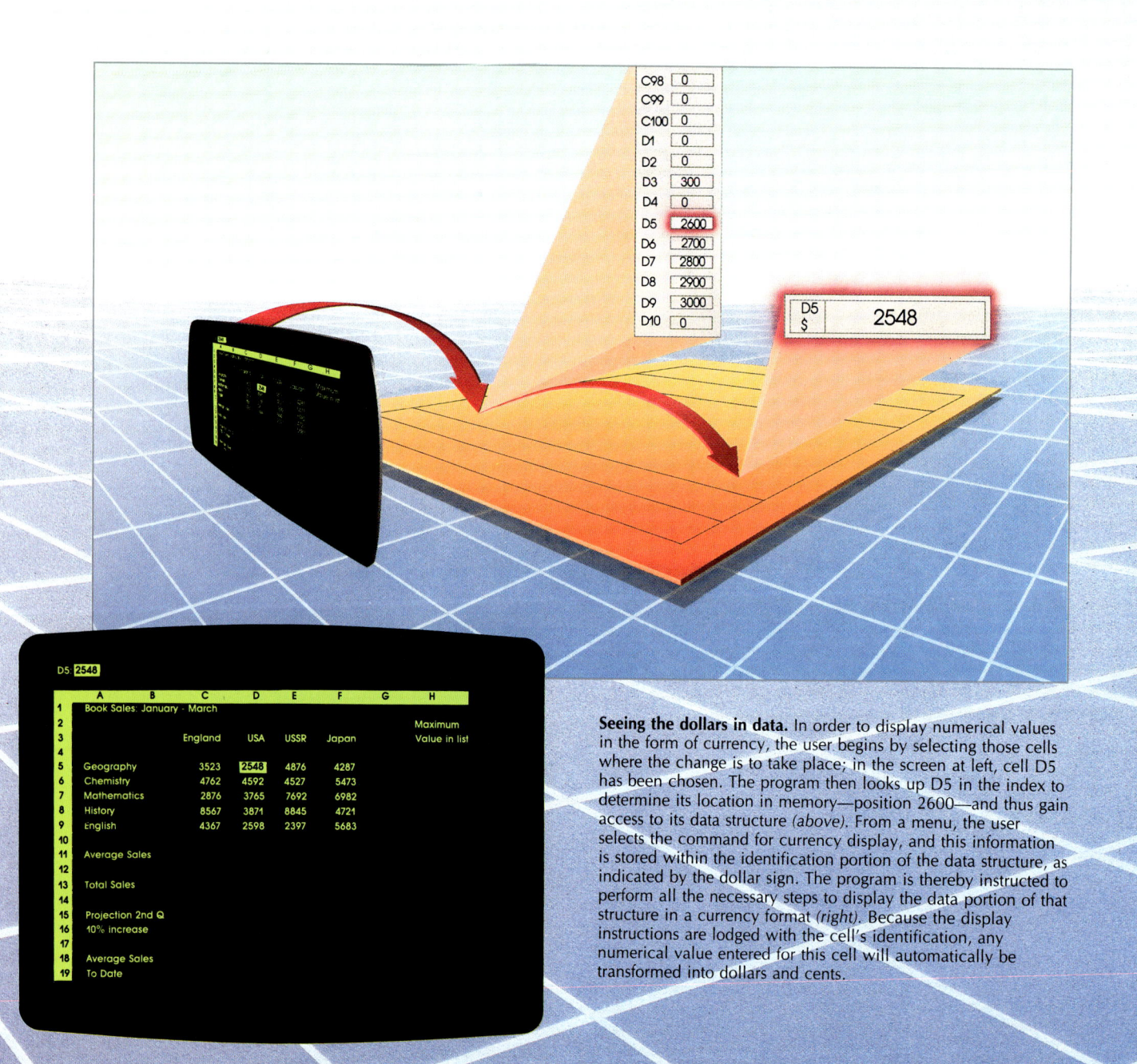

Seeing the dollars in data. In order to display numerical values in the form of currency, the user begins by selecting those cells where the change is to take place; in the screen at left, cell D5 has been chosen. The program then looks up D5 in the index to determine its location in memory—position 2600—and thus gain access to its data structure *(above)*. From a menu, the user selects the command for currency display, and this information is stored within the identification portion of the data structure, as indicated by the dollar sign. The program is thereby instructed to perform all the necessary steps to display the data portion of that structure in a currency format *(right)*. Because the display instructions are lodged with the cell's identification, any numerical value entered for this cell will automatically be transformed into dollars and cents.

quire a variety of special treatments, from currency signs and two-place decimals *(below)* to the standard fiscal idiom of parentheses to represent negative values.

The coding that automatically produces such changes is invoked with simple commands or selections from a menu, and the effects can be applied to one or a few cells or to all the figures in an entire spreadsheet. The process is essentially one of changing for selected cells the standard settings, known as defaults, that determine how data will normally be displayed. As illustrated below, changing one default may necessitate fine-tuning another: As a cell's setting is changed to currency format, which adds extra symbols, its column must be widened because, unlike labels, numerical entries are not permitted to run into neighboring cells.

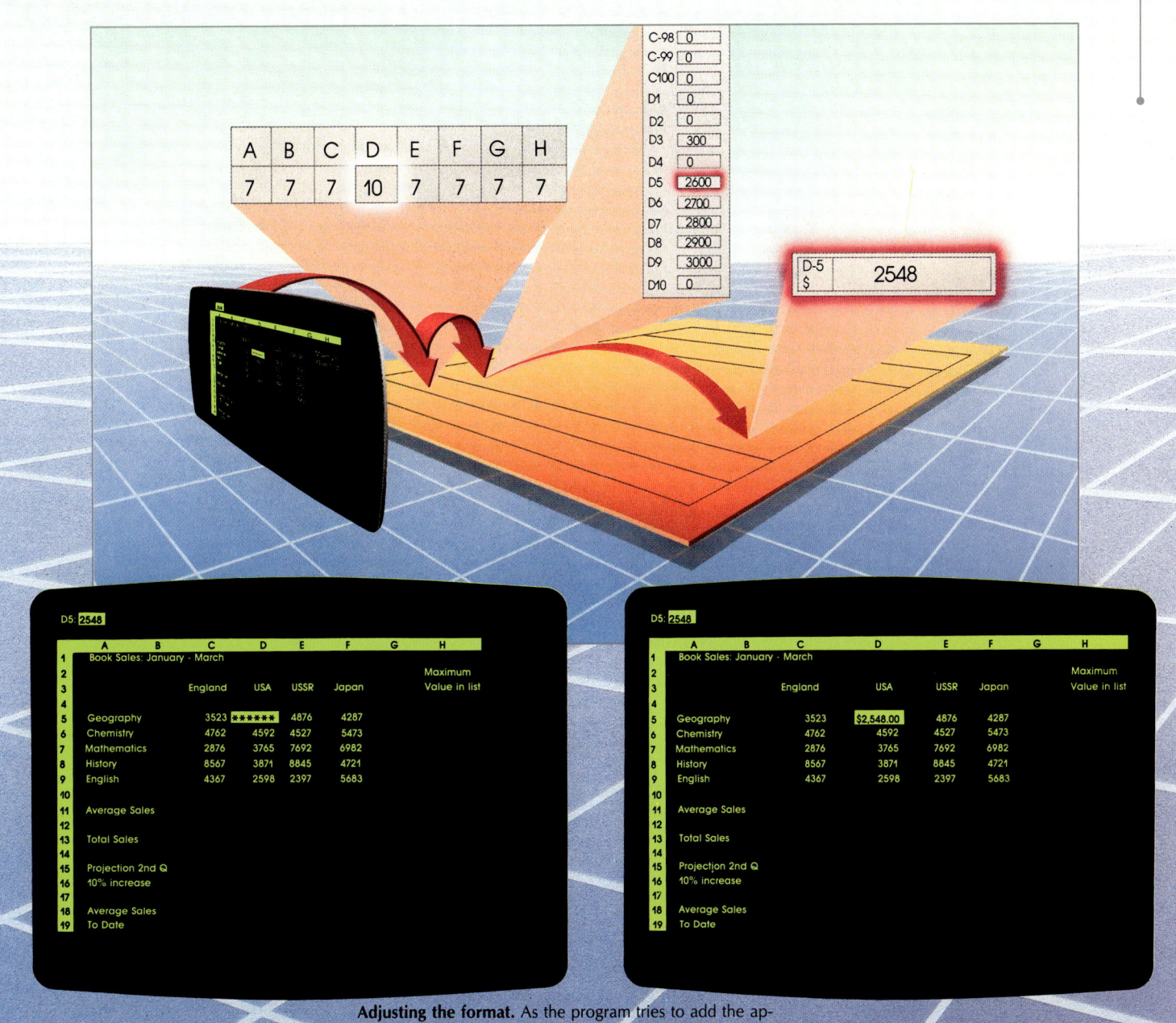

Adjusting the format. As the program tries to add the appropriate currency symbols to the data for cell D5, it runs into a problem: Column D, currently set at seven spaces, is too narrow. The program displays a row of asterisks in the cell *(above, left)*, indicating that the standard setting, or default, for column width needs to be changed. The defaults for every column are stored in the program memory, as represented by the double row of boxes at top. The user has just changed the width of column D to ten, and the program can now display the cell *(right)*, inserting a dollar sign, a comma for thousands, and a decimal point and two zeros for cents.

Wizards of Number-Crunching

A Computational Powerhouse

The most valuable aspect of any spreadsheet program is its ability to perform all sorts of calculations on stored data, from simple arithmetic to complex statistical analyses. Entering formulas is as easy as entering values or labels, and there are few limits on how the dozens of mathematical functions that a program performs can be combined.

As always, the programming is designed to make things as simple as possible. Although a formula for averaging, for example, could be entered longhand as a sequence of additions divided by the total number of entries, a built-in averaging function takes care of all the details automatically. The user need only indicate which cells the function encompasses, employing the range command to save listing cells individually. Ranges can define rows, columns, an individual cell, or blocks of cells by their two outermost entries. In the example below, the range covers the five entries in column C. Had the range been stated as C5..D9, a two-column block of ten cells would have been defined.

Among other conveniences, when a formula is copied from one column to another, the program adjusts the targeted range accordingly; the formula for C11, for example, if copied to D11, would average column D. A single, perhaps complex, computation can thus process many different sets of data without having to be rewritten each time.

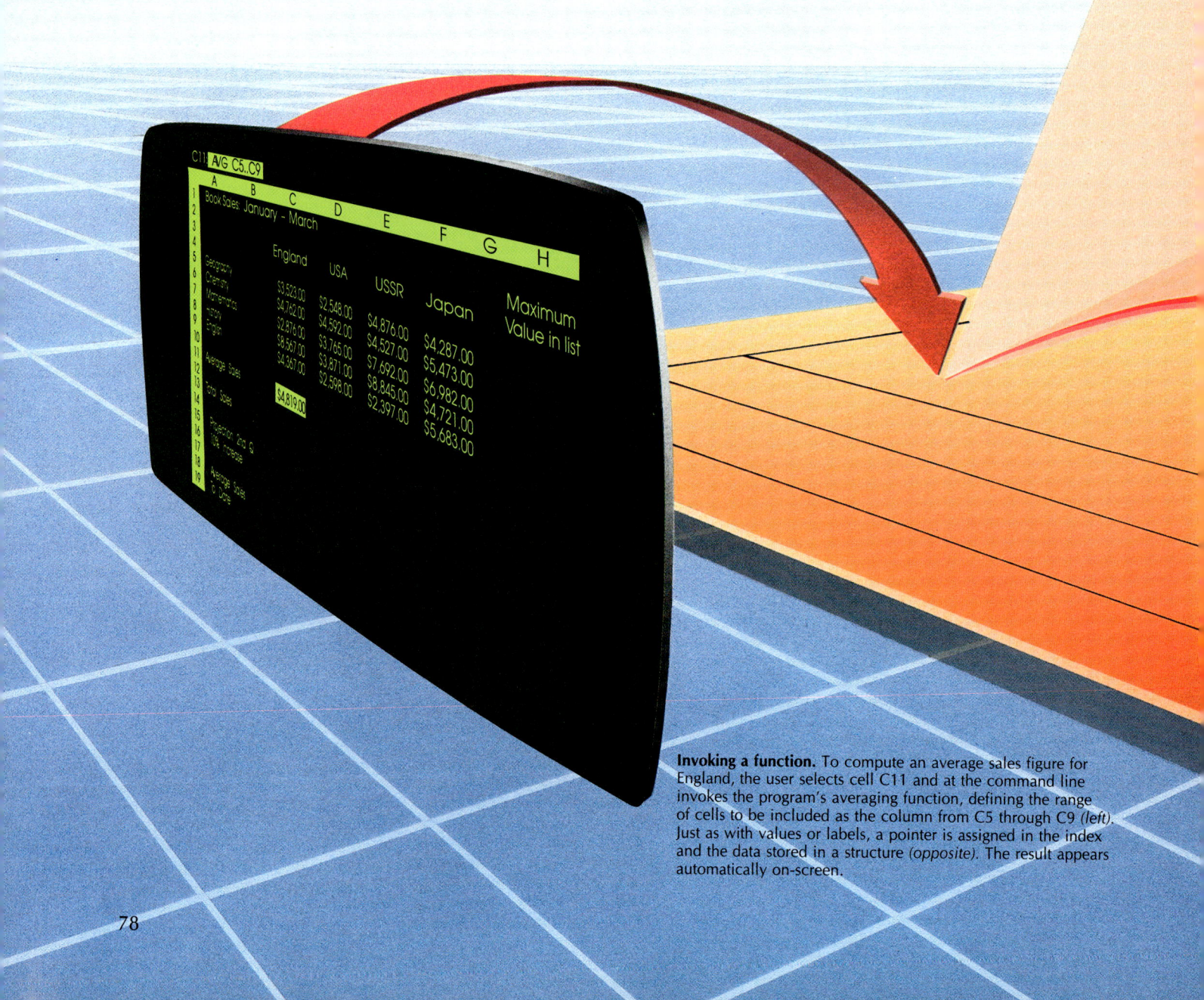

Invoking a function. To compute an average sales figure for England, the user selects cell C11 and at the command line invokes the program's averaging function, defining the range of cells to be included as the column from C5 through C9 *(left)*. Just as with values or labels, a pointer is assigned in the index and the data stored in a structure *(opposite)*. The result appears automatically on-screen.

A specially defined structure. When the data for cell C11 is loaded at memory address 4100, an *F* is placed in the identification portion of the structure *(below)*, denoting that the structure contains a function. This tells the program to find in its memory the appropriate instructions for that function and, once the calculations are complete, to display the result rather than what was entered at the command line. As the function runs, the program will hop from the C11 structure to the index and then to those structures where the values for each cell listed in the formula are stored.

Wizards of Number-Crunching

A Shortcut to Updated Results

As more and more formulas are worked into a spreadsheet, an intricate weave of relationships among cells develops and complicates one of the program's most basic tasks—updating calculations as new information is entered. Frequently, changing the value of one cell can set in motion a long chain of recalculations, especially when formulas themselves are interconnected and the alteration has many indirect consequences. A program that missed even one out of dozens of relationships would be utterly worthless, its error compounding every time new data was entered.

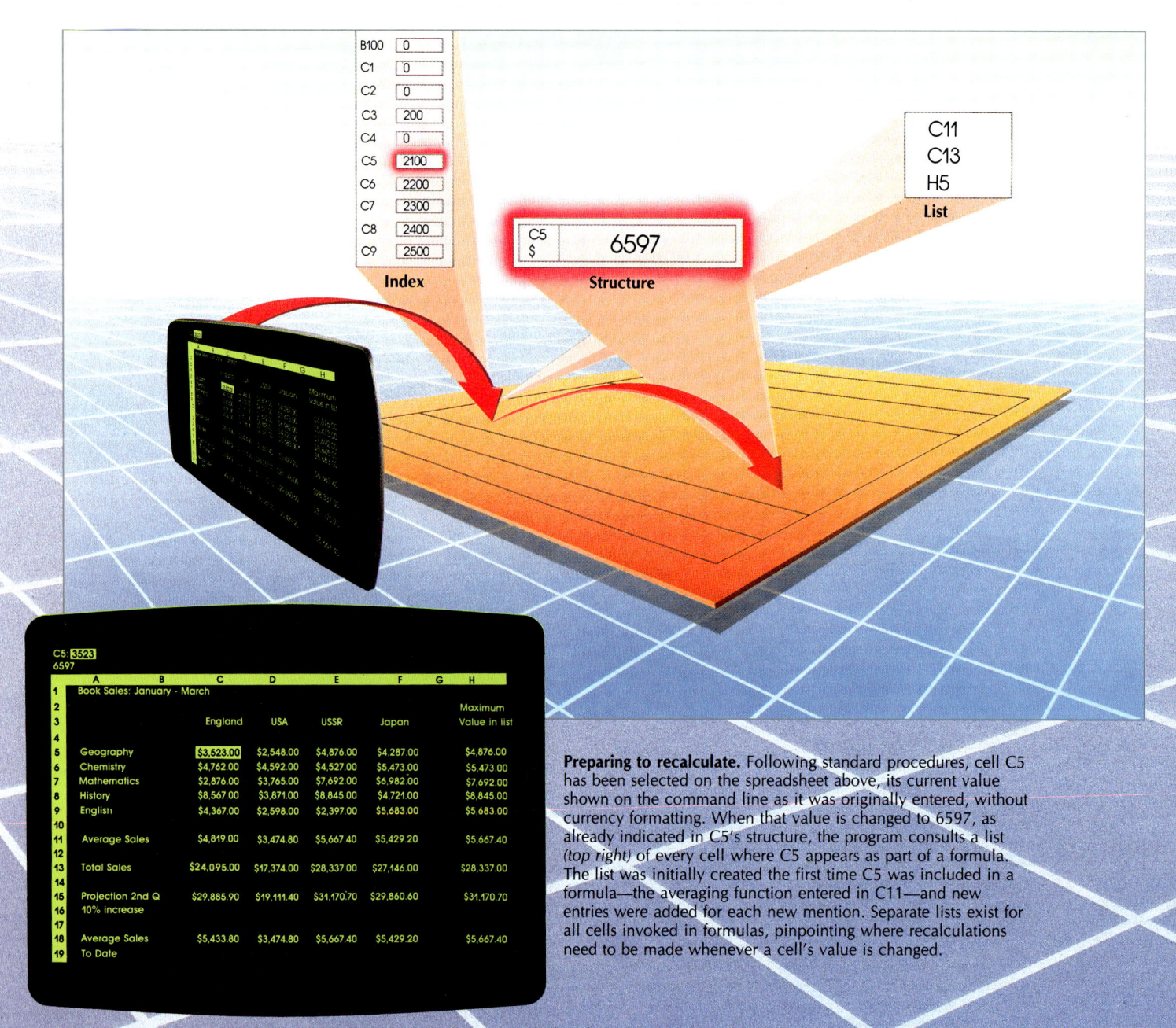

Preparing to recalculate. Following standard procedures, cell C5 has been selected on the spreadsheet above, its current value shown on the command line as it was originally entered, without currency formatting. When that value is changed to 6597, as already indicated in C5's structure, the program consults a list *(top right)* of every cell where C5 appears as part of a formula. The list was initially created the first time C5 was included in a formula—the averaging function entered in C11—and new entries were added for each new mention. Separate lists exist for all cells invoked in formulas, pinpointing where recalculations need to be made whenever a cell's value is changed.

One of the earliest methods of ensuring that no oversights occur was to design the program to recalculate every formula throughout the spreadsheet whenever a value was changed, regardless of whether that formula was affected. Although it was reliable, this approach could be quite time-consuming, particularly if a whole series of changes were being entered. To help speed things along, some program designers introduced a special function that allowed the user to enter multiple changes before invoking the recalculation procedure; even with this improvement, the computer often still had to plow needlessly through totally unrelated computations.

A more efficient tactic, illustrated below, makes use of relatively small amounts of the spreadsheet's available memory to keep track of each cell's relationships, listing them as formulas are created. Recalculations can then be aimed at affected cells only.

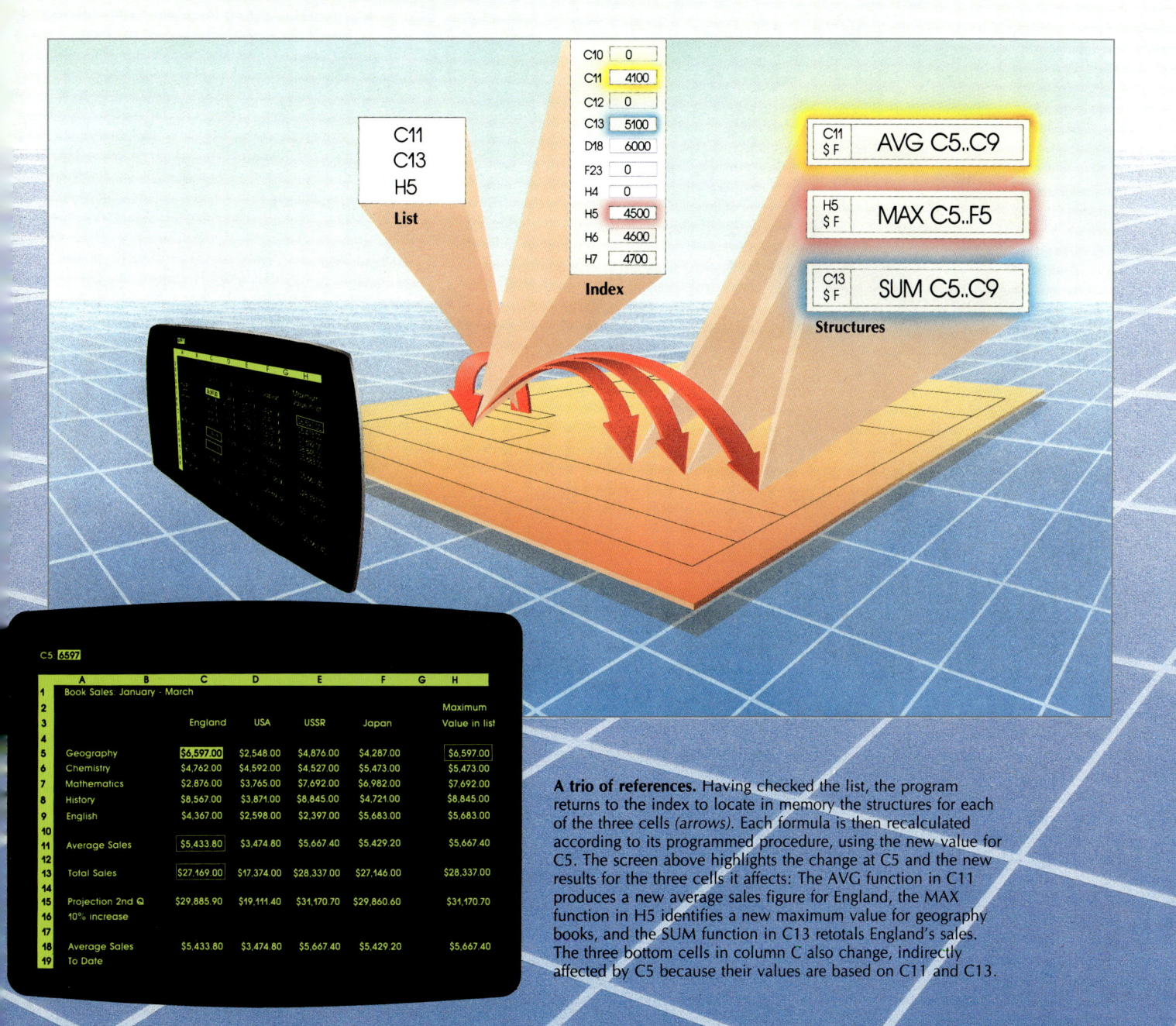

A trio of references. Having checked the list, the program returns to the index to locate in memory the structures for each of the three cells *(arrows)*. Each formula is then recalculated according to its programmed procedure, using the new value for C5. The screen above highlights the change at C5 and the new results for the three cells it affects: The AVG function in C11 produces a new average sales figure for England, the MAX function in H5 identifies a new maximum value for geography books, and the SUM function in C13 retotals England's sales. The three bottom cells in column C also change, indirectly affected by C5 because their values are based on C11 and C13.

81

Wizards of Number-Crunching

Pathways between Spreadsheets

For a variety of reasons, data is often best handled in a series of separate spreadsheets rather than in a single, all-encompassing giant. Smaller spreadsheets are less likely to strain the resources of a personal computer's internal working memory; once a particular work sheet has been completed, it can be stored out of the way on disk, clearing the memory decks for the next creation. Smaller spreadsheets are also usually simpler in structure, less prone to error, and easier to diagnose if problems arise. In a large spreadsheet, formulas often become extremely complex, and mistakes are not only harder to trace but can be more devastating in effect.

Operating in a smaller framework requires programming techniques that enable spreadsheets to share information, as in the example below. The process begins when the user names a cell or range of cells in the current work sheet, intending to carry the values or results of formulas to a second sheet. The first sheet is then stored to disk and the second created or loaded into the computer's working memory. At the selected location, the user enters the name of the range and which work sheet it comes from. The program searches the disk and brings the original sheet into memory, locating the appropriate structures and supplying their contents to the new sheet. The first sheet is then returned to disk.

The computer's memory must, of course, be able to hold two spreadsheets at once, but links can be passed on in this fashion to numerous sheets, one pair at a time.

A chain of dependent cells. The four screens at left represent four separate spreadsheets that track book sales over the four quarters of the year. The structure and formulas in the top section of the first work sheet *(far left)* were copied wholesale to subsequent sheets, with the main heading changed and new values inserted. The last three or four rows, which reflect an accrual of information from one spreadsheet to the next, depend on a series of links between cells in different sheets. The arrows at left represent the three types of connections, which actually involve all the cells in all of these rows during each exchange: A projection made on the first spreadsheet about sales in the second quarter becomes input to the second spreadsheet for calculating how much actual sales varied from the estimate; and both average and total sales are kept up to date through links with previous sheets.

Wizards of Number-Crunching

Graphic Perspectives on Spreadsheet Data

Although they are perfectly suited to the recordkeeping and data-manipulation tasks for which they are designed, a spreadsheet's rows and columns are often less than ideal at revealing the story behind the numbers. To compensate, spreadsheet programs generally include graphics capabilities that enable users to visualize the relationships among selected items of information, turning unenlightening ranks of figures into eye-pleasing charts and graphs that help make the significant statistics stand out.

The process of converting numbers into images involves additional manipulations of a spreadsheet's values, performed through algorithms stored in the program's memory that take into account the dimensions of the screen and the type of display selected, such as bar graph, plotted line, or pie chart. These intricate procedures, as well as the program's skillful maneuvering through multiple pointer indexes when data comes from more than one spreadsheet *(below)*, are entirely hidden from the user, who simply selects a graphics option from the menu and names ranges of cells.

A fringe benefit of visual representations is their ability to unmask errors. If one value in a series of plotted points is way out of line with all the others, it indicates more clearly than figures in a spreadsheet row or column that a mistake may have been made.

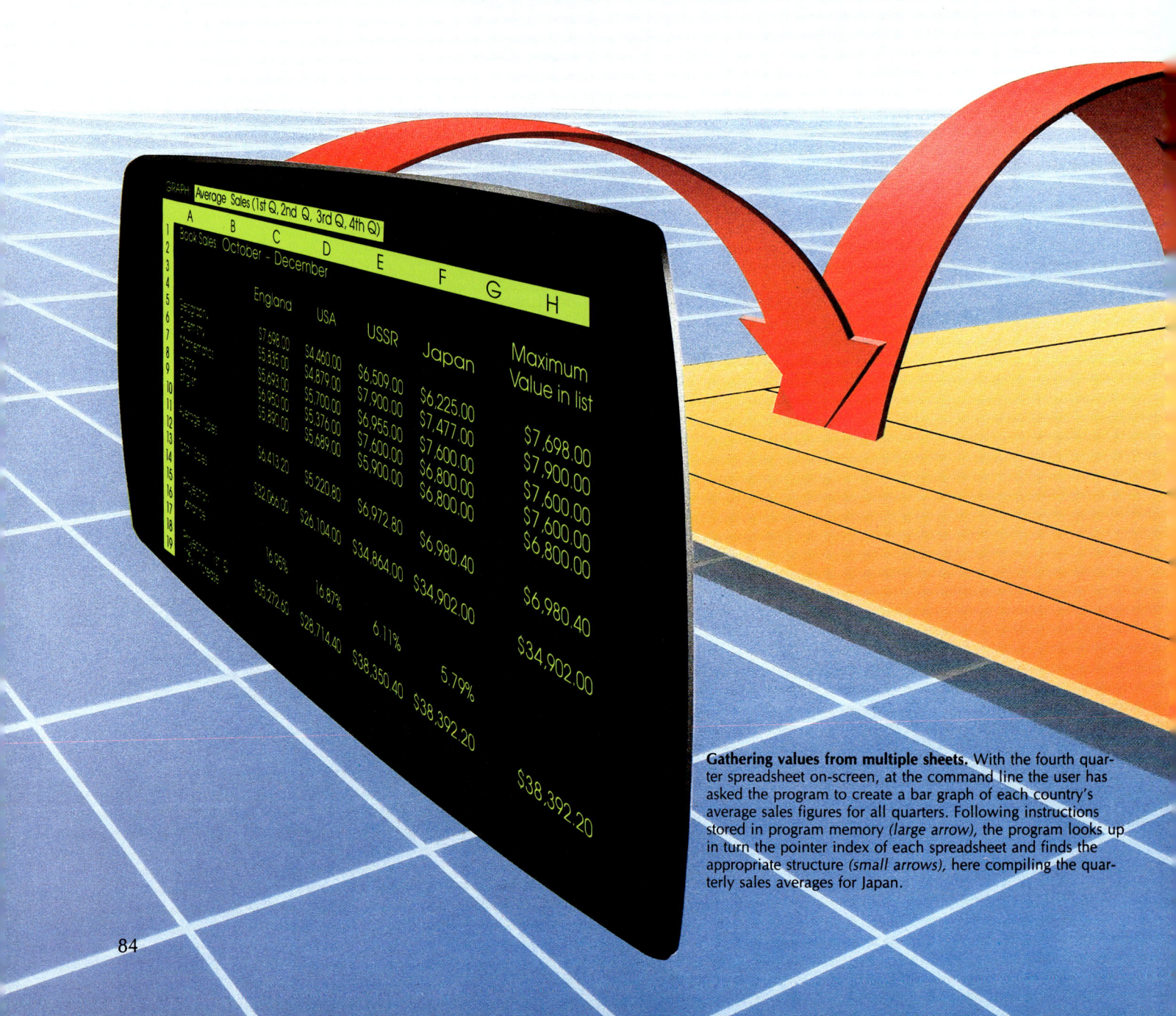

Gathering values from multiple sheets. With the fourth quarter spreadsheet on-screen, at the command line the user has asked the program to create a bar graph of each country's average sales figures for all quarters. Following instructions stored in program memory *(large arrow)*, the program looks up in turn the pointer index of each spreadsheet and finds the appropriate structure *(small arrows)*, here compiling the quarterly sales averages for Japan.

84

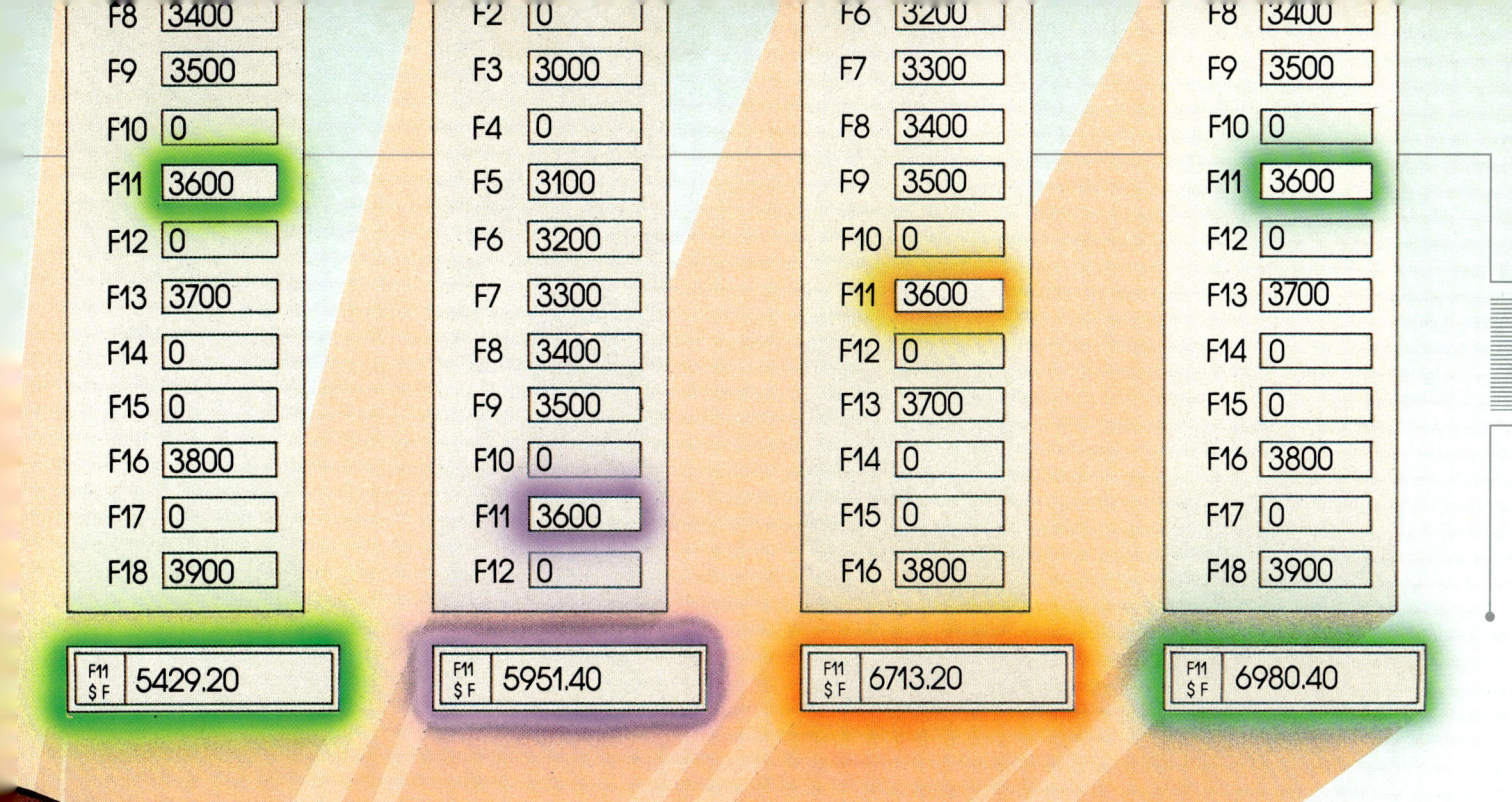

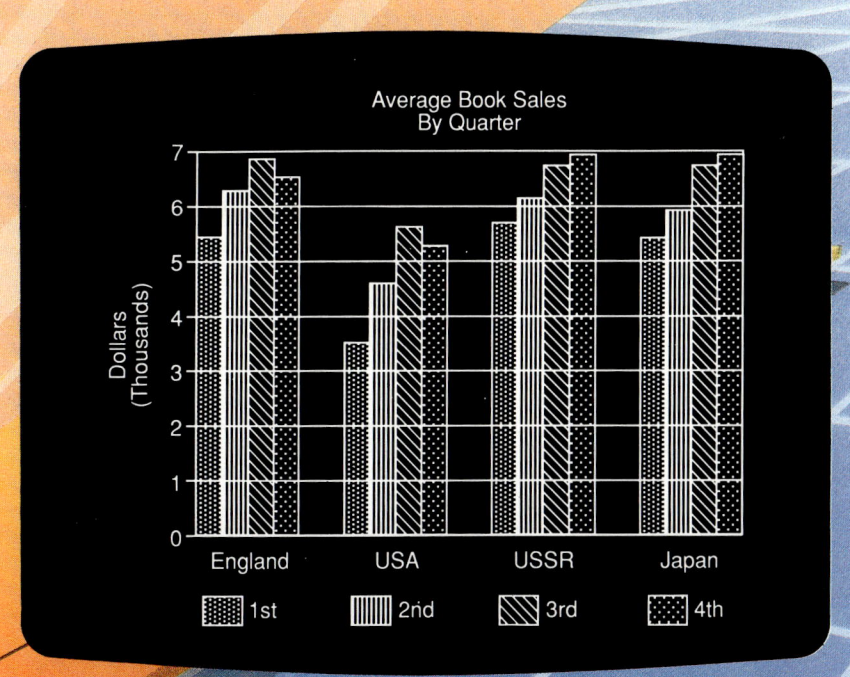

F8	3400
F9	3500
F10	0
F11	3600
F12	0
F13	3700
F14	0
F15	0
F16	3800
F17	0
F18	3900

F2	0
F3	3000
F4	0
F5	3100
F6	3200
F7	3300
F8	3400
F9	3500
F10	0
F11	3600
F12	0

F6	3200
F7	3300
F8	3400
F9	3500
F10	0
F11	3600
F12	0
F13	3700
F14	0
F15	0
F16	3800

F8	3400
F9	3500
F10	0
F11	3600
F12	0
F13	3700
F14	0
F15	0
F16	3800
F17	0
F18	3900

F11 $F	5429.20
F11 $F	5951.40
F11 $F	6713.20
F11 $F	6980.40

Average Book Sales By Quarter

Dollars (Thousands) — England, USA, USSR, Japan — 1st, 2nd, 3rd, 4th

Graphing the results. Once all the average sales figures have been compiled, the program invokes an algorithm that creates a vertical scale related to the screen's dimensions and based on the highest figure in the group—Japan's fourth quarter average of nearly $7,000 *(top right)*. The algorithm then calculates each figure's position on the scale, creating a bar graph that gives a quick picture of annual trends and comparative averages from country to country. Other comparisons could have been charted merely by naming different combinations of cells.

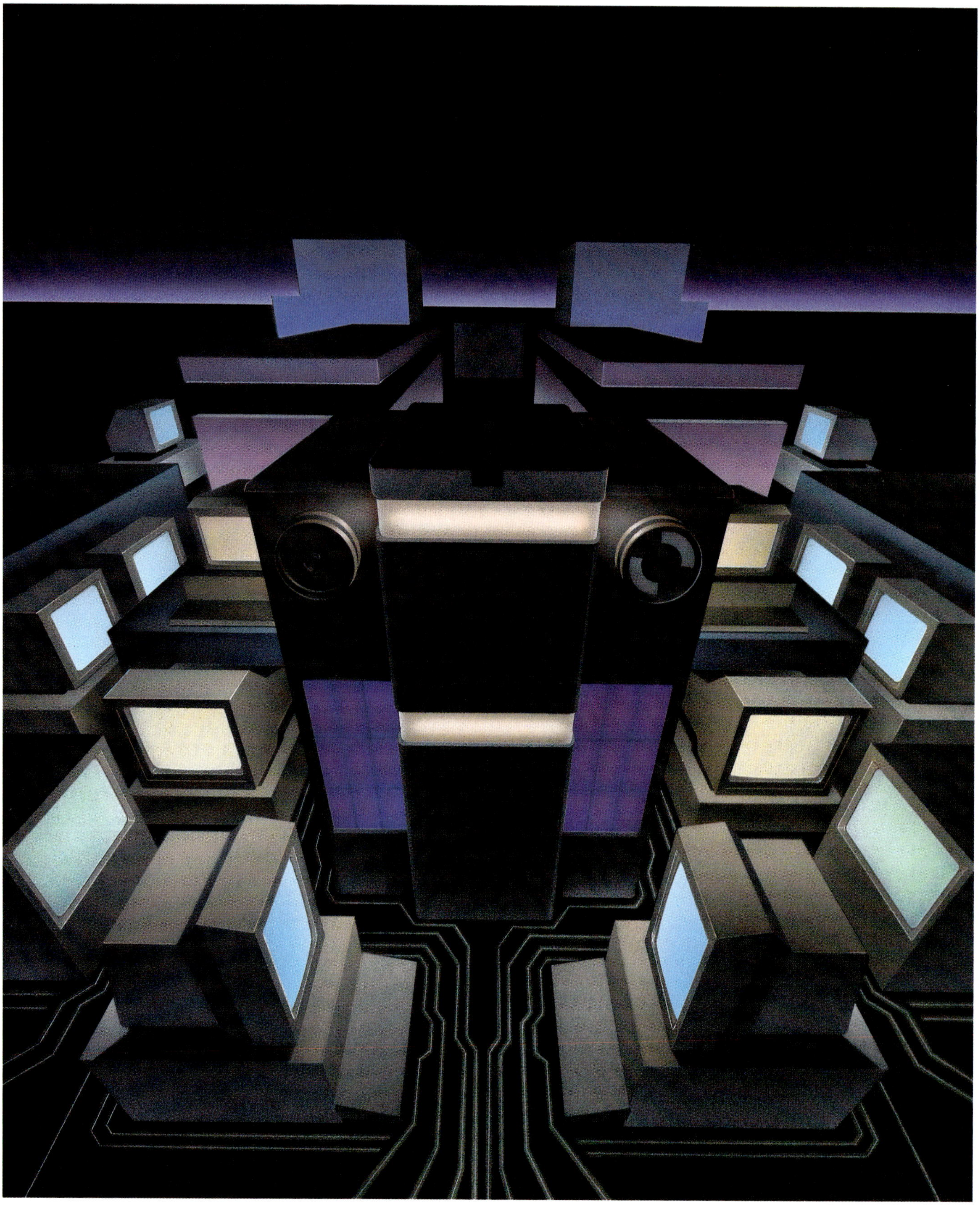

Challenging the Mainframe

In 1985, with the United States petroleum industry in a slump, oil-related businesses nationwide were forced to retrench. Fish Engineering & Construction, Inc., a Houston firm specializing in the design and building of petrochemical refineries, felt the economic pinch keenly, and company president Jim Boyd was on the prowl for economies. First to go was the corporate jet. With that cash hemorrhage stanched, the most objectionable expense was the $280,000 that Fish Engineering spent each year on its IBM 4341 computer and its data-processing staff. The company relied on this small mainframe principally for keeping records and preparing technical specifications for plants under development. Engineers and clerical workers tapped into the 4341 by means of ten so-called dumb terminals, which derived their power entirely from the central computer. Surveying the situation, Boyd began to wonder if some other configuration might suffice.

The outlook seemed bleak. One consultant advised that a computer any smaller than the IBM would be incapable of the work expected of it. An IBM sales representative suggested upgrading to an even larger and more expensive model. However, Boyd had recently become an aficionado of personal computers, and he knew that others in the company had already begun to use them in their work. Although the machines were less powerful than the mainframe, he and his staff were carefully watching trends in the microcomputer world and felt sure that PCs would soon be capable of handling their needs.

In late 1985, Fish took the plunge and bought a dozen personal computers—mostly Deskpro 286s from Compaq Computer Corporation—and joined them in a network. When the more powerful Deskpro 386 became available in September 1986, Fish snapped up several of them. Within three short years, the company would see business rebound and its personal computer network expand to 130 stations.

Predating IBM's PS/2 Model 80 by more than a year, the Deskpro 386 was the first microcomputer built around Intel Corporation's powerful 80386 microprocessor. In the mid-1980s, as the 80386 chip was being designed at Intel, Compaq had just begun planning a new generation of personal computers. Having employed Intel microprocessors in all its earlier computers and seeing enormous promise in the new one, the hard-charging Houston company arranged to confer with the chipmaker as the circuitry took shape. Compaq hoped to ensure that its evolving product would have maximum compatibility with existing peripherals and software. During the entire course of the chip's development, engineers from the two companies consulted over the features that the new microprocessor would comprise.

In every respect, the 80386 was an elegantly engineered marvel. Designed to execute program instructions and move data to and from memory in thirty-two-bit chunks, the 80386 could perform the same operations with eight-bit or sixteen-bit parcels, assuring the software and hardware compatibility so important to Compaq. With a thirty-two-bit memory address, the chip could address 256 times the memory accessible to Intel's preceding generation of microprocessors with its twenty-four-bit address. And the 80386 was astonishingly fast. Operating at a clock speed of sixteen megahertz (MHz), it could execute up to four million instructions per second—a measure of computer speed known as MIPS. Subsequent versions of the chip would clock at twenty and twenty-five megahertz, yielding an even more impressive top performance of six to seven MIPS, and ultimately, clock speed would rise to thirty-three megahertz. A reviewer summed up the response to the new chip: "Twelve years ago when the 8080 microprocessor first became available, not everyone agreed that it could power a small computer. With the 80386, there's no longer any doubt about what it was designed for and what we can use it for. The 80386 is for doing work. Lots of it."

At Fish Engineering, the speed of the 80386 microprocessor led to a significant increase in productivity. Because the IBM 4341 sauntered along at the rate of about one MIPS, the effective speed for each worker with ten terminals attached to the machine was approximately forty times less than the power provided by the four-MIPS Compaqs. Furthermore, the price of the 4341 had been in the neighborhood of $25,000 per terminal; for the Compaq 386s, Fish Engineering spent less than $10,000 per terminal. That figure included the installation of a network to tie all the machines to a centralized program- and data-storage facility with a capacity of 300 megabytes (300 million bytes)—as well as to printers and other peripheral equipment. In addition, the cost of keeping Fish's computer system up and running dropped more than 75 percent the first year to $65,000.

Fish dedicated fifty Compaq 386s to computer-aided design (CAD) and computer-aided engineering. Equipped with oversized, crisp-imaged monitors, these computers enabled the company's engineers to prepare electrical charts, piping diagrams, and flow sheets electronically rather than manually. Such capabilities would have been prohibitively expensive to duplicate on the 4341, which was basically a glorified bookkeeping and calculating machine. For example, there was no program for the IBM machine at a reasonable price that would operate a plotter, so plans and diagrams had to be rendered by hand.

Switching to microcomputers eliminated this costly and time-consuming step. At every stage, the engineers can send copies of drawings to their colleagues over the network. In the field, Fish engineers who supervise plant construction carry portable Compaq computers right onto building sites in order to track men and materials. Advances such as these permitted Fish Engineering to lower its prices to customers by as much as four percent.

A GIANT STEP UPWARD
Soon after bringing out its Deskpro 386, Compaq Computer had company in pioneering the microcomputer stratosphere. Dell Computer and other firms jumped on the Compaq bandwagon with their own PCs based on Intel's 80386 chips. In IBM's new PS/2 line, the Model 80 incorporated the 80386 microprocessor. Apple introduced the Macintosh II, powered by the 68020, an advanced thirty-two-bit chip from Motorola that was comparable in many ways to the Intel microprocessor. As these computers and others like them became available, they helped to further obscure distinctions between different tiers of computing that had evolved during the preceding two decades or so.

In the beginning, there was only one kind of computer—the mainframe. Over the years, mainframe central processing units, built of many integrated circuits spread over numerous circuit boards, became increasingly potent. Almost regardless of cost, they were designed with the intention of wringing the most MIPS possible from succeeding generations of technology. Just as extracting the last horsepower from a race-car engine results in a power plant that costs many times as much as the one in the average automobile, optimizing the CPU performance made for expensive electronics.

Rapid access to huge stores of data was another consideration—and one requiring expensive "smart" disk drives that, instead of handling requests for information as they arrived from the processing unit, rearranged them to minimize time spent searching for the next parcel of data on the disk. Mainframes also had operating systems that facilitated communications with many terminals. Computers with these capabilities could command high prices in the scientific community because blinding speed enabled the machines to solve increasingly complex problems in physics, chemistry, and astronomy. In the business world, speed permitted a mainframe to serve many users at once by giving each a short turn on the CPU.

In 1960, Digital Equipment Corporation moved into the lower end of these markets by introducing the minicomputer. Less powerful than a mainframe, the machines suited many enterprises the way Baby Bear's chair fit Goldilocks—just right. Although DEC's first computer, the PDP-1, cost a hefty $120,000, the price of a mini plummeted in 1963 with the arrival of the PDP-8. At $18,000 each, the PDP-8 was so inexpensive that small companies and departments of large corporations could get into the computing game for a reasonable price. Other organizations could afford to outfit individual engineers and scientists with machines of their own. Professionals who shared a mainframe to help design machinery or solve the mysteries of science, for example, might have to wait hours to receive the results of their labors from the data-processing center. A personal minicomputer could reduce this enforced idleness to minutes, substantially increasing productivity.

Sensing an opportunity, companies such as Apollo Computer outside Boston and Sun Microsystems in California began producing machines called work stations, which they optimized for the computer-intensive graphics programs common in engineering. Beginning in 1980, Apollo introduced a line of such work stations built around Motorola's 68000 series of microprocessors. Soon thereafter, Sun Microsystems introduced competing machines. At prices ranging between $20,000 and $80,000, such computers offered better performance for less money than a general-purpose minicomputer.

A CONFUSING HIERARCHY

The arrival of thirty-two-bit PCs such as the Deskpro 386, the Macintosh II, and the PS/2 Model 80 further complicated the computing landscape, creating yet another stratum of processing power. In this fast-changing terrain, personal computers such as the IBM PC, the AT, and their imitators—all operating at speeds of one MIPS or less—occupied the lowest stratigraphic level. Atop the PCs lay graphics work stations for engineers. With innards resembling a cross between a PC and a minicomputer, they processed two million to eight million instructions per second, performance comparable to a variety of minicomputers.

Machines at the upper end of this second layer overlapped the lower regions of the next tier, which was occupied by mainframes. Although many of these computers operated at speeds in the neighborhood of fifty MIPS, the boundary between minis and mainframes was hard to distinguish. For example, the one-MIPS IBM 4341 that Fish Engineering retired in 1986 was considered by some to be a small mainframe and by others to be a very large minicomputer. Regardless of classification, it was nearly worthless by then. Fish sold the machine for parts, netting less than $2,000.

Like social-climbing nouveaux riches, personal computers leaped up the computing ladder. By 1988, Motorola had speeded its 68000 series of microprocessors into the minicomputer and work-station range of six to seven MIPS, as Intel had done with its 80386 microprocessor. And even more powerful chips—the so-called reduced instruction set microprocessors—were on the horizon. Based on well-known methods for optimizing speed that had fallen into disfavor with computer designers, such chips are inherently much faster than ordinary microprocessors. They promised performance well within the mainframe stratum. And at a projected cost of about $600 per MIPS, such machines would tantalize users with enormous computing power at a bargain rate compared to mainframes, which commonly sell for about $120,000 per MIPS.

When Fish Engineering purchased its first thirty-two-bit computers in 1986, the company was one of only a handful of enterprises willing to risk trading the tried-and-true mainframe for a largely untested concept—a network of interconnected microprocessors. During the following two years, however, many other organizations, in fields as diverse as finance, the lumber business, architecture, and ship design, joined the engineering company in pioneering the personal-computer alternative.

TO EACH HIS OWN
At the Wall Street firm Shearson Lehman Hutton, for example, traders in the fast-paced auction of over-the-counter stocks were slowed in their work by a system of dumb terminals that displayed market information. Pairs of Shearson traders shared a suite of hardware that consisted of four terminals and four keyboards. Competition for use of the keyboards to call for the latest stock

quotations, market statistics, technical analyses, and other information often delayed the brokers' reaction to changing market conditions—a serious problem. As David Serena, vice president for trading at Shearson, noted: "Thirty seconds is an enormous amount of time in our business."

A move in 1988 to a new building in New York City's World Financial Center presented Shearson with an opportunity to streamline the delivery of trading information to its agents. Instead of sharing equipment, each trader was given a thirty-two-bit personal computer equipped with a high-resolution monitor that was large enough to display information from as many as four services simultaneously in separate areas, or windows—each of which could be enlarged to fill the entire screen.

The PCs offered a number of speed advantages. And unlike dumb terminals, they could be programmed to automatically update the monitor with fresh data, largely eliminating the need to query information services by keyboard for the latest facts. Confronted by a single monitor and keyboard instead of four—and relieved of sharing equipment with a partner—each trader could respond to the marketplace much more swiftly. And there was an unexpected bonus: restarting a personal computer after a system failure took only fifteen seconds, one-sixth as long as the old system.

Integrating the display of information onto a single monitor, however helpful, hardly exhausts Shearson's ambitions for personal computers in its trading operations. For example, customized software will enable the machines to monitor incoming data and sound an alert, say, when the price of a particular stock begins to fall or rise. Or the computers can be programmed with a stock-trading expert system that will signal the traders when changes in interest rates and the price of a commodity such as oil, for example, combine to create an opportunity to buy or sell a stock for a profit.

High-powered micros have also helped the Weyerhaeuser Company, the world's largest timber company, to better husband its fourteen million acres of forests in the United States and Canada. Weyerhaeuser augmented its mainframe computer with 2,000 personal computers installed in sawmills, warehouses, and headquarters offices. The computers help keep tabs on trees throughout their history, from seedling to finished lumber. For example, calculating shipping charges for products sent by truck and rail across North America entails complex computations involving a multitude of transportation companies, rates, regulations, and tariffs. "All these details affect the cost of a single shipment," says Bruce Sanchez, senior sales representative for Weyerhaeuser Information Systems. "A computerized freight-modeling system is an economic necessity." So complicated are such assessments that they had always been a job for a mainframe. But in an effort to decentralize and thereby speed this work, Weyerhaeuser developed a shipping-charge program for its thirty-two-bit personal computers. It worked so well that the company named it ExcelleRate and began selling it to other businesses.

Weyerhaeuser is also experimenting with the use of its speediest desktop machines to glean from satellite photographs clues about the age and health of forests. To inventory timberlands without this technology, crews must scour the woods in surveys that take months to complete. In Weyerhaeuser's tests, a photograph is loaded into a personal computer through a digitizer. Then the PC compares the picture to a database containing results of ground-level surveys of the same areas. Details in the photographs are related to species, height, and probable age of timber stands as confirmed by human observation. The correlations thus established are used to interpret satellite pictures of thousands of timberland acres that have never been surveyed on foot. To display a satellite photograph on the screen, the computer must process more than 38 million bytes of data, yet the twenty-megahertz microcomputers used in the Weyerhaeuser tests can present such an image in little more than a minute, a speed that compares favorably with the performance of graphics work stations.

DESIGNER'S AMANUENSIS
The ability of personal computers to exhibit two-dimensional images such as photographs or engineering drawings lies behind one of the machines' most remarkable applications—computer-aided design and drafting. Developed in the early 1980s, CAD for microprocessors soon became a billion-dollar business. By the time thirty-two-bit PCs came along, many thousands of microcomputer CAD systems were in use everywhere from high-school drafting classes to top-secret military laboratories. Programs ranged from the modest to the ornate.

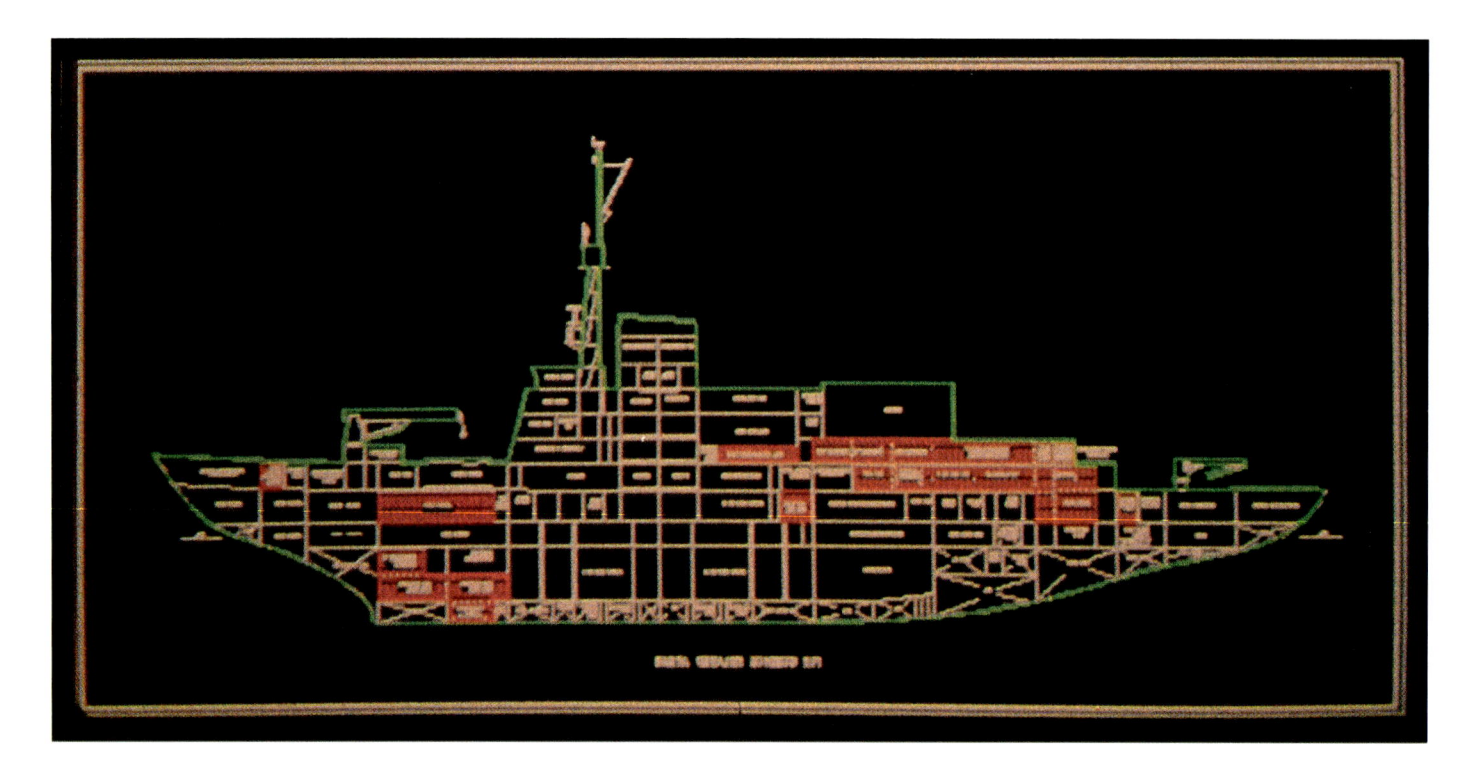

AutoSketch, for example, turned out simple, two dimensional drawings; written for the basic IBM PC and clones, the program cost less than $100. At the pinnacle of this kind of software were programs for IBM ATs and other 80286 machines that rendered much more complex two-dimensional shapes; such programs cost as much as $3,500.

Even the best of this software could be almost painfully slow on the computers that it was written for when called upon to deal with complicated drawings. But when run on a thirty-two-bit machine, the same programs did their work in a trice. As a result, many organizations that depended on electronic drafting assistance chose personal computers rather than minis as their tool. Such was the decision reached by the U.S. Coast Guard's Naval Engineering Division after an in-depth study of available CAD systems.

Naval Engineering's full-time charge is to keep the Coast Guard fleet trim and up-to-date. Doing so entails not only refurbishing a wide range of ships—from an antique, three-masted windjammer to a modern cutter—but designing new vessels as well. These responsibilities involve the meticulous drafting of ship plans. For many decades, the staff had done this by hand, sometimes rediagraming a vessel several times before passing the drawings on to shipyards for bids. A minicomputer installed in the division's Washington, D.C., headquarters in 1980 took over some of the time-consuming manual drafting, but not all members of the staff had access to the machine, and there was still a great deal of pen-and-ink work to be done.

By late 1986, the minicomputer had been orphaned by its manufacturer (parts and service were no longer available), and a committee mustered to choose a replacement. Finding minicomputers too expensive at $30,000 to $50,000 per terminal, the committee opted to buy eight thirty-two-bit personal computers built around the 80386 microprocessor; they cost $9,000 apiece.

As a result, the Naval Engineering Division's experts now work on personal computers, assembling 17,000-ton ships on the screen with the click of a mouse. A designer can select from an array of standard elements such as hatch

A 17,000-ton polar icebreaker takes shape on the screen of a personal computer at Coast Guard headquarters in Washington, D.C. Details of more than sixty systems of the new ship, from plumbing to electronics, are managed by computer-aided design (CAD) software that saves engineers an average of thirty-nine hours per drawing compared to manual drafting techniques.

covers and bulkheads, scale them to the desired size, and fit them into place in seconds, then remove them or alter them at will. Zooming in on a chosen part is as simple as highlighting it on the screen. To transfer a single component from another vessel, a designer calls up the pertinent plan, copies the piece, and adds it to the evolving blueprints. A drawing that took forty minutes to appear on the screen with the old minicomputer system flashes into view in less than thirty seconds.

The Coast Guard estimates that productivity has risen 30 percent since the arrival of the PCs. Shipbuilders, too, are expected to rely increasingly on microcomputers. Having a system that dovetails with those of contractors may save Naval Engineering up to $400,000 a year by reducing the need for redrawing plans by hand as shipbuilders and the Coast Guard collaborate in moving a design toward its final form.

A NEW APPROACH TO INTERIORS

A similar urge to eliminate repetitive, manual redrafts led the award-winning interior designer Gary Whitney down the road to microcomputer CAD. Whitney was among the first in his profession to envision the use of computers at the earliest stages of a project, rather than saving them for churning out technically perfect working drawings at the end.

As director of design for a division of 3D/International, a Houston firm, Whitney had designed hotels and corporate headquarters from Hong Kong to Dubai and had concluded that traditional methods had a major flaw. In each of the several steps required to turn a rough sketch into a finished room "each person literally had to begin with a clean piece of paper." If a designer went to a computer instead of a sketch pad as ideas for a project began to coalesce, Whitney thought, the first rough vision could become the armature for all future drawings, including the final blueprint. He was certain that such an approach would yield considerable savings.

In pursuit of this vision, he left 3D/International in 1987 to form The Whitney Group. His new offices had not a single drawing board. Instead, there was a network of Compaq Deskpros loaded with a $4,000 CAD program named Bentley. At first, the notion of working on a screen instead of a sketch pad intimidated Whitney's team of designers. Unaccustomed to computers, the designers felt that the cool, electronic screen crimped the imagination. But their resistance soon ebbed, and within a year, Whitney could assert: "This is a 100 percent CAD office. The monitor is our paper, the mouse is our pencil, and the delete button is our eraser."

The Whitney Group soon won commissions to design an office building in Houston, interiors for a San Antonio insurance company, and a $25 million resort in the U.S. Virgin Islands, all billed at a lower rate than the industry standard because of the built-in efficiencies of working electronically. Whitney says the computers have cut design time for major projects in half. Economies such as these have attracted the attention of other designers and even architects eager to eliminate redundancy and boost output. Small firms especially like CAD on microcomputers because it gives them capabilities previously reserved for larger rivals that were prosperous enough to afford minicomputers or work stations. The Whitney Group's founder has become a much sought-after speaker, and interior designers looking to get started in the field "beat the door down trying to get in here," he says, "because anybody who wants to be competitive in the industry wants to learn this new language."

THE DEMANDS OF ENGINEERS
While draftsmen and designers are satisfied with two-dimensional CAD programs, mechanical engineers, chemists investigating molecules, and other researchers in a wide variety of disciplines covet software that is capable of rendering and handling shapes as if they were three-dimensional solids, rotating them for a view of the back or the top. For a computer program to determine which parts of the object are obscured by others requires an astronomical number of calculations—so many that the feat was long reserved for mainframes and minicomputers.

Personal computers built around thirty-two-bit microprocessors, however, are able to make short work of these computations when teamed with specialty chips known as math coprocessors. Motorola produces the 68881 coprocessor to accompany its 68020 chip, and Intel pairs its 80387 math chip with the 80386 microprocessor. The purpose of these coprocessors is to perform floating-point arithmetic. This technique speeds calculations by reducing the number of steps needed to handle numbers larger than can be accommodated by the microprocessor's thirty-two-bit word length. In one test, for example, a thirty-two-bit microcomputer without a coprocessor took eight minutes to display an image of a beach ball; use of the math chip reduced the wait to less than thirty seconds.

Taking advantage of this speed, dozens of 3-D programs became available for the souped-up micros. The bestselling AutoCad, which constructed see-through wire-frame models—images composed of pencil-thin lines—was extended by a program called AutoShade that covered the skeletons with a skin of color to make the shapes seem solid. Another program, named RoboSolid, had a library of simple solids. These building blocks, called primitives, could be linked to form complex models that RoboSolid could analyze for a selection of properties, including mass, volume, and center of gravity.

Although the 3-D programs were for the moment less capable than the software available for the expensive work stations popular among engineers and scientists, builders of these machines saw personal computers threatening to encroach on their turf—and a green one it was. In 1986, sales of work stations had ballooned to $1.5 billion a year, and forecasters expected sales to continue climbing. Sensing that the best defense might be a strong offense, Sun Microsystems announced in 1988 that the 80386 was "too smart to be used in a personal computer," and took aim at the high-end PCs by introducing the Sun386i work station. Inside were Intel's 80386 and 80387 processors.

Sun intended to challenge PCs on their home ground—the business market. Like other work-station builders, the company had never succeeded in the corporate arena because businesses tended to have an aversion to the UNIX operating system. UNIX is favored by the typical work-station customer because of certain advantages it has over MS-DOS, the operating system used by most personal computers built around Intel microprocessors. For example, UNIX is especially adept at dissolving communications barriers between different machines and at letting a computer divide its attention between multiple tasks.

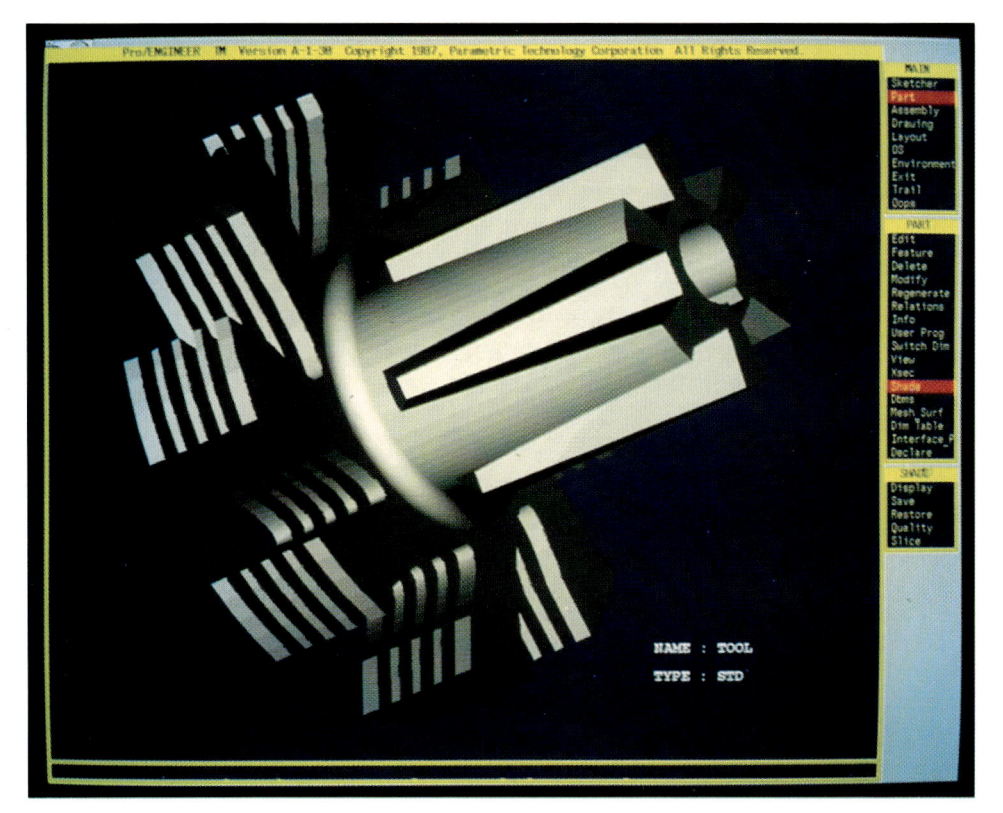

This image of a cutting tool, with five-tiered blades and a grooved shank, was produced by the parametric modeling program Pro/Engineer. Subtle shadings clarify the object's contours, which the software can create by combining two-dimensional side, top, and end views stored in the computer.

However, the operating system is so difficult to learn that it has been called "user surly." The 386i was designed to overcome this problem by making UNIX run programs written for MS-DOS. The tactic worked. Almost immediately, the Sun386i began contributing significantly to the company's revenues. At an annual rate of nearly two billion dollars, money was rolling into Sun faster than to all workstation builders combined just a couple of years earlier.

At the same time, 3-D software for computers based on microprocessors improved by leaps and bounds, in some instances becoming the equal of programs available for minicomputers. A case in point is an innovative solid-modeling program called Pro/Engineer, sold by the Waltham, Massachusetts, company Parametric Technology Corporation. Originally written for Apollo and Sun work stations containing Motorola's 68000-series chips, Pro/Engineer was reworked to run on the Sun386i's 80386 microprocessor as well.

Company founder Samuel Geisberg is a mathematician who immigrated to the United States from the Soviet Union in 1974. Almost immediately, he became involved in developing CAD software, and in 1985 he started his own firm outside Boston. Geisberg began his new venture by rethinking the whole problem of solids modeling from the point of view of an engineer. He realized that it wasn't enough for the software to create objects that looked realistic. A good program must also accommodate an engineer's thought processes and work habits. Ideally, it would allow a designer to express ideas in a familiar language. Instead of having to translate features such as holes and slots into the geometry of cylinders and cubes, an engineer should be able to deal directly in such concepts.

Geisberg also wanted his software to link parts of models to one another so that a change in one would lead to logical changes in others. A block drawn with a hole through it provides a simple example. In most programs, if the engineer decides to lengthen the block, the hole must be adjusted in a separate step. Geisberg's program offered a simpler process. If the opening were labeled a "through hole," in the parlance of engineers, it would automatically lengthen with the block. Designated a "blind hole," it would hold its depth.

Pro/Engineer came out in 1987 and, though regarded as "a major breakthrough in the way designers interact with design systems," received criticisms that drove Geisberg to fine-tune his work. However, a revised version of the program released in 1988 satisfied the reviewers. One hailed the new Pro/Engineer as "possibly the best design system on today's market."

Pro/Engineer is emblematic of the PC's progress up the computing ladder, and more is to come. Computers based on microprocessor technology, it seems, will inevitably offer more power at a much lower cost per user than sharing a minicomputer or a mainframe. Microprocessors may be speeded up by a variety of means. Smaller circuit elements can be placed closer together so that electrons have less distance to travel during processing. Chips consisting of transistors only one micrometer (a millionth of a meter) wide are available, but future microprocessors may be built from components as small as one-quarter micrometer across. Transistors made with the semiconductor gallium arsenide are inherently faster-operating than similar components of silicon. Experimental electronic devices based on a phenomenon called quantum tunneling, which can switch from on to off in as little as two trillionths of a second, presage perhaps a thousandfold increase in computer speed.

But as these technologies are being cultivated, another has already blossomed. In early 1986, IBM introduced a personal computer called the RT PC. The RT stood for RISC Technology, RISC being shorthand for Reduced Instruction Set Computer. This machine made use of an idea that an IBM research team under the direction of John Cocke had incorporated into an experimental minicomputer back in the mid-1970s. Given the name 801 (after the building in which it took shape), the computer capitalized on an observation made by Cocke and his team as they searched for inexpensive ways to make computers run faster: The simplest 20 percent of a computer's instruction set—fundamental operations such as add, load from memory, and store in memory—did 80 percent of the work. As explained on pages 99-103, the mere existence of hundreds of complicated, little-used instructions slowed execution of the simple ones. Furthermore, because instructions varied in length and differed in their paths through the computer's logic circuitry, the processor had to finish one instruction before it could begin the next.

The RT PC instruction set had fewer than half the usual complement, making the machine fast, but not spectacularly so. Other RISC designs appeared from Motorola, Intel, Hewlett-Packard, Sun Microsystems, and a California firm appropriately named MIPS. Some of the chips had as few as one-quarter the instructions of the RT. They mimicked complex instructions by combining simpler ones, each of which was identical in length to the others and followed the same route through the logic circuitry. These factors and others permitted RISC architecture to begin processing a new instruction almost as soon as the preceding one had been started, vastly increasing speed. Sun Microsystem's SPARCstation 1, for example, cost only $9,000 and streaked along at twelve MIPS.

ROLES FOR MAINFRAMES
Such performance tends to further blur the old distinctions among computers based primarily on processing speed. The term mainframe, for example, may come to mean simply a powerful computer serving as a central resource shared by many users. Applications of this kind will almost certainly persist in enterprises that depend on databases so enormous that it would be uneconomical

Speed from Simplicity

A microprocessor is known by its instruction set, the repertoire of capabilities built into the chip that are reused hundreds of thousands of times in various combinations to create a typical computer program. Small instruction sets were the rule in the earliest chips. Each instruction adds to the circuitry that must be built into the microprocessor, and chipmaking technology of the day was so primitive that only a few instructions could be squeezed onto a piece of silicon. There was, for example, always an add instruction, but there was rarely one for multiplication. To multiply 101 by 11, a programmer had to instruct the processor to shift the first number one place to the left to simulate multiplying by 10, then to add 101. Larger numbers required additional shift and add operations.

As chip-fabricating techniques improved, more instructions could be fitted onto the chip, much to the delight of software writers. Soon they could tell a microprocessor not only to multiply and divide in one instruction, but to perform all manner of operations that had formerly been extremely complicated to program. For example, moving a block of data such as a paragraph from one place in memory to another could now be done with a single instruction; formerly, a programmer had to move the data one byte at a time.

Eventually, these complex instructions numbered in the hundreds, far too many to be wired directly onto a microprocessor. So they were defined as combinations of a smaller set of simpler instructions that could be accommodated on the chip—and circuitry for an interpreter, called microcode, was added to the microprocessor to decipher them. Like an overdeveloped bureaucracy, however, such processors lose in efficiency what they gain in complexity. Running instructions through an interpreter costs valuable time, the more so because no instruction, not even the simplest, can bypass it.

This kind of chip architecture is called a Complex Instruction Set Computer (CISC), and it is found in most personal computers. In practice, however, most of the complex instructions are rarely used, so they have been banished to make a more streamlined architecture called a Reduced Instruction Set Computer, or RISC *(left)*. With less than one-fourth the instructions of a CISC chip, a RISC microprocessor has room to wire all its instructions onto the chip and can thus forgo an interpreter.

As explained on the following pages, eliminating the interpreter is just one of the ways that designers speed processing in a RISC chip. Its memory usage is also streamlined compared to that of a CISC processor. In a typical CISC system, most instructions may transfer data to or from the computer's main-memory banks, which lie far from the processor. A CISC addition instruction, for example, might add the contents of two memory locations and place the sum in a third. Because frequent references to memory are time-consuming, RISC designs minimize such delays by increasing the number of quickly tapped on-chip memory locations called registers, where work in progress can be temporarily stored.

Perhaps the greatest advantage of the RISC concept is its capacity for a processing technique called pipelining. This approach permits loading of a new instruction into the processor while preceding orders are still being carried out. For every tick, or "cycle," of the computer's internal clock, a procession of instructions advances through the chip's logic circuitry, one station at a time. Once a program is under way, pipelining can accept a new instruction with each tick of the clock. In contrast, CISC systems are largely unsuited to pipelining. Their longer, more complicated instructions are nonlinear. That is, they tend to backtrack through the chip's logic and would collide with any other instruction following too close behind. As a result, a CISC chip can accept, on average, no more than one instruction every five or six clock cycles.

Speed from Simplicity

Contrasting Architectures

Even microprocessors as different as RISC and CISC chips have much in common. Both, for example, are usually programmed in a high-level language such as FORTRAN or Pascal. This version of the software is prepared for the chip by another program called a compiler. Both microprocessors also include circuitry wired into the chip for at least a portion of the instruction set. These so-called hard-wired instructions serve, in effect, as controllers that direct data through the

An essential conversion. Before software written for a CISC chip can be executed, a compiler translates it into a machine-oriented dialect known as an assembly language. As these instructions enter a CISC microprocessor, they are matched against the computer's full instruction set, which is stored permanently on the chip. The outcome of the comparison is an address in the interpreter where the instruction may be found.

A second translation. The interpreter converts CISC assembly-language instructions into sequences of simpler commands called executable instructions that the machine's logic circuits can respond to.

Following instructions. The chip has four logic-function areas. One fetches the next step of the program to the microcode interpreter; the other three carry out sequences of executable instructions. Of these, the Arithmetic Logic Unit (ALU) performs calculations; another contains circuitry for transferring data to or from the computer's main memory; and the last writes data into and reads it from on-chip registers. Microregisters are used to temporarily store interim results produced by a sequence of executable instructions for later use within the same series. Execution registers hold final results that may be needed by a subsequent series.

microprocessor's logic circuits as the computer executes a program. CISC and RISC chips are also identical in their logic circuits, which are shown here as separate areas for clarity.

Despite the similarities, important differences arise from the microprocessors' instruction sets. The more complicated instructions of CISC microprocessors like the one shown at left are too elaborate for direct execution by the chip's logic circuits. Each must therefore pass through the microcode. This circuitry serves as an interpreter to convert assembly-language instructions into sequences of simpler commands.

In a RISC device *(below)*, instructions are so elementary that they can be directly executed without recourse to microcode. Lacking such an interpreter and having fewer built-in instructions, RISC chips offer ample space for other useful circuits, yet they generally have smaller dimensions than CISC microprocessors.

A more capable compiler. The RISC system shown here employs a special kind of compiler to translate high-level programs into its much simpler assembly language. Known as an optimizing compiler, it reorganizes program instructions to take best advantage of the RISC chip's pipelining feature.

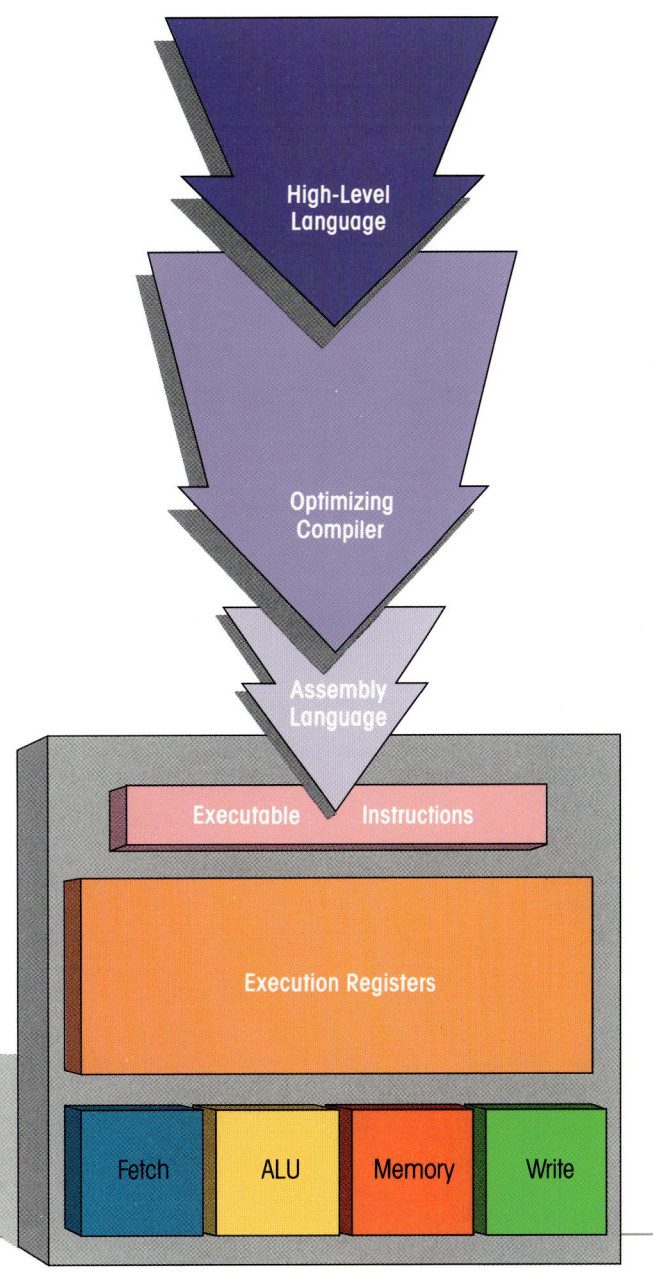

Direct action. Unlike CISC assembly-language instructions, commands to a RISC microprocessor are so simple that they need no interpreter and can be carried out instantly by the processor's logic circuits. A consequence of this simplicity is that RISC instructions produce no interim results, eliminating the need for microregisters and making space for additional execution registers.

Speed from Simplicity

The Power of Pipelining

The illustrations on these pages explain how the differences in instruction sets inhibit pipelining in CISC processors *(upper diagram)* and promote it in RISC chips. In this example, the RISC chip runs through a simple program in about half the time required by the CISC design, as indicated by the timer on the next page ticking off clock cycles.

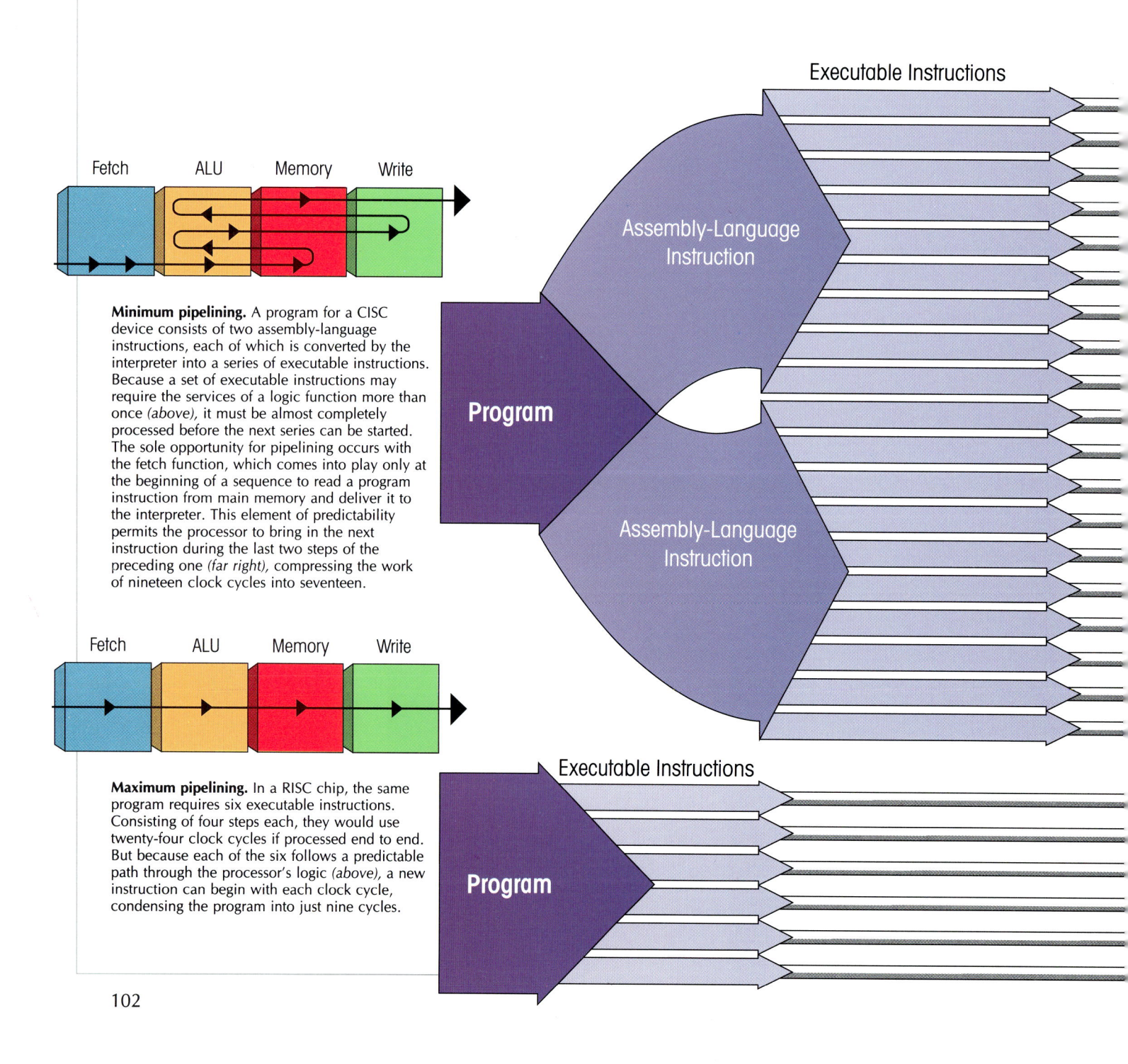

Minimum pipelining. A program for a CISC device consists of two assembly-language instructions, each of which is converted by the interpreter into a series of executable instructions. Because a set of executable instructions may require the services of a logic function more than once *(above)*, it must be almost completely processed before the next series can be started. The sole opportunity for pipelining occurs with the fetch function, which comes into play only at the beginning of a sequence to read a program instruction from main memory and deliver it to the interpreter. This element of predictability permits the processor to bring in the next instruction during the last two steps of the preceding one *(far right)*, compressing the work of nineteen clock cycles into seventeen.

Maximum pipelining. In a RISC chip, the same program requires six executable instructions. Consisting of four steps each, they would use twenty-four clock cycles if processed end to end. But because each of the six follows a predictable path through the processor's logic *(above)*, a new instruction can begin with each clock cycle, condensing the program into just nine cycles.

In reality, the RISC chip is even faster because the program, which is comparable to performing a pair of simple additions, is compiled directly from a high-level language into executable instructions. In effect, the RISC processor gets a head start on the CISC chip, which cannot send executable instructions to its logic circuitry until an intermediate layer of assembly-language commands is decoded by the interpreter.

Although the speed difference illustrated here is typical of the two kinds of processors, the benefits of RISC over CISC vary, depending on the skill of the chip designer and other factors, from little improvement over a CISC chip to three times its speed and more.

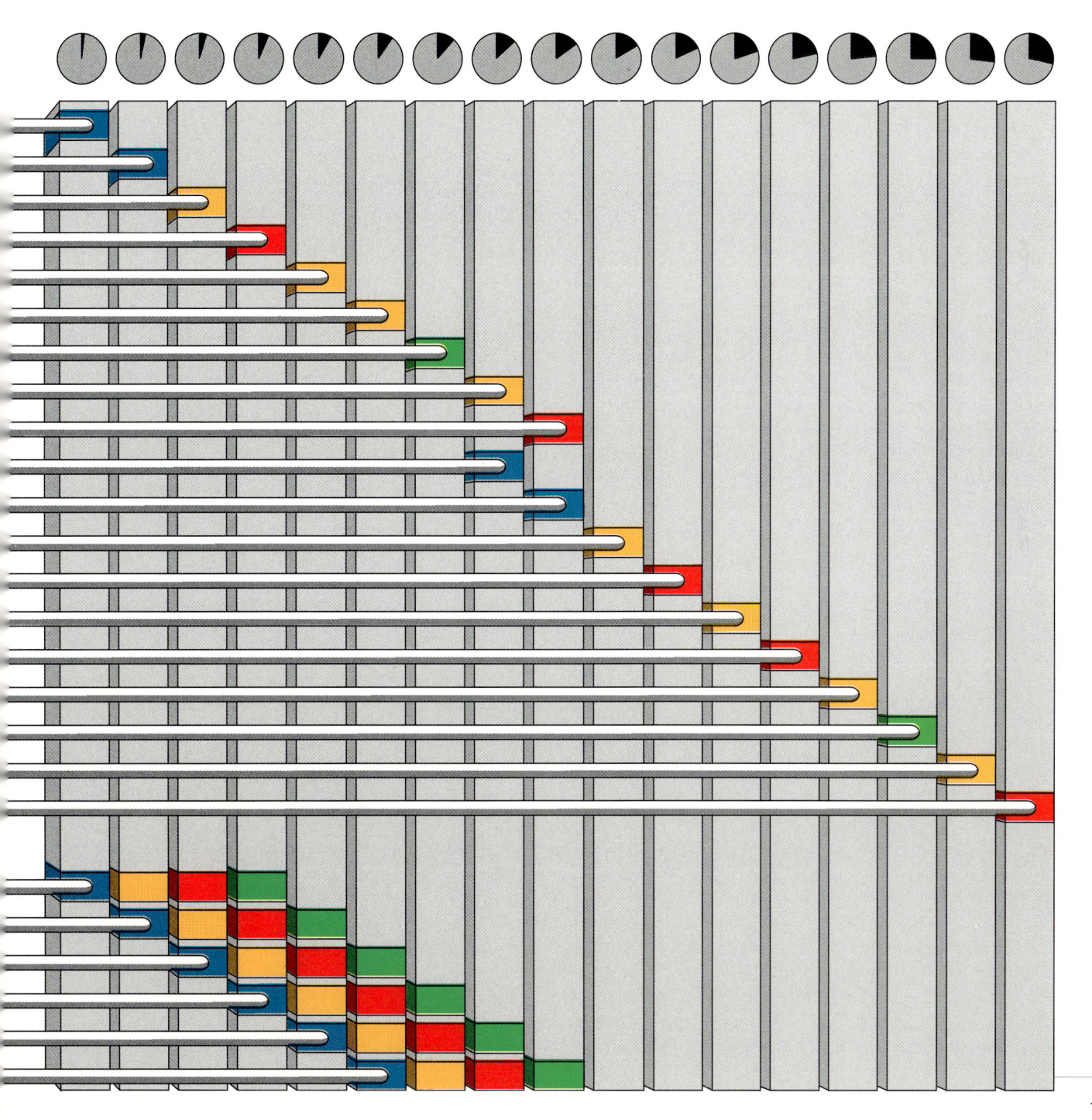

to replicate and distribute them. One stockbrokerage firm on New York City's Wall Street, for example, has several hundred disk drives to keep financial histories of thousands of stocks on line for instant reference; each drive has a capacity of more than a gigabyte. Data-processing managers speak of such huge installations as disk farms.

The costs of assembling a disk farm will likely remain high enough to encourage continued centralization, but the designs of the "mainframes" in control of these resources may be quite different from the computer architectures that have traditionally been assigned this role. In 1987, American Airlines' parent company, AMR Inc., launched Confirm, a new hotel-reservation system. Like the airline's flight-reservation network, Confirm required a central processor that each second could juggle a host of requests for information and maintain a vast database of bookings. At first, a conventional mainframe seemed the way to go, but in the end, AMR acquired its hardware from a company named Sequent Computer Systems of Beaverton, Oregon.

Called the Balance B21, AMR's new computer had three circuit boards, each holding two Intel 80386 microprocessors. Sharing memory and working in a style known as parallel processing—in which each of the chips handles part of a job—the computer can hit peak speeds of twenty-four MIPS. Sequent engineers have ganged as many as thirty of the thirty-two-bit chips into one machine for a speed of 120 MIPS. Called the S81, the machine supports 1,000 terminals and costs about $1 million. A mainframe capable of serving as many users can have a price tag ten times as high.

Microprocessor technology, imaginatively and economically employed by Sequent, permitted AMR to avoid conventional mainframe computers yet satisfy a mainframe-scale need for computer power. In the form of conventional PCs, microprocessors are expected to shoulder part of the computing burden of mainframes harnessed to even larger applications than Confirm. For example, to keep track of six million reservations made up to a year in advance, the Apollo reservation system that United Airlines shares with five other companies requires a data-storage facility capable of handling 900 gigabytes of information. Apollo's disk farm comprises 750 drives. They are installed in several rooms, one big enough for a game of football. The nineteen mainframe computers at the core of this service handle 70,000 terminals, from which emanate a barrage of 1,400 queries each second.

Years ago, the system's managers realized that an attractive way around traffic jams would be to insert smaller computers between the mainframes and the travel agents who use Apollo to make reservations. Frequently requested information (a travel agent in San Francisco may ask often about flights to Los Angeles, for example, but rarely for the schedule between Chicago and Atlanta) could be stored in these computers, which would save the mainframes the trouble of handling routine queries.

Strains on Apollo approached the crisis point in the early 1980s. As air travel picked up, United was forced to add more and more terminals to the automated booking system, which it owned outright at the time. The network's complement of IBM 3090 mainframes, Big Blue's most powerful model, was increased more than once to deal with the surge in requests for flight information. Recalls one executive, "We were always dependent on IBM or some other vendor to provide us with the latest big piece of hardware or some advance in storage technology that would give us the needed capacity. We were continually up against a wall." In particular, when United sought to add smaller mainframes to the system, they were told that no such option existed. IBM simply had not made its biggest computers compatible with its smaller ones.

SOFTWARE TO THE RESCUE
Finally, United turned to its own resources. At the airline's behest, Apollo programmers began development of a system for connecting the 3090s to more modest IBM mainframes. In two years, the job was finished. The resulting software, called the Open Systems Manager, overcame incompatibilities between different operating systems so that computers, both large and small, could run the reservation-system programs.

IBM ultimately rose to the challenge presented by United's Open Systems Manager software with a plan called Systems Application Architecture (SAA). The idea behind SAA is not only to have all classes of mainframes communicating with one another but to extend this capability across the full range of IBM computers, including PS/2 models. Anticipating such a development, United and other airlines installed personal computers in travel agents' offices. Initially these machines served as little more than dumb terminals, but eventually they are expected to assume some of the mainframes' responsibilities.

IBM has expressed confidence that SAA and other plans afoot will keep the conventional mainframe competitive for years to come, but industry observers are not so sure. Instead, they say, mainframe builders may share the earlier experience of minicomputer manufacturers, who in the mid-1980s had seen the market for their machines attacked on two flanks—by work stations in the technical community and, in the business world, by networks built around powerful PCs serving as central repositories of programs and data.

One consequence of this melee was a two-year lull in computer sales that began in late 1984. At the time, the inactivity was widely regarded as nothing more than an economic fluctuation following a three-decade boom. But three years later, IBM, DEC, and Unisys once again all reported disappointing revenues from mainframes, leading a number of analysts to wonder whether the earlier slowdown had in reality marked a turning point in the commercial history of computers: a permanent shift toward microprocessor-powered personal computers and away from the expensive old-line minicomputer and mainframe architectures.

And the pressure is likely to become even greater. Computer specialists assert that the promise of the 80386 generation of personal computers has barely been tapped, primarily because advances in hardware have utterly outstripped the ability of software writers to keep up. For the most part, these machines are running programs that were written for eight-bit computers such as the original IBM PC. Such software cannot, for example, take advantage of the thirty-two-bit path between the microprocessor and memory—which would offer a fourfold gain in speed. The most common operating system for these machines, MS-DOS, also lacks the ability to harness the full power of thirty-two-bit chips.

As software begins to catch up with hardware, microcomputers will become an even better value. But microprocessor developments proceed apace. Intel has unveiled the next in its line of microprocessors—the 80486. Fully compatible with the software written for all its predecessors, the new chip runs up to four times as fast as the 80386. An even faster chip—the 80586—is in the works. Perhaps most dazzling are the RISC chips. Unlike other lines of processors, which have huge libraries of software written for old models that will run on the more recent ones, these chips require all-new software. Consequently, programs written for the machines can be expected to take full advantage of their astounding speed. Running at fifty MIPS, a RISC computer is as fast as many mainframes and initially might cost around $30,000 to the average mainframe's several million. If personal-computer prices continue to fall as they have since the early 1980s, almost anyone might be able to afford a mainframe for the desk.

Placing all that computing power in the hands of one individual might seem extravagant—until the idea is put in perspective. Less than a decade ago, 256K was considered to be a lot of memory for a personal computer. Now that a PC operating system like OS/2 requires more than six times that amount, such a notion has become almost quaint. "Fast" has been redefined, too. Personal computers that operated at one MIPS once seemed speedy enough for mundane tasks such as word processing, but rare is the writer who would not appreciate a four-MIPS machine. "No amount of MIPS is sufficient in the long run," says Mitchell Kapor, who founded Lotus Development Corporation, producers of the spreadsheet program 1-2-3. "There are already things that users would really like to have that strain the capabilities of even fast 80386s. To have the crispest display, updating instantly, you want something faster." Built into printers for desktop publishing, a fifty-MIPS microprocessor might shorten from six minutes to less than one minute the time needed to print a page. Given such processing speed, a personal computer might acquire voice-recognition capabilities that could take dictation and turn it into a flawlessly typed letter. Or, as shown on the following pages, supernetworks might evolve, in which PCs would become gateways to a global village of computing.

A Universal Network

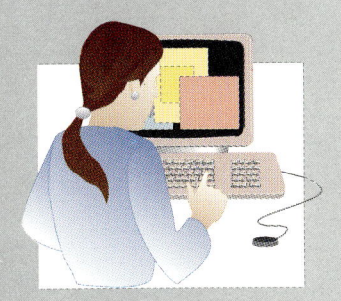

Although a powerful entity on its own, the personal computer becomes a tool of virtually unlimited capabilities when it serves as a gateway to other computers. Networks that link PCs to one another and to larger machines not only facilitate terminal-to-terminal exchanges of information but also enable users of small-scale machines to harness the processing muscle of such giants as supercomputers, running programs that would overwhelm the relatively meager resources of their own computers.

The ideal of distributed computing, in which a wide variety of computers carry out tasks for each other and share data with little apparent effort, is not easily achieved. For most of the history of computing, networks could only be formed among computers built by the same manufacturer or with compatible hardware designs and processing techniques. Exchanges between different types of computers were practically nonexistent.

In 1984, researchers at the Massachusetts Institute of Technology—itself an owner of a menagerie of computing hardware—set out to overcome the barrier of incompatibility. Backed by the Digital Equipment Corporation and IBM, they designed a sophisticated package of software, known as the X Window system, that integrates all of the university's high-resolution graphics terminals and mainframes. A person at one terminal can request access to any other computer on the network and thereby run several different programs simultaneously. The system's basic approach is to display the output from different computers in different windows on a single computer screen.

As outlined on the following pages, the X Window system employs an intricate array of procedures, but the essential ingredient is a communications standard, or universal language, for all network interchanges. As a result, each type of computer need only be fluent in two languages—its own and the network's.

A Universal Network

An Interplay of Computer Resources

Communications have always been an essential element in the computing environment. Within even a single personal computer, information is continually on the move, flowing from an input device such as a keyboard or a mouse to memory and processing circuitry and from there to a screen, printer, or storage disk. These exchanges often require special procedures, say, for translating relatively comprehensible commands typed at the keyboard into the binary language that the computer's electronic circuits understand.

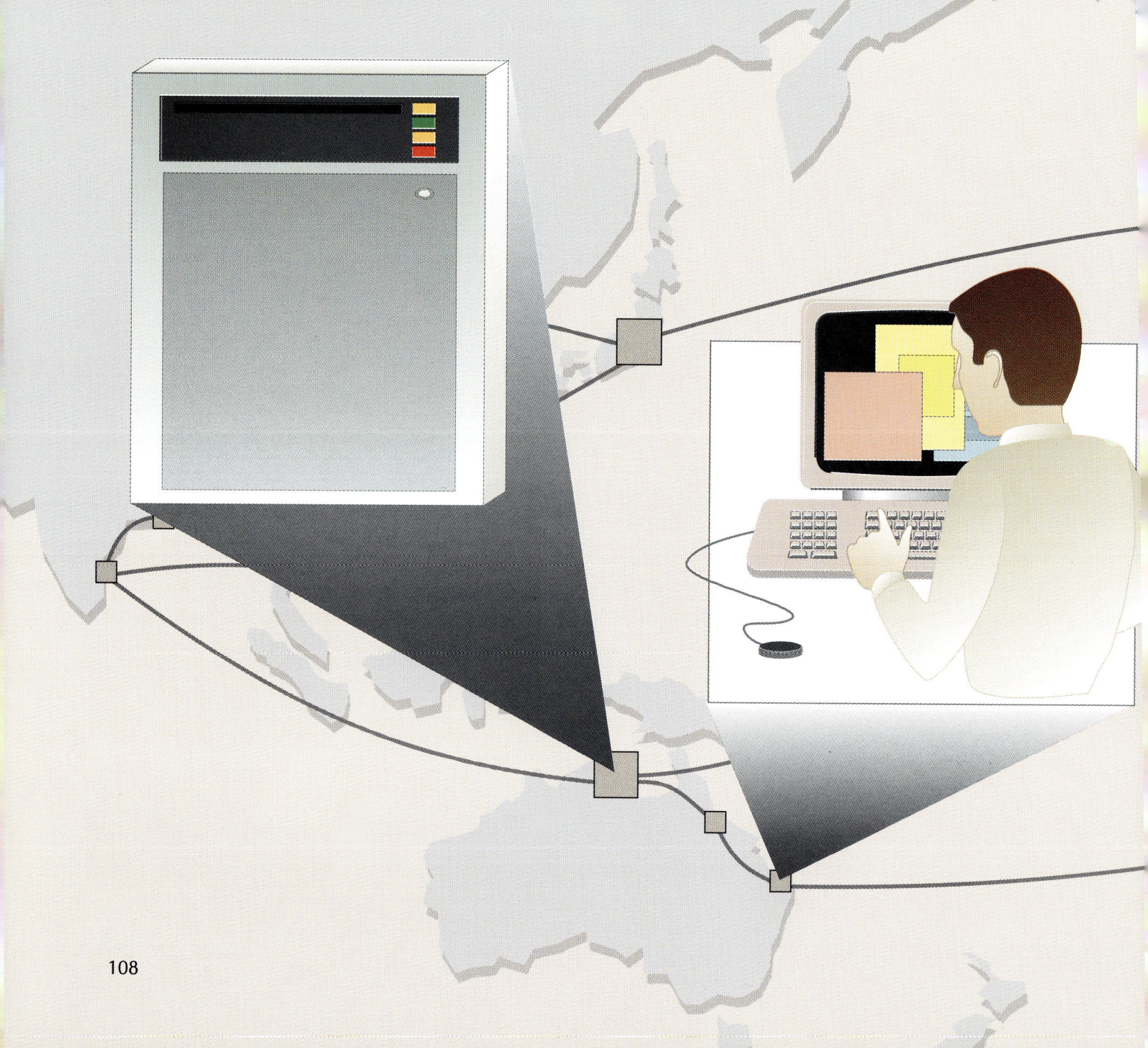

The same principles apply when several computers communicate with one another. The simplest systems, known as local area networks, typically employ standard electronic transmission lines—copper wire, coaxial cables, and the like—to connect personal computers, mainframes, and peripheral devices in the same location, such as an office building. Because these machines usually speak the same language, the network's chief task is ensuring that messages get to the right place and that they do not interfere with one another along the way.

Global networks, such as the one illustrated below, require more sophisticated approaches. The communications themselves involve more exotic media, such as microwave links for relaying messages hundreds of miles overland and satellites for bridging the vast expanses of oceans. More complex yet is overcoming the incompatibilities between different types of computers. Here is where the X Window system proves its worth. In the example on pages 118 and 119, oceanographers in Australia and North America are preparing for an upcoming conference. They not only need to share work produced on their own personal computers but also must incorporate the results of programs run on mainframes hundreds of miles away. Although the various computers involved are as different as apples and oranges, all the necessary information appears almost instantly in overlapping windows on the users' screens, with the intricacies of the process hidden from view.

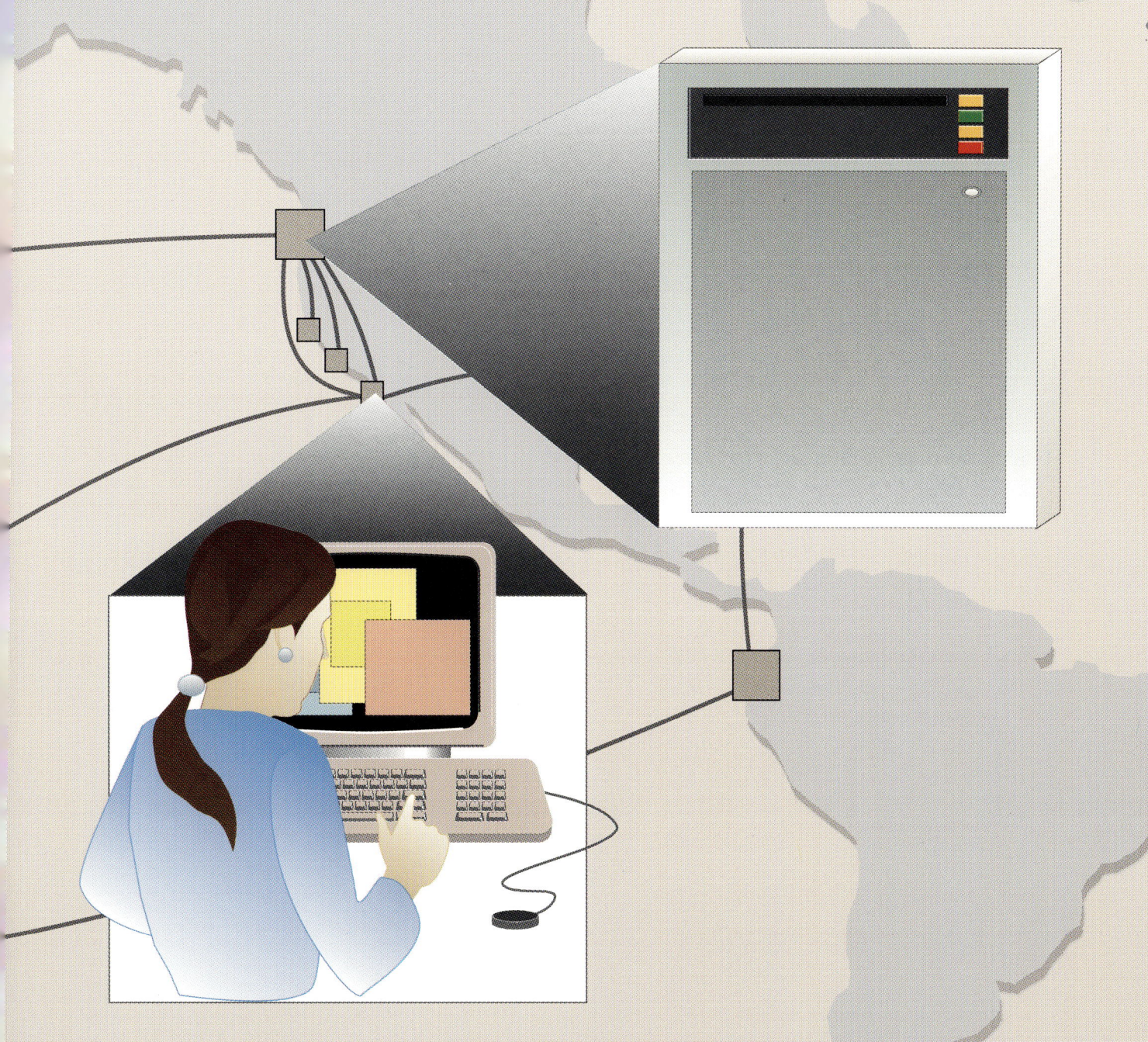

A Universal Network

Software Layers to Disguise Differences

To achieve an apparently effortless flow of information, the X Window system establishes within every computer layers of software that, in effect, isolate each machine from all the details of network communication. An individual computer is thus able to go about its business as if every other computer with which it interacts is designed in exactly the same way and follows precisely the same procedures for running programs and manipulating data.

These software layers handle two distinct tasks: sending information through the network and receiving information

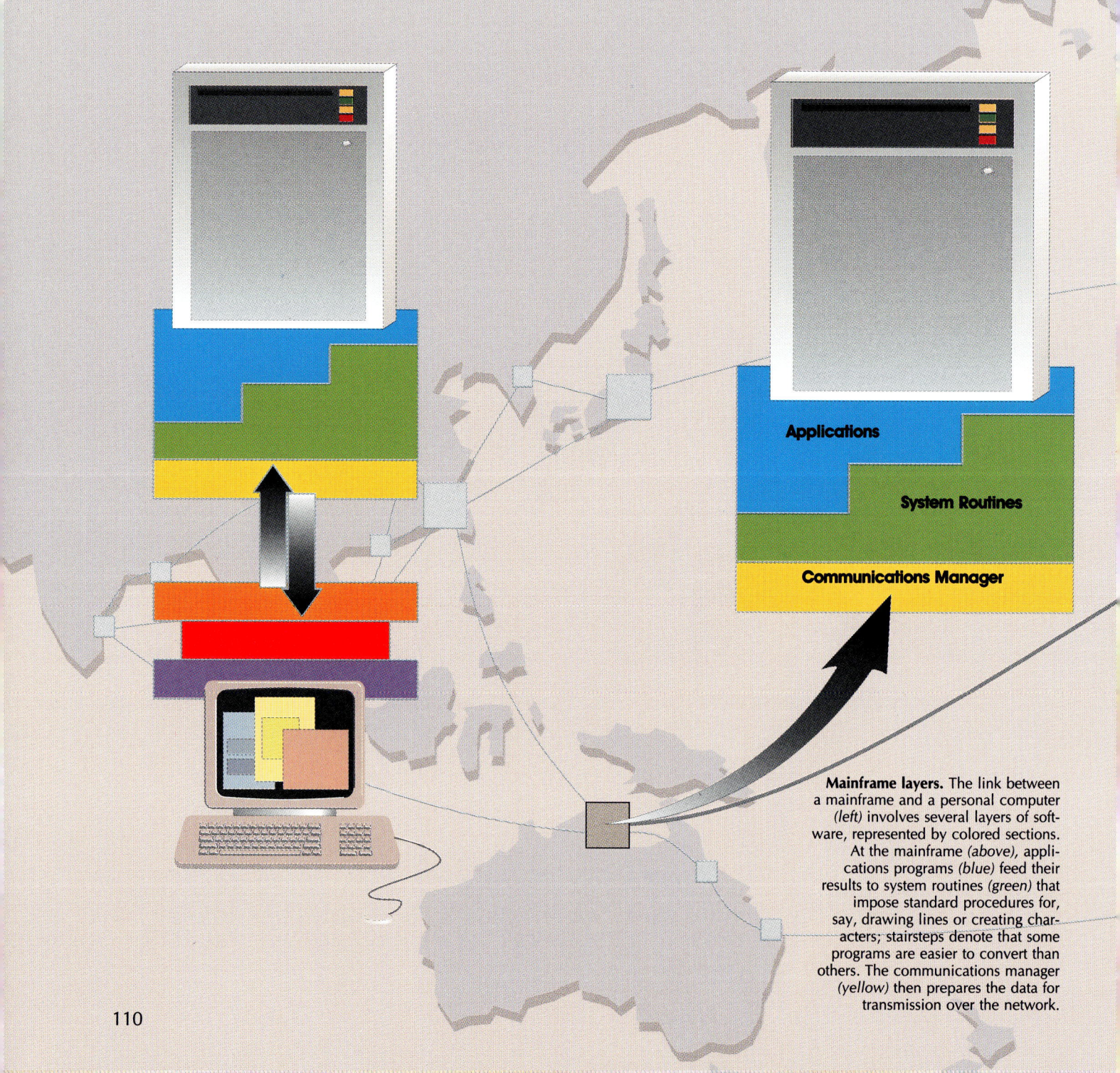

Mainframe layers. The link between a mainframe and a personal computer *(left)* involves several layers of software, represented by colored sections. At the mainframe *(above)*, applications programs *(blue)* feed their results to system routines *(green)* that impose standard procedures for, say, drawing lines or creating characters; stairsteps denote that some programs are easier to convert than others. The communications manager *(yellow)* then prepares the data for transmission over the network.

from it. Because computers can be both senders and recipients, layers to execute both chores must be present. In a typical scenario, a PC user might request results from a program loaded on a mainframe. The program itself, specifically tailored to that mainframe, resides in the sending computer's first software layer. The second layer consists of a library of routines that are common to the entire network; the routines constitute the foundation of the X Window system's versatility. No matter what the form of the program's output—a bar graph, a numerical table, or even lines of text—this second layer transforms the data into standard coding that will draw the results pixel by pixel on the receiving screen. A third layer then performs the necessary formatting chores for actually transmitting the data through the network.

A similar arrangement exists at the receiving end, where layers closest to the network act as data managers, identifying incoming coding, translating it as necessary for the receiver's hardware, and apportioning instructions from different programs—including those in the receiver's own software layer—to different windows.

Displaying results on-screen. Data arriving from other computers is handled first by the receiving computer's system manager *(orange)*, which coordinates all activities and takes care of translating the information into the proper format for its computer. The window manager *(red)* allocates screen space, assigning data to specific windows and rearranging windows as needed. The receiving computer's own applications software *(purple)* is also monitored by the system and window managers.

A Universal Network

Rules for Organizing Network Messages

The essence of any network is its protocol—the procedural standards it sets for the transmission of messages. In order for the information from one computer to reach the right destination and be interpreted properly, the digital signals that actually travel over wires and cables or through the air via microwaves or radio waves must be organized according to the network's established conventions, regardless of the messages' actual contents.

The routines in a sending computer's second software layer simplify matters by ensuring that messages from different

Lines of Programming That Define a Cursor

Listed at right are the parameters of the X Window system's routine for creating a cursor. The specific cursor being designed is given a name—cid—so that it can easily be distinguished from other cursors that might appear in other windows. The cursor's shape is generated on a pixmap, an array of bits that represent the brightness values of the thousands of picture elements, or pixels, of which a screen is composed; the "source" line defines the general shape, such as a square or an arrow, and the "mask" line refines it. Foreground and background colors are fashioned from combinations of red, green, and blue, and the cursor's starting position is defined in terms of horizontal and vertical screen coordinates, labeled x and y. The designation CARD16 indicates that each color and coordinate will be represented by a sixteen-bit number.

Packaging a routine's instructions. The row of blocks below represents a data package thirty-two bytes long, organized according to the protocol for sending messages over the network. For the cursor-generating routine above, the first eight bytes, marked "header" and "name," would contain, among other information, code identifying the type of routine and labeling this specific instance. Succeeding bytes would supply actual values for the pixels to be turned on to fashion the cursor's shape and color, and for the coordinates of its initial position on the screen.

| Header | Name | Shape Designators |

kinds of computers are first translated into the X Window system's standard formats. The instructions for fashioning a cursor, as outlined below, are a case in point: Although there are many different styles of cursor, ranging from a plain square to an arrow, a paintbrush, or even a miniature hand with a pointing finger, the design characteristics are the same; variations are created by inserting different values for shape and color variables.

The protocol itself, which is defined within the instructions of the communications manager, is a carefully determined method for packaging the coded information prepared by these system routines.

Of key importance are the first few bytes of data at the beginning of one of these packages, which indicate the type of routine and how long the package will be, and which identify both the destination and the source. This allows system managers at receiving computers to keep straight what may be multiple messages arriving from many different sources and to determine right away precisely which procedures to follow for interpreting the rest of the message.

CreateCursor

cid: CURSOR

source: PIXMAP
mask: PIXMAP
fore—red, fore—green, fore—blue: CARD16
back—red, back—green, back—blue: CARD16
x,y: CARD16

Color Designators · Position

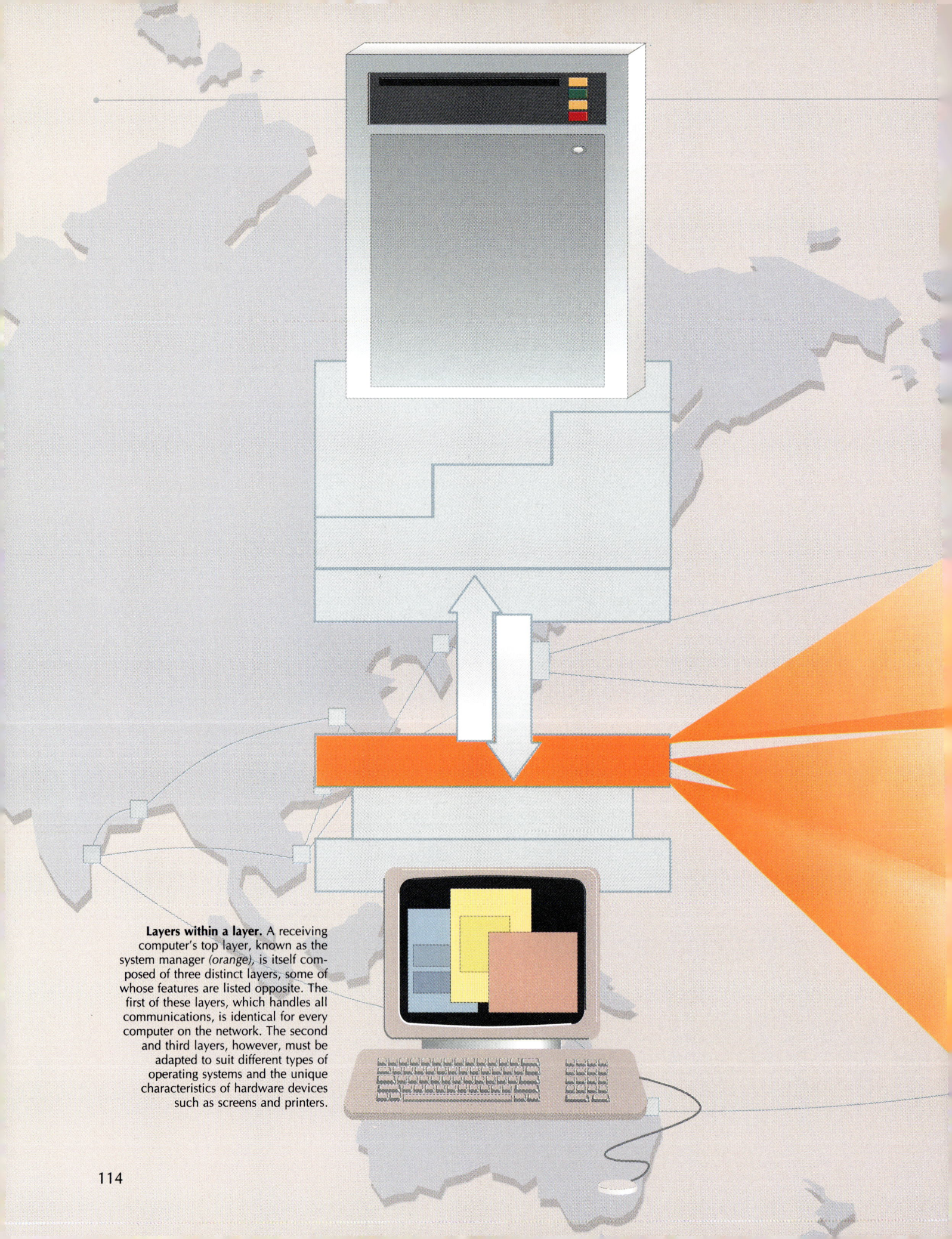

Layers within a layer. A receiving computer's top layer, known as the system manager *(orange)*, is itself composed of three distinct layers, some of whose features are listed opposite. The first of these layers, which handles all communications, is identical for every computer on the network. The second and third layers, however, must be adapted to suit different types of operating systems and the unique characteristics of hardware devices such as screens and printers.

A Universal Network

Three-Part Anatomy of a System Manager

Just as outgoing packets of data must be converted from their original form for transmission over the network, incoming messages must be reconverted for the type of machine on which they will be displayed. The process requires attending to many tasks, distributed among three layers of software *(below)* that together make up the receiving computer's system manager.

The top layer, which is the counterpart of a sending computer's communications manager, is a generic piece of software, at home on any computer. It plays the role of dispatcher, keeping tabs on the continual stream of data packages on the network, identifying those addressed to its computer, and maintaining communications with computers whose data is being displayed in its own computer's windows. If, for example, the user types new text or changes the position of a cursor in a window, this layer prepares and forwards a message to the appropriate computer where the actual processing takes place.

The next two layers must be specially developed for the computer on which they are loaded. Before any data can be displayed, it has to be tailored to the computer's operating system—the set of programs that controls computer operations. The operating-system-dependent layer converts incoming messages into a command language that the circuitry of the computer will understand. The other customized layer, known as the hardware-dependent layer, performs the final step, creating the proper code for the computer's peripheral devices—its printer, screen, and other output equipment.

GENERIC LAYER

*Manages communications through the network, relaying messages to and from remote software applications.
*Serves all open connections between sending computers and the receiving work station.
*Manages requests for processor time.
*Monitors communications for errors.

OPERATING-SYSTEM-DEPENDENT LAYER

*Translates data formats into format understood by the work station's operating system.
*Allocates work station's memory and decides when to use local memory and when to use remote memory.
*Manipulates fonts for text displays.

HARDWARE-DEPENDENT LAYER

*Drives all hardware devices associated with the work station.
*Makes allowances for hardware variations, adjusting formats for black-and-white or color graphics terminals, mouse or puck, or different keyboard configurations.
*Forwards user commands entered via hardware devices to operating-system-dependent layer.

A Universal Network

Managing Multiple Screen Views

The heart of the X Window system is its ability to provide access to many different programs, running on many different computers, through window displays on a single screen. Merely by moving the cursor from one window to another, the user can shift from editing with a word processor in the PC, for example, to entering scientific data for evaluation by sophisticated software in a distant mainframe. As explained previously, the process depends on a complex variety of network interchanges and data conversions, but coordinating

Establishing a window hierarchy. A receiving computer's window manager *(above, left)* allocates screen space to programs and data from other computers, and each window it creates becomes part of a hierarchy akin to a family tree *(right)*. Called the root, the entire screen is, in effect, the ancestor of all subsequent windows. At the next level are parent windows, each representing a separate computer; they are initially stacked on-screen in their order of precedence in the hierarchy, from left to right. Windows created within a parent are known as children and may include aids such as menus, as well as portions of other windows that have been copied or transferred with "cut-and-paste" operations. In this example, the middle window's first child overlaps the second child on-screen because the user has requested that order.

116

the display of results is an intricate task in itself, requiring the dedicated services of a separate body of software procedures known as the window manager.

The window manager's chief responsibility is organizing the presentation of windows on the screen, usually stacking them in order of precedence so that the most recently opened window appears in full view. Although a sending computer may include in its data package suggestions about the size of window it needs, the window manager may decide differently, being guided instead by programmed policy for doling out space. Some of its decisions can, however, be overruled by the user through commands entered at the keyboard or with a mouse, to suit individual preferences or the requirements of a particular situation. As demand or user requests dictate, the manager automatically resizes windows or rearranges their stack order.

The next two pages describe a hypothetical example of the full system in operation on a global network.

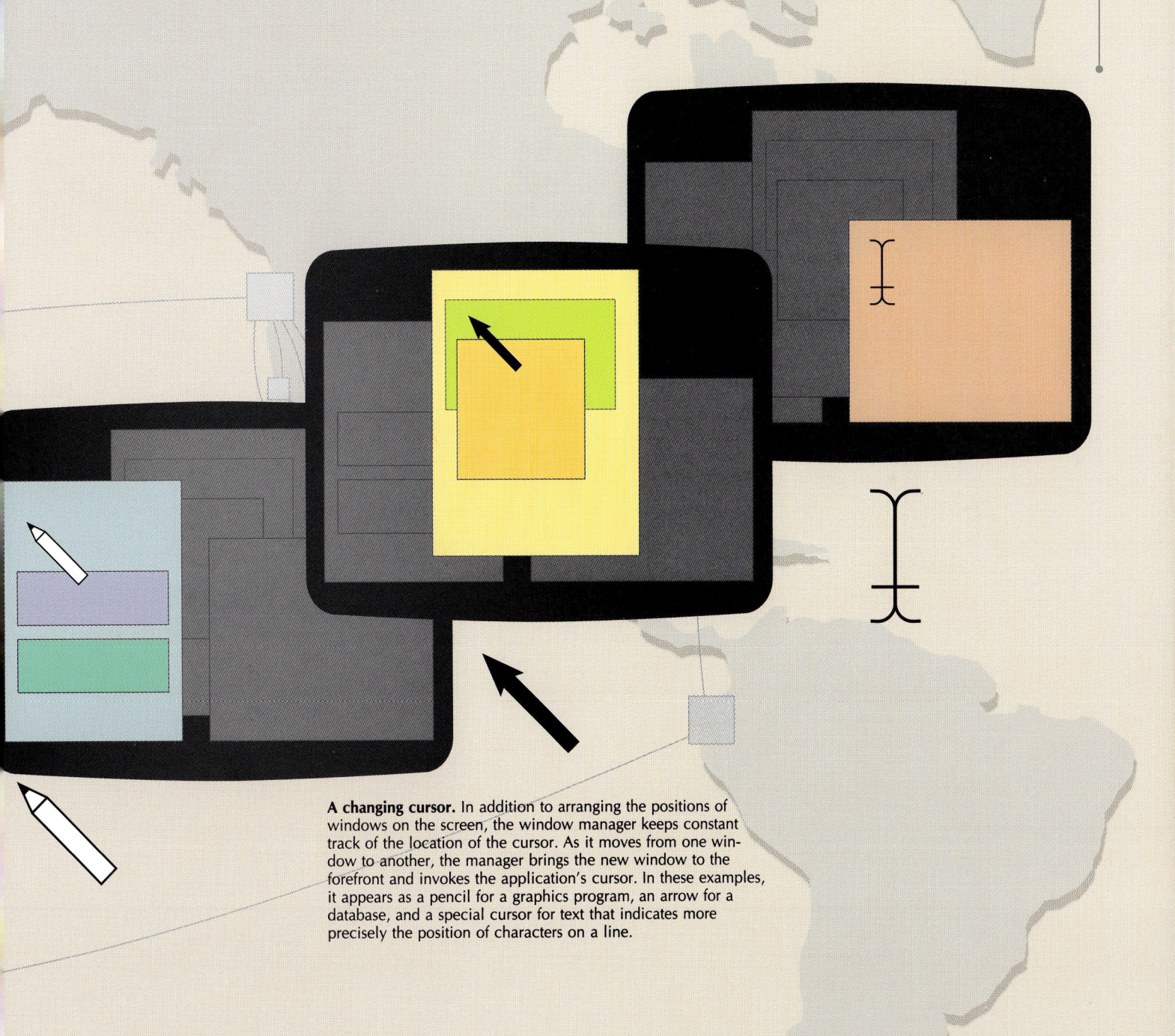

A changing cursor. In addition to arranging the positions of windows on the screen, the window manager keeps constant track of the location of the cursor. As it moves from one window to another, the manager brings the new window to the forefront and invokes the application's cursor. In these examples, it appears as a pencil for a graphics program, an arrow for a database, and a special cursor for text that indicates more precisely the position of characters on a line.

117

A Universal Network

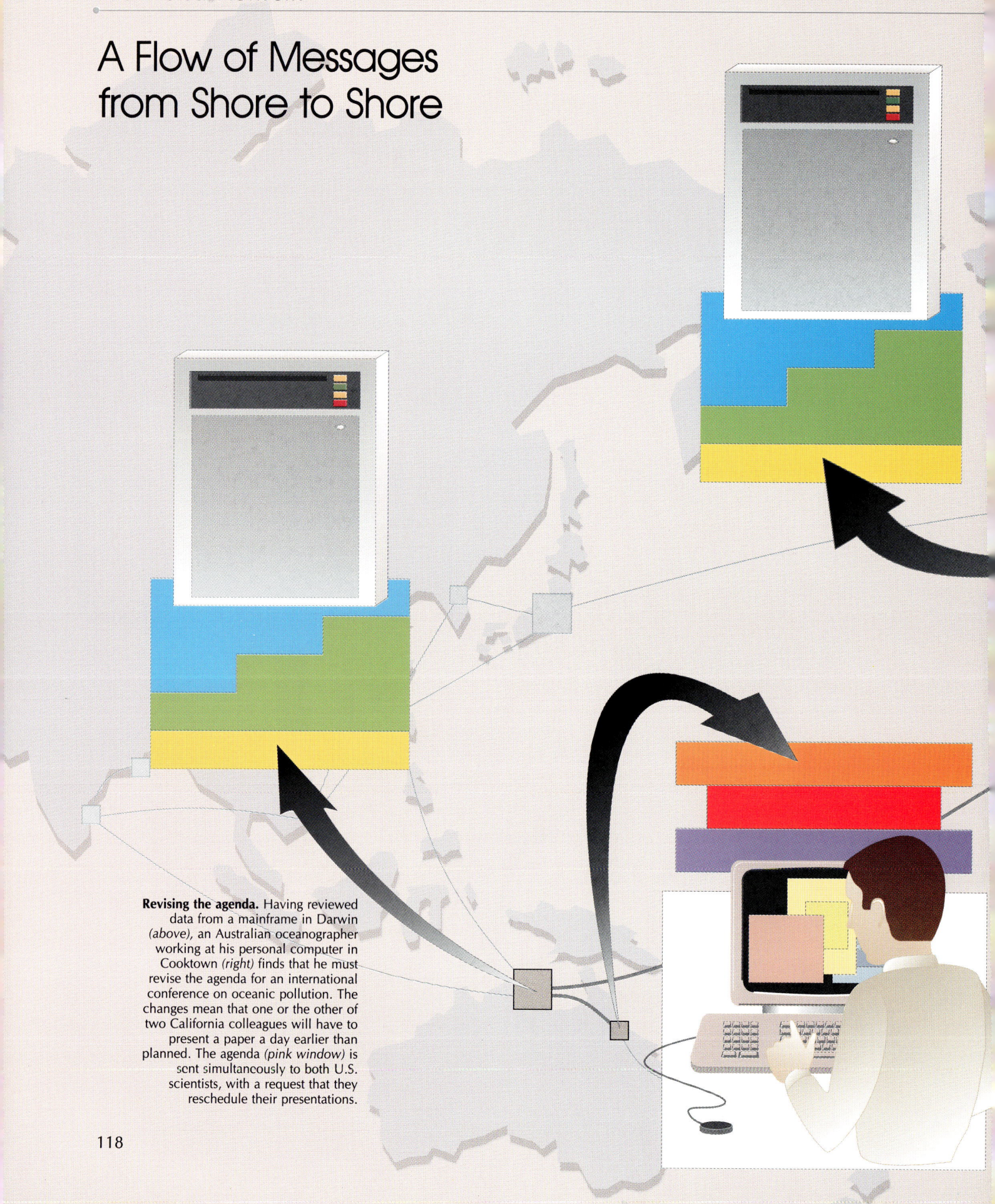

A Flow of Messages from Shore to Shore

Revising the agenda. Having reviewed data from a mainframe in Darwin *(above)*, an Australian oceanographer working at his personal computer in Cooktown *(right)* finds that he must revise the agenda for an international conference on oceanic pollution. The changes mean that one or the other of two California colleagues will have to present a paper a day earlier than planned. The agenda *(pink window)* is sent simultaneously to both U.S. scientists, with a request that they reschedule their presentations.

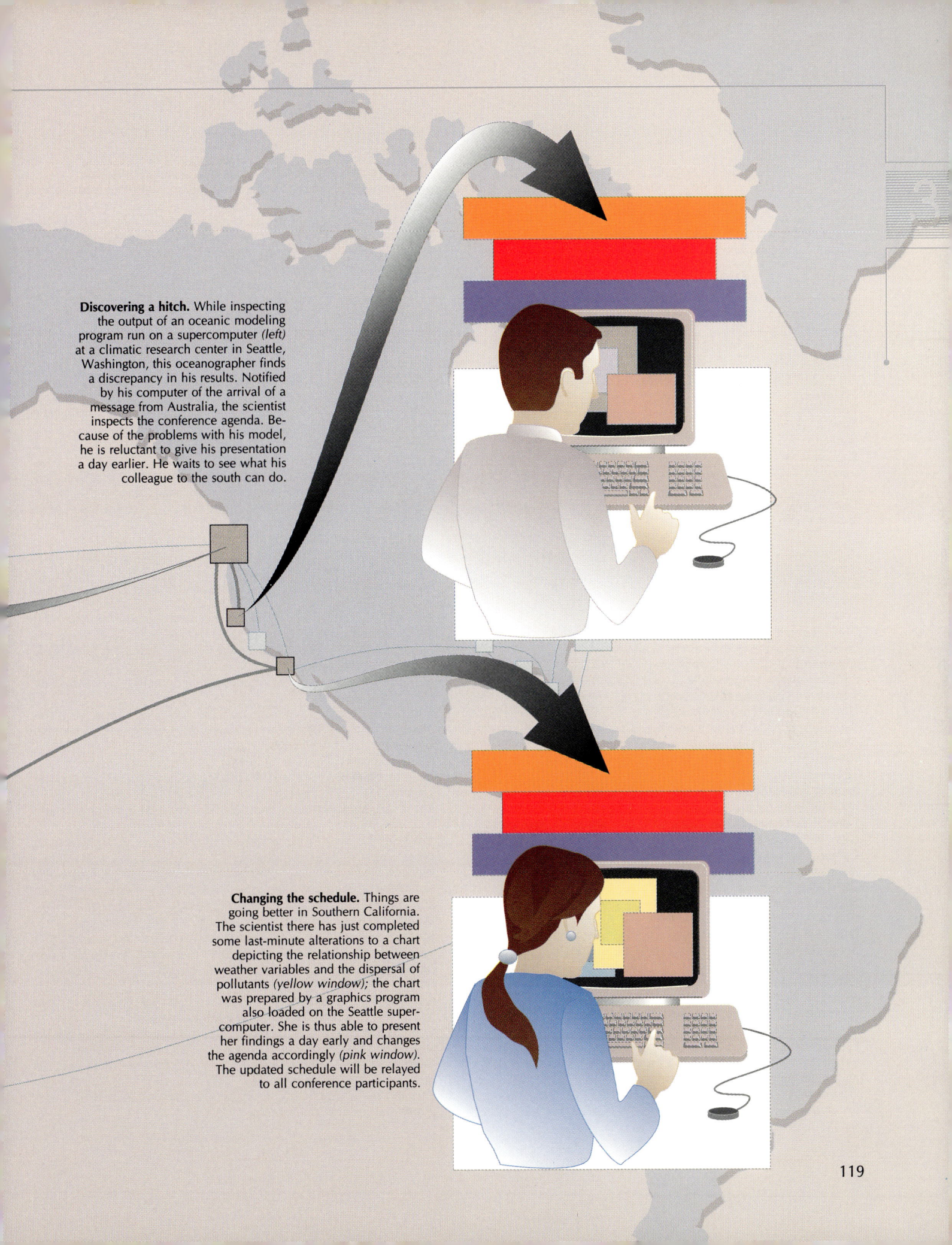

Discovering a hitch. While inspecting the output of an oceanic modeling program run on a supercomputer *(left)* at a climatic research center in Seattle, Washington, this oceanographer finds a discrepancy in his results. Notified by his computer of the arrival of a message from Australia, the scientist inspects the conference agenda. Because of the problems with his model, he is reluctant to give his presentation a day earlier. He waits to see what his colleague to the south can do.

Changing the schedule. Things are going better in Southern California. The scientist there has just completed some last-minute alterations to a chart depicting the relationship between weather variables and the dispersal of pollutants *(yellow window)*; the chart was prepared by a graphics program also loaded on the Seattle supercomputer. She is thus able to present her findings a day early and changes the agenda accordingly *(pink window)*. The updated schedule will be relayed to all conference participants.

Glossary

Address: the location of a specific cell in a computer's memory.

ASCII: the acronym for American Standard Code for Information Interchange, a widely used system for encoding letters, numerals, punctuation marks, and signs as binary numbers.

Assembly language: a low-level programming language, specific to a given computer, that uses short mnemonics corresponding directly to machine instructions.

Binary code: a system for representing information by combinations of two symbols, such as one and zero, true and false, or the presence or absence of voltage.

Binary number system: a number system that uses two as its base and expresses numbers as strings of zeros and ones.

Bit: the smallest unit of information in a digital computer, equivalent to a single zero or one. The word "bit" is a contraction of "binary digit."

Bus: a set of wires for carrying signals through a computer.

Byte: a sequence of eight bits treated as a unit for computation or storage.

Cathode-ray tube (CRT): a television-like display device with a screen that lights up where it is struck from the inside by a beam of electrons.

Central processing unit (CPU): the part of a computer that interprets and executes instructions.

Chip: an integrated circuit on a square of silicon or other semiconductor material, made up of thousands of transistors and other electronic components.

Circuit: an electrical network through which current can flow.

Circuit board: the board, often fiberglass, on which electronic components are mounted.

Clock: a device, usually timed by vibrations of a quartz crystal, that coordinates a computer's operations.

Command: a statement, such as "print" or "copy," that sets in motion a preprogrammed sequence of instructions to a computer.

Compiler: a program that converts a program written in a high-level language into either machine code or assembly language, holding the instructions in memory without executing them. The compiled program is stored for use at any later time.

Computer-aided design (CAD): the use of a computer to create or modify a design.

Computer-aided manufacture (CAM): the use of a computer in the manufacturing of a product.

Control unit: the circuits in the CPU that sequence, interpret, and carry out instructions.

Cursor: the movable spot of light that indicates a point of action or attention on a computer screen.

Database: an organized collection of facts about a subject.

Digital: pertaining to the representation, manipulation, or transmission of data by discrete signals.

Disk: a round magnetized plate, usually made of plastic or metal, organized into concentric tracks and pie-shaped sectors for storing data.

Disk drive: the mechanism that rotates a storage disk and reads or records data.

Electron: a negatively charged particle that orbits the nucleus of an atom.

Fetch instruction: the first phase of a typical instruction cycle, in which the control unit retrieves a program instruction from memory and loads it into the CPU.

Floppy disk: a small, flexible disk used to store information or instructions.

Hardware: the physical apparatus of a computer system.

Hard-wired: built in by the manufacturer and therefore incapable of being altered by programming.

High-level language: a programming language that approximates human language more closely than does machine code or assembly language, and in which one statement may invoke several machine-code or assembly-language instructions.

Icon: a symbol that may represent a program, files of data, or a procedure on a display screen.

Input: information fed into a computer.

Instruction: an order in elementary machine language specifying an operation to be carried out by the computer. A set of instructions forms a program.

Integrated circuit: an electronic circuit all of whose components are formed on a single piece of semiconductor material, usually silicon.

Kilobyte (K byte): 1,024 bytes (1,024 being one K, or two to the tenth power); often used as a measure of memory capacity.

Language: a set of rules or conventions to describe a process to a computer.

Laser printer: a printer that employs particles of dry ink, which cling in the desired pattern to electrically charged paper.

Liquid crystal display (LCD): a digital display mechanism made up of character-forming segments of a liquid crystal material sandwiched between polarizing and reflecting pieces of glass.

Machine code: a set of binary digits that can be directly understood by a computer without translation.

Mainframe computer: the largest type of computer, usually capable of serving many users simultaneously.

Memory: the principal work space inside a computer in which instructions and data can be recorded or from which it is retrieved; the term applies to internal storage facilities as opposed to external storage, such as disks or tapes.

Menu: a list of commands, functions, or graphic symbols shown on a display screen.

Microcomputer: a desktop or portable computer, based on a microprocessor and meant for a single user; often called a personal computer.

Microprocessor: a single chip that contains all the elements of a computer's central processing unit; sometimes called a computer on a chip.

Minicomputer: a midsize computer smaller than a mainframe and usually with much more memory than a microcomputer.

MIPS: millions of instructions per second; used as a measure of processing speed for computers.

Modem: a device that enables data to be transmitted between computers, generally over telephone lines. The word "modem" is an abbreviation for "modulator/demodulator."

Monitor: a television-like output device for displaying data.

Mouse: a hand-held input device that, when rolled across a flat surface, causes a cursor to move in a corresponding way on a display screen.

Object-oriented language: a type of programming language that represents information in units called objects, each containing data and a set of operations to manipulate that data.

Operating system: a set of programs used to control, assist, or supervise all other programs that run on a computer system.

Output: the data returned by a computer either directly to the user or to some form of storage.

Parallel: pertaining to data or instructions processed several bits at a time, rather than one bit at a time.

Peripheral: any device that is used for input or output functions in conjunction with a computer.
Pipelining: a processing technique that allows a CPU or a processor to work on more than one instruction at a time.
Pixel: short for "picture element"; one of the thousands of points on a computer screen from which digital images are formed.
Power supply: a device for converting external alternating current into the direct-current voltages needed to run a computer's electronic circuits.
Program: a sequence of instructions for performing a certain operation or solving a problem by computer.
Programming language: a set of words, letters, numerals, and abbreviated mnemonics, regulated by a specific syntax, used to describe a program to a computer.
Random-access memory (RAM): a form of temporary internal storage whose contents can be retrieved and altered by the user.
Read-only memory (ROM): permanent internal memory containing data or operating instructions that can be read but not altered by the user.
Register: a special circuit in the central processing unit that can either hold a value or perform an arithmetical or logical operation.
Semiconductor: a solid crystalline substance whose electrical conductivity falls between that of a metal and an insulator.
Serial: pertaining to data or instructions that are processed in sequence, one bit at a time, rather than in parallel (several bits at a time).
Silicon: an abundant semiconducting element from which computer chips are made.
Software: programs that enable a computer to do useful work.
Spreadsheet: software that simulates electronically the rows and columns of a ledger sheet, with a capacity for defining mathematical relationships between figures in particular positions on the ledger. Spreadsheets are used for accounting and for financial analysis and modeling.
Terminal: a device composed of a keyboard for putting data into a computer and a video screen or printer for receiving data from the computer.
Time-sharing: the simultaneous use of a computer by more than one person.
Window: a partitioned section of a video screen that displays the contents of a data file or the workings of an application program, while other data or programs are visible on other portions of the screen.
Word: the basic storage unit of a computer's operation; a sequence of bits—commonly from eight to thirty-two—occupying a single location and processed as a unit by the computer.
Word processing: the use of a computer for creating, displaying, editing, storing, and printing text.

Bibliography

Books
Alternative Computers, by the Editors of Time-Life Books (Understanding Computers series). Alexandria, Virginia: Time-Life Books, 1989.
Augarten, Stan, *Bit by Bit: An Illustrated History of Computers.* New York: Ticknor & Fields, 1984.
The Chipmakers, by the Editors of Time-Life Books (Understanding Computers series). Alexandria, Virginia: Time-Life Books, 1988.
Chposky, James, and Ted Leonsis, *Blue Magic: The People, Power and Politics behind the IBM Personal Computer.* New York: Facts On File Publications, 1988.
Computer Basics. by the Editors of Time-Life Books (Understanding Computers series). Alexandria, Virginia: Time-Life Books, 1985.
Computer Languages, by the Editors of Time-Life Books (Understanding Computers series). Alexandria, Virginia: Time-Life Books, 1986.
Freiberger, Paul, and Michael Swaine, *Fire in the Valley: The Making of the Personal Computer.* Berkeley, California: Osborne/McGraw-Hill, 1984.
Input/Output, by the Editors of Time-Life Books (Understanding Computers series). Alexandria, Virginia: Time-Life Books, 1986.
Isaacson, Dr. Portia, and Dr. Egil Juliussen, *IBM's Billion Dollar Baby: The Personal Computer.* Richardson, Texas: Future Computing, Inc., 1981.
Jourdain, Robert, *Programmer's Problem Solver for the IBM PC, XT & AT.* New York: Prentice Hall Press, 1986.
Kane, Gerry, *MIPS R2000 RISC Architecture.* Englewood Cliffs, New Jersey: Prentice Hall, 1987.
Lafore, Robert, *Turbo C: Programming for the IBM.* Indianapolis, Indiana: Howard W. Sams & Company, 1987.
Lammers, Susan, ed., *Programmers at Work.* Bellevue, Washington: Microsoft Press, 1986.
Levering, Robert, Michael Katz, and Milton Moskowitz, *The Computer Entrepreneurs: Who's Making It Big and How in America's Upstart Industry.* New York: New American Library, 1984.
Littman, Jonathan, *Once Upon a Time in ComputerLand.* Los Angeles, California: Price Stern Sloan, Inc., 1987.
Malone, Michael S., *The Big Score: The Billion-Dollar Story of Silicon Valley.* Garden City, New York: Doubleday & Company, 1985.
Moritz, Michael, *The Little Kingdom; The Private Story of Apple Computer.* New York: William Morrow and Company, 1984.
Osborne, Adam, and John Dvorak, *Hypergrowth: The Rise and Fall of Osborne Computer Corporation.* Berkeley, California: Idthekkethan Publishing Co., 1984.
Ralston, Anthony, and Edwin D. Reilly, Jr., eds., *Encyclopedia of Computer Science and Engineering.* 2d ed. New York: Van Nostrand Reinhold Company, 1983.
Reid, Glenn C., *PostScript Language: Program Design.* Reading, Massachusetts: Addison-Wesley Publishing Company, 1988.

Schildt, Herbert:
C: The Complete Reference. Berkeley, California: Osborne/McGraw-Hill, 1987.
C: Power User's Guide. Berkeley, California: Osborne/McGraw-Hill, 1988.
Schustack, Steve, Variations in C. Bellevue, Washington: Microsoft Press, 1985.
Sculley, John, and John A. Byrne, Odyssey: Pepsi to Apple . . . A Journey of Adventure, Ideas, and the Future. New York: Harper & Row, Publishers, 1987.
Slater, Robert, Portraits in Silicon. Cambridge, Massachusetts: The MIT Press, 1987.
Software, by the Editors of Time-Life Books (Understanding Computers series). Alexandria, Virginia: Time-Life Books, 1985.
Stallings, William, Computer Organization and Architecture. New York: Macmillan Publishing Company, 1986.
Stevens, Al, Turbo C: Memory-Resident Utilities, Screen I/O and Programming Techniques. Portland, Oregon: MIS: Press, 1987.

Periodicals
"Abundant Spreadsheet Choices." Personal Computing, September 1988.
Ahl, David H.:
"Ascent of the Personal Computer." Creative Computing, November 1984.
"The First Decade of Personal Computing." Creative Computing, November 1984.
"The First West Coast Computer Faire." Creative Computing, September/October, 1977.
"Analyzing Data from All the Angles." PC Magazine, October 27, 1987.
Anderson, John J., "Hello. Mr. Chips." Creative Computing, June 1985.
Apiki, Steve, and Stan Diehl, "PostScript Printers Come of Age." BYTE, September 1988.
"Apple vs. IBM." Fortune, February 18, 1985.
Bairstow, Jeffrey, "Personal Workstations Redefine Desktop Computing." High Technology, March 1987.
Baran, Nick, "Two Worlds Converge." BYTE, February 1989.
Barrett, Jon, and Kirk Reistroffer, "Designing a Raster-Image Processor." BYTE, May 1987.
Beale, Stephen, James Cavuoto, and Aileen Abernathy, "A Touch of Gray." MacUser, February 1989.
Belitsos, Byron, "MIS Pilots the Air Wars." Computer Decisions, March 1988.
Bender, Eric, "The Blue Sky's the Limit." PC World, June 1987.
"Big Blue Adds to Its Arsenal." Newsweek, August 27, 1984.
Brody, Herb, "RISC-y Business." High Technology Business, August 1988.
"The BYTE Awards." BYTE, January 1989.
"Can Bill Lowe Put IBM's PC Unit into Pinstripes?" Business Week, January 20, 1986.
Castro, Janice, "Kicking Junior Out of the Family." Time, April 1, 1985.
"Challenging 1-2-3 on Price & Power." PC Magazine, October 27, 1987.
Cocks, Jay, "The Updated Book of Jobs." Time, January 3, 1983.

"The Coming Shakeout in Personal Computers." Business Week, November 22, 1982.
"Compaq: An IBM Clone Meets the Real Thing." Fortune, April 16, 1984.
"Compaq's Gutsy Bid to Be More Than an IBM Copycat." Business Week, July 9, 1984.
Curran, Lawrence J., and Richard S. Shuford, "IBM's Estridge." BYTE, November 1983.
"The Datamation 100: Company Profiles." Datamation, June 15, 1988.
Davis, Jo Ellen, and Geoff Lewis, "Compaq is Trying to Steal a March on IBM." Business Week, September 22, 1986.
Day, Michael, "IBM Fights to Make Micro Channel an Industry Standard." LAN TIMES, December 1988.
Ditlea, Steve:
"Spreadsheets Can Be Hazardous to Your Health." Personal Computing. January 1987.
"Word Processing." Personal Computing, October 1986.
"An Easy-Come, Easy-Go World." Time, September 5, 1983.
Elmer-Dewitt, Philip:
"The Next Major Battleground." Time, April 25, 1988.
"Soul of the Next Machine." Time, October 24, 1988.
Faflick, Philip, "The Hottest-Selling Hardware." Time, January 3, 1983.
Farber, Daniel, "Rosing Outlines Sun's Strategy." MacWEEK, March 7, 1989.
Fersko-Weiss, Henry, "How to Link Spreadsheets." PC, July 15, 1985.
Flanagan, Patrick, "A Critical System Takes Shape." Computer Decisions, October 1988.
Friedrich, Otto, "The Computer Moves In." Time, January 3, 1983.
Furger, Roberta, "Redefining the Laptop." Infoworld. November 7, 1988.
"The Future of High-Performance Personal Systems." MIPS, February 1989.
Gannes, Stuart:
"Back-to-Basics Computers with Sports-Car Speed." Fortune, September 30, 1985.
"Sun's Sizzling Race to the Top." Fortune, August 17, 1987.
Garvey, Ruth S., "Computers in Sports: By Land, Sea and Air!" Toshiba MicroLife, winter 1988.
"The Giant Takes Command." Newsweek, July 11, 1983.
Glogau, Jordan, "High-End Halftoning." PostScript Language Journal, June 1987.
Goldstein, Mark L., "An Industry Legend—At 21." Industry Week, April 20, 1987.
Guengerich, Steven, and Steven Papermaster, " 'Throwing Out the Mainframe': It Can Work, But It's Not Easy." PC Week, March 24, 1987.
Guglielmo, Connie, "The Soul of a Not-So-New Machine." MacWEEK, January 17, 1989.
Guterman, Jimmy, "Sun '386 Machines Run Unix and DOS." PC Week, April 12, 1988.
Hafner, Katherine M., "Polishing the Apple II to Keep Its Classroom Lead." Business Week, September 22, 1986.
Hafner, Katherine M., and Richard Brandt, "Steve Jobs: Can He Do It Again?" Business Week, October 24, 1988.
Hafner, Katherine M., and Geoff Lewis, "The Knockoffs Head for

a Knockdown Fight with IBM." *Business Week.* December 21, 1987.
Hennessey, John, "VLSI RISC Processors." *VLSI Systems Design,* October 1985.
Hillkirk, John, "Michael Dell: Whiz Kid Combines Computer Competence, Financial Finesse." *USA Today,* February 15, 1988.
Honan, Patrick, "Compaq Computer Corporation: Upholding the Standard." *Personal Computing,* August 1988.
"How Compaq's Portable Leaped Ahead of the Pack." *Business Week,* August 15, 1983.
"How the PC Project Changed the Way IBM Thinks." *Business Week,* October 3, 1983.
Hyde, Randall L., "Overview of Memory Management." *BYTE,* April 1988.
"IBM Joins the Race in Personal Computers." *Business Week,* August 24, 1981.
"The IBM PC AT." *BYTE,* October 1984.
"IBM's 'Junior' Will Stabilize a Chaotic Market." *Business Week,* November 14, 1983.
"IBM's Personal Computer Spawns an Industry." *Business Week,* August 15, 1983.
"IBM Wants a Bite of the Apple." *Newsweek,* August 24, 1981.
Iles, Amanda, "The Fountain of Ingenuity at PARC." *MacWEEK,* April 5, 1985.
"Intel's New 80860 CPU Aims to Be a Cray on a Chip." *BYTE,* April 1989.
"An Interview: The Macintosh Design Team." *BYTE,* February 1984.
Johnson, Thomas L., "The RISC/CISC Melting Pot." *BYTE,* April 1987.
Joyce, Ed, and David E. Essex, "Building Compatibility: An Interview with Jonathan Joseph, Director of Compatibility Software Products, Phoenix Technologies Ltd." *PCResource,* 1987.
Kneale, Dennis:
  "IBM's AT Computer Puts Pressure on Rivals and Rest of Its PC Line." *Wall Street Journal,* October 17, 1984.
  "IBM Competitors Scramble to Produce Clones of Firm's Personal Computer AT." *Wall Street Journal,* April 17, 1985.
Kneale, Dennis, Hank Gilman, and Paul B. Carroll, "IBM Unveils Family of New PCs, Fueling Competition in Industry." *Wall Street Journal,* April 3, 1987.
Kull, David, "SAA: Master Plan or Grand Illusion?" *Computer & Communications Decisions,* June 1987.
Lancaster, Don, "Hardware Hacker." *Radio-Electronics,* May 1988.
Leibowitz, Michael R., "Workstation Wars: The Battle of the Big 7." *High Technology Business,* November 1987.
Lewis, Geoff, "The PC Wars: IBM vs. the Clones." *Business Week,* July 28, 1986.
Lockwood, Russ, "The Many Faces of a 386." *Personal Computing,* July 1988.
Lombardi, John, "Heavy Duty Word Processing." *Infoworld,* January 23, 1989.
Lowe, William C., "The PC in Retrospect." *Personal Computing,* October 1986.
Magnet, Myron, "Clive Sinclair's Little Computer That Could." *Fortune,* March 8, 1982.
Marcom, John, Jr., "IBM Shipments of PC Version are Curtailed." *Wall Street Journal,* December 17, 1984.
Markoff, John:
  "In an Age When Tiny Is All, Big Computers Are Hurting." *New York Times,* April 4, 1989.
  "Spreadsheet Rivalry Heats Up." *New York Times.* January 17, 1989.
Markoff, John, and Ezra Shapiro, "Macintosh's Other Designers." *BYTE,* August 1984.
Morgan, Chris, Gregg Williams, and Phil Lemmons, "An Interview with Wayne Rosing, Bruce Daniels, and Larry Tesler." *BYTE,* February 1983.
Morrow, George, "Bus Wars." *Infoworld,* November 14, 1988.
Nash, J. Madeleine, "Power Station in a Pizza Box." *Time,* April 24, 1989.
O'Reilly, Brian, "Compaq's Grip on IBM's Slippery Tail." *Fortune,* February 18, 1985.
O'Reilly, Francis J., "Tandy Survives Personal Computer Shakedown." *Westchester Business Journal,* March 2, 1987.
"Other Maestros of the Micro." *Time,* January 3, 1983.
Patterson, David A., "Reduced Instruction Set Computers." *Communications of the ACM,* January 1985.
Pearson, Ronald, "Lies, Damned Lies and Spreadsheets." *BYTE,* December 1988.
Pelli, Denis G., "Programming in PostScript." *BYTE,* May 1987.
Pepper, Jon, "Shearson Gets a Jump on the Market with Personal Workstations for Traders." *PC Week,* August 22, 1988.
Perry, Tekla S., " 'PostScript' Prints Anything: A Case History." *IEEE Spectrum,* May 1988.
"Personal Computers: And the Winner Is IBM." *Business Week,* October 3, 1983.
"Personal Computers: IBM Will Keep Knocking Heads." *Business Week,* January 14, 1985.
Petzold, Charles, "Intel's 32-Bit Wonder: The 80386 Microprocessor." *PC Magazine,* November 25, 1986.
Port, Otis, et al., "Intel: The Next Revolution." *Business Week,* September 26, 1988.
Porter, Stephen, "The Flexible Solid." *Computer Graphics World,* June 1988.
Robinson, Phillip:
  "Closing the Gap between PCs and Workstations." *Infoworld,* December 12, 1988.
  "How Much of a RISC?" *BYTE,* April 1987.
Rottenberg, David, "King of the Clones." *Boston Magazine,* June 1987.
Rubin, Charles A., "Moving Up with Spreadsheet Math." *Personal Computing,* January 1985.
Schlender, Brenton R.:
  "Apple Era behind Him, Steve Jobs Tries Again, Using a New System." *Wall Street Journal,* October 13, 1988.
  "Intel Introduces a Chip Packing Huge Power and Wide Ambitions." *Wall Street Journal,* February 28, 1989.
Seybold, John W., "The Desktop Publishing Phenomenon." *BYTE,* May 1987.
"Software: The New Driving Force." *Business Week,* February 27, 1984.
"Steve Jobs Comes Back." *Newsweek,* October 24, 1988.
Stipp, David, "Phoenix Software Rises to Prominence." *Wall Street Journal,* May 3, 1985.
Stone, Paula S., "Move to PCs Saves Fish from Drowning."

Infoworld, January 4, 1988.
Tannenbaum, Jeffrey A., "Small Businesses Learn That a Computer without Software Is 'Dumb Hunk of Iron.'" *Wall Street Journal,* April 2, 1980.
Taylor, Alexander, "Small-Computer Shootout." *Time,* March 2, 1981.
Thompson, Tom, "Sun's New Workstation: The Sun 386i." *BYTE,* July 1988.
Thompson, Tom, and Nick Baran, "The NeXT Computer." *BYTE,* November 1988.
Uttal, Bro:
"The Coming Struggle in Personal Computers." *Fortune,* January 29, 1981.
"A Computer Gadfly's Triumph." *Fortune,* March 8, 1982.
Vasilopoulos, Audrey, "Solid Modeling Made Easy." *Computer Graphics World,* January 1989.
Verity, John W., and Geoff Lewis, "Computers: The New Look. The Mainframe Era is Fading—and the Micro is Taking Command." *Business Week,* November 30, 1987.
Walkenbach, John, et al., "By the Numbers." *Infoworld,* January 16, 1989.
Walske, Steven, "Solid Models Link Design and Manufacturing." *Machine Design,* July 7, 1988.
Webster, Bruce F.:
"The Macintosh." *BYTE,* August 1984.
"The Macintosh II." *BYTE,* October 1987.
Wiegner, Kathleen K., "They Are Not There Waiting for the Plane to Land." *Forbes,* June 27, 1988.
Williams, Gregg:
"The Apple Macintosh Computer." *BYTE,* February 1984.
"The Lisa Computer System." *BYTE,* February 1983.
Williams, Gregg, and Rob Moore, "The Apple Story, Part 1: Early History." *BYTE,* December 1984.

Wohlers, Terry:
"CADD Catches 32-Bit Wave." *Computer Graphics World,* June 1987.
"The Leap to 3D." *Computer Graphics World,* March 1988.
Wood, Patrick, "Halftones and the Image Operator." *PostScript Language Journal,* June 1987.

Other Sources

Datapro 70. Delran, New Jersey: Datapro Research Corporation/McGraw-Hill, 1989.
Datapro Reports on IBM Products. Delran, New Jersey: Datapro Research Corporation/McGraw-Hill, 1985.
Datapro Reports on Word Processing. Delran, New Jersey: Datapro Research Corporation/McGraw-Hill, December 1988.
"The Firm That Dropped the Drawing Board." Company literature. Houston, Texas: The Whitney Group, no date.
LOTUS 1-2-3: Getting Started Manual Release 2.01. Cambridge, Massachusetts: Lotus Development Corporation, 1986.
"Origins of an Architecture: 801/RISC." *IBM Research Highlights.* Number 1, 1986.
"A Revolution in Progress." Santa Clara, California: Intel Corporation, 1984.
RISC Technology Backgrounder. MIPS Computer Systems, Inc., Sunnyvale, California, March 28, 1988.
"U.S. Coast Guard Uses PC-Based CAD System to Design and Upgrade Its Fleet." Application note. Houston, Texas: Compaq Computer Corporation, no date.
"Weyerhaeuser Turns to Compaq Computers to Help Manage Its Vast Forests." Application note. Houston, Texas: Compaq Computer Corporation, no date.
"The Whitney Group Breaks Mold of Traditional Design Practice." Application note. Houston, Texas: Compaq Computer Corporation, no date.

Picture Credits

Credits for the illustrations that appear in this volume are listed below. Credits from left to right are separated by semicolons; from top to bottom they are separated by dashes.

Cover: Art by Fred Devita. 6: Art by Fred Devita. 9: Courtesy Apple Computer, Inc. 11: Art by Matt McMullen; courtesy Apple Computer, Inc.; courtesy Software Arts, Inc.; Eric Hartmann/Magnum. 12, 13: Art by Matt McMullen; © 1985 Andrew Popper; courtesy Apple Computer, Inc.; courtesy International Business Machines Corporation; courtesy Compaq Computer Corporation; Diana Walker/*Time*. 16, 17: Mickey Pflegler/*Time*; © Nubar Alexanian/Woodfin Camp & Associates, Inc. 18, 19: Art by Fred Devita. 20, 21: Art by Alfred Kamajian. 22, 23: Art by Fred Devita. 25: © Bob Straus. 26: Steve Sellers, courtesy Toshiba America Information Systems, Inc./Computer Systems Division. 29-43: Art by Matt McMullen. 44: Art by Fred Devita. 46: © Jim Wilson/Woodfin Camp & Associates, Inc. 48, 49: Courtesy Apple Computer, Inc. 50-57: Computer-generated art by Time-Life Books. 59: © 1984 Matt Herron/Black Star. 64-67: Art by Fred Devita. 69-85: Art by Stephen Bauer. 86-93: Art by Fred Devita. 94: Dennis Brack/Black Star, courtesy Compaq Computer Corporation. 97: © Jon Chomitz, courtesy Parametric Technology Corporation. 99: Courtesy Integrated Device Technology, Inc. 100-103: Art by Time-Life Books. 107-119: Computer-generated art by Time-Life Books.

Acknowledgments

The editors wish to thank: **In Canada:** Calgary: Michael R. Williams, University of Calgary; **In the United States:** Arizona—Thatcher: Don Lancaster, Synergetics; California—Berkeley: Garth A. Gibson and Robert L. Miller, University of California; Freemont: Jackie Rae, Waterside Associates; Hillsborough: George Morrow; Mountain View: Thomas G. Baffico, Liz Marie Bond, Brenda Hansen, and Glen C. Reid, Adobe Systems Incorporated; San Jose: DataQuest Incorporated; Connecticut—Ridgefield: James Blackwell, Blackwell Consulting; Maryland—Kensington: Jane Gruenebaum; Massachusetts—Carlyle: Peter Baumgartner, Petra Associates; Mississippi—Norwood: Jonathon Joseph, Phoenix Technologies Ltd.; Nevada—Incline Village: Egil Juliussen; New Hampshire—Nashua: Linda Giragosian, Darlene Hrycuna Skupien, and Richard Treadway, Digital Equipment Corporation; New Jersey—Carlstadt: Cort Hollan, Applied Graphics Technologies; New York—Albany: Isabel Nirenberg, State University of New York; New York: Steve Terry, Electronic Directions; Pennsylvania—Malvern: Albert J. Charpentier, Ensoniq, Inc.; Pittsburgh: Brian Harrison, Carnegie-Mellon University; Texas—Austin: Charles Melear, Motorola Semiconductor, Inc.; Houston: Peter Heyne, Compaq Computer Corporation; Utah—Orem: Allan Brown, WordPerfect Corporation; Virginia—Alexandria: Stephen A. Campbell, Darby Graphics, Inc.; Reston: L. Scott Randall, Image Technology; Washington—Seattle: John D. Nelson, Aldus Corporation; Bob Wallace, Quicksoft Inc.

Index

A
Adobe Systems: PostScript, 51
Ahl, David: 10
Aldus Corporation: 67
Alpert, Martin: 18
Alto: 59-60
AMR: Confirm system, 104
Apollo Computer: 89
Apple Computer Company: 45-46; and enthusiasts, 47-48; logos, *9;* reshaping after Macintosh, 65-68; strategy, 47, 67-68; working environment, 48-49, 62
Apple LaserWriter: 68
Apple Lisa: 49, 58, 59, 60-61, 63; canceled, 66; graphical interface, 59-60; software, 61, 63
Apple Macintosh: *12,* 65; developers, *48-49;* development, 58-60, 61-65; Mac Plus, 68; Mac II, 68, 89; marketing, 64-65; memory, 64; software, 65; user interface, 59-60, 64, 68
Apple II: *7, 11,* 18; early success, 8, 47; engineering, 45; software, 47; and VisiCalc, 10
Apple III (Sara): 49, 58
Atkinson, Bill: *49, 59,* 60, 61, 64
AutoCad: 96
AutoSketch: 94

B
Banana printers: 24
Bentley: 95
BIOS: copiers of IBM PC, 22-24
Boyd, Jim: 87
Bricklin, Daniel: 9, *11*
BusinessLand: 25

C
Canion, Rod: 22, *25*
Cary, Frank: 11, 16
CISC (Complex Instruction Set Computer): 99; architecture, *100;* and pipelining, *102-103*
Clones, IBM PC: 23-25
Cocke, John: 98
Coleman, Dennis: 39
Colvin, Neil: 24
Commodore International: PET, 9
Compaq Computer Corporation: 22-23, 28, 68, 87; and 80386 machines, 87-88, 89
Compilers: CISC and RISC, *100-101*
Computer-aided design (CAD): for interior design, 95-96; on micros, 88-89; for ship design, 93, *94,* 95; 3-D, 96, *97,* 98
Computer-aided engineering (CAE): on micros, 88-89, *97,* 98
ComputerLand: 16, 25
Computers: cost vs. speed, 91; hierarchy of power, 89-91; linking different classes, 105; mainframe sales, 105; reclassifying, 98, 104; RISC, 91, 98, 106
Coprocessor: mathematical: 96
Corona Data Systems: 23-24
CP/M: 16
Cromemco: 9

D
Data General: and microcomputers, 10
Dell, Michael: and Dell Computer, 24-25, 89
Desktop publishing: *50-51;* page-description language, *50-53;* printing by, *56-57;* and scanned images, *54-55*
Digital Equipment Corporation: and minicomputers, 90; and personal computers, 10
Disk farms: 104

E
Eagle Computer: 23, 24
Eggebrecht, Lewis: 13, 14
EISA (Extended Industry Standard Architecture): 28
Elephant Memory Systems: 24
Engelbart, Douglas: 59
Epson Corporation: 16
Espinoza, Chris: 62
Estridge, Philip Donald: *11,* 14, 15, 16, 17, 27
Excel: 68

F
Fish Engineering & Construction, Inc.: 87, 88-89, 91
Frankston, Robert: 9, *11*

G
Gates, William, III: *17,* 67
Geisberg, Samuel: 97
Gorin, Ralph: 39
Graphical interface: 59-50

H
Hallock, Robert: 10
Harris, Jim: 22
Hertzfeld, Andy: 47-48, 62, 64

Hewlett-Packard: and microcomputers, 10; RISC machine, 98
Hypercard: 59

I
IBM: Dirty Dozen, 11-13; and early microcomputers, 8, 10; Entry Level Systems unit, 10, 11-12, 25; 4341, 88, 91; 5100 series, 10; restructuring of microcomputer division, 25; and RISC technology, 98; Systems Application Architecture (SAA), 105
IBM PC: *11;* Acorn, 14; aftermarket, 18-19; approach to building and selling, 15-16; AT, *12,* 25; BIOS, 22, 23, 24; compatibles to, 19, 22-25; debut, 16-17; early planning, 11-14; microprocessor, 12-13; open architecture, 14, 15; operating system, 15; Project Chess, 14; RT PC, 98; software, 19
IBM PS/2: 27; 80386 models, 89; industry reaction to, 28; Micro Channel Architecture, 28; protection from clones, 27-28
Icons: 60
Intel: 8086, 12; 8088, 13; 80286, 25; 80386, 27, 87-88; 80387, 96; 80486, 104; RISC processor, 98

J
Jobs, Steven: 7, *46,* 62-63; and Apple, 7, 45-46, 59, 60, 61-62, 65, 66, 67; and NeXT, 7, 67

K
Kapor, Mitchell: *12,* 67, 106
Kay, Alan: 59
Kildall, Gary: *16*

L
Leading Edge Products: 24
Lotus 1-2-3: 12, 19
Lowe, William: 8, 10-14, 18, 25

M
MacPaint: 59, 65
MacWrite: 65
Mainframe: lull in sales, 105; redefined, 98, 104
Mandel, Alfred: 67
Markkula, A. C. (Mike): 18, 46, 47, 60, 61, 63
Memory: addressing, 20-21; registers on RISC processor, 99
Microcode: 99, 100

Microcomputers: 7-8; growth of market, 18; organizations using, 88, 91-96; power of, 20-21
Microprocessors: CISC, 99; clock speed, 20-21, 88, 98; Intel, 12-13, 25, 27, 87-88, 96; math coprocessors, 96; memory capacity, 20, 21, 88; and microchip technology, 98; Motorola, 60-61, 68, 89, 96; recent advances, 106; RISC, 91, 98, 106; word size, 12-13, 20-21, 87-88
MicroSoft: and Apple Macintosh, 68; and IBM PC, 15
Milestones in personal computers: *11-13*
MIPS: RISC machine, 98
M.I.T. (Massachusetts Institute of Technology): X Window, 107, *108-119*
Morrow, George: 10
Motorola: RISC processor, 98; 68000, 61-62; 68020, 68, 89; 68881, 68, 96
Mouse interface: 59
Murto, Bill: 22

N
Networks: local vs. global, 108-109; X Window, 107, *108-119*
NeXT: 7
North Star: 9

O
Ohio Scientific: 9
Open architecture: 14
Operating systems: limitations of MS-DOS, 105; MS-DOS vs. UNIX, 96-97
Osborne, Adam: 8, 22; Osborne I, 23

P
Page-description language (PDL): *51-53*; and printing, *56-57*; and scanned images, *54-55*
PageMaker: 68
Papajohn, Ted: 22
Parametric Technology Corporation: 97
Phoenix Software Associates Ltd.: 24, 25
Pipelining: 99, 101, *102-103*
Pointers: *34-35*
Portable computers: Compaq, 23, *25*; laptop, *26*; Osborne, 22-23

PostScript: *50-57*
Processor Technology: 9
Pro/Engineer: 97-98

Q
Quickdraw: 61, 64

R
Raskin, Jef: 58, 60, 61-62
Reservations systems: 104-105
RISC (Reduced Instruction Set Computer): 91, 98, 99, 106; architecture, 100, *101*; pipelining, *102-103*
Roach, John: 18
RoboSolid: 96
Rothmueller, Ken: 60, 61

S
Sanchez, Bruce: 93
Sanders, Wendell: 58
Scan codes: 30
SCI Systems: 15
Scott, Michael: 46, 47, 60, 61
Sculley, John: 63, 65, 66-67, 68
Sears, Roebuck and Company: 16
Sequent Computer Systems: Balance B21, 104; S81, 104
Shane, Michael: 24
Shearson Lehman Hutton: 91-92
Smalltalk: 59
Smith, Burrell: *49*, 62
Software, microcomputer: *See* specific applications
Sparks, H. L.: 16
Spreadsheets: 69; calculations, *78-81*; formatting, *76-77*; graphics, *84-85*; linking, *82-83*; Lotus 1-2-3, 12, 19, 69; memory use, *74-75*; scrolling, *72-73*; structure, *70-71*; VisiCalc, 9-10
Stanford Research Institute (SRI): 59
Sun Microsystems: 90, 96-97; SPARCstation 1, 98
Sydnes, Bill: 13, 14

T
Tandon Corporation: 15
Tandy Radio Shack: 68; TRS-80, 9, 18
Tecmar, Inc.: 18-19
Texas Instruments (TI): and microcomputers, 10
3D/International: 95
Tramiel, Jack: 9

U
United Airlines: Apollo system, 104-105; Open Systems Manager, 105
UNIX: and MS-DOS, 96-97
U.S. Coast Guard: and CAD blueprints, 94-95

V
Video display: character-based, 31, *32*; graphics-based, 32, *33*; memory-mapped video, *40-41*
VisiCalc: 9, 11, 17

W
Weyerhaeuser Company: 92-93; ExcelleRate, 93
Whitney, Gary: 95; The Whitney Group, 95
Wigginton, Randy: 62
Wilkie, Dan: 15
Windows: *40-41*; 59
Word processors: 29; display, 31, *32-33*; formatting documents, *36-37*; mail merge, *42-43*; memory use, *30-31*; pointers, *34-35*; spelling checkers, *38-39*; windows, *40-41*. *See also* Desktop publishing
Work stations: 90; and personal computers, 96
Wozniak, Steven: 45, *46*, 66, 68
WYSIWYG: 36

X
X Window: 107, *108-119*; protocol, *112-113*; software, *110-111*; system manager, *114-115*; window manager, *116-117*
Xerox PARC (Palo Alto Research Center): Alto, 59-60; PARC, 59, 60; Star, 60

Y
Young, Richard: 16

Z
Zenith Electronics Corporation: 15, 68

Time-Life Books Inc.
is a wholly owned subsidiary of
TIME INCORPORATED

Editor-in-Chief: Jason McManus
Chairman and Chief Executive Officer:
J. Richard Munro
President and Chief Operating Officer:
N. J. Nicholas, Jr.
Editorial Director: Richard B. Stolley

THE TIME INC. BOOK COMPANY

President and Chief Executive Officer: Kelso F. Sutton
President, Time Inc. Books Direct:
Christopher T. Linen

TIME-LIFE BOOKS INC.

EDITOR: George Constable
Executive Editor: Ellen Phillips
Director of Design: Louis Klein
Director of Editorial Resources: Phyllis K. Wise
Editorial Board: Russell B. Adams, Jr., Dale M. Brown, Roberta Conlan, Thomas H. Flaherty, Lee Hassig, Donia Ann Steele, Rosalind Stubenberg
Director of Photography and Research:
John Conrad Weiser
Assistant Director of Editorial Resources:
Elise Ritter Gibson

PRESIDENT: John M. Fahey, Jr.
Senior Vice Presidents: Robert M. DeSena, James L. Mercer, Paul R. Stewart, Joseph J. Ward
Vice Presidents: Stephen L. Bair, Stephen L. Goldstein, Juanita T. James, Andrew P. Kaplan, Carol Kaplan, Susan J. Maruyama, Robert H. Smith
Supervisor of Quality Control: James King

PUBLISHER: Joseph J. Ward

Editorial Operations
Copy Chief: Diane Ullius
Production: Celia Beattie
Library: Louise D. Forstall

Correspondents: Elisabeth Kraemer-Singh (Bonn); Christine Hinze (London); Christina Lieberman (New York); Maria Vincenza Aloisi (Paris); Ann Natanson (Rome); Dick Berry (Tokyo). Valuable assistance was also provided by: Elizabeth Brown (New York).

UNDERSTANDING COMPUTERS

SERIES DIRECTOR: Lee Hassig
Series Administrator: Gwen C. Mullen (acting)

Editorial Staff for *The Personal Computer*
Designers: Robert K. Herndon, Cynthia Richardson, Lorraine D. Rivard
Associate Editors: Pictures—Susan V. Kelly;
Text—Robert A. Doyle (principal), Allan Fallow
Researchers: Katya Sharpe Cooke, Flora J. Garcia, Patrick J. Gordon, Tucker Jones, Roxie France-Nuriddin
Writers: Margery A. duMond, Esther Ferington, Robert M. S. Somerville
Copy Coordinator: Elizabeth Graham
Picture Coordinator: Robert H. Wooldridge, Jr.
Editorial Assistant: Susan L. Finken

Special Contributors: Mark Bello, Gina Maranto, Jim Merritt, Eugene Rodgers (text); Maureen M. McHugh (research); Mel Ingber (index).

THE CONSULTANTS

DAVID AHL founded *Creative Computing,* a monthly magazine that chronicled the microcomputer world from 1974 through 1985. He is now a freelance journalist working from his home in Morristown, New Jersey.

ALAN T. COOKE is a management consultant for the accounting firm of Grant Thornton. His background is in accounting and the decision sciences, with special interests in management-information systems and programming.

AARON GOLDBERG is a vice president at International Data Corporation in Framingham, Massachusetts. He has been tracking the personal-computer market for the company since 1979.

MARK D. HILL is assistant professor of computer sciences at the University of Wisconsin at Madison, and a recipient of the 1989 Presidential Young Investigator Award. His current research interests are performance and implementation factors in computer-memory systems.

WALTER S. KEY works as consultant in the area of factory and office automation, specializing in the introduction of the microcomputer to the workplace.

FREDERICK B. MAXWELL, a microcontroller specialist, is presently working under contract to the United States Postal Service in its Process Control Division in Landover, Maryland.

EZRA SHAPIRO is a freelance writer who specializes in microcomputer topics and contributes frequently to *BYTE, MacWEEK,* and other industry publications. He lives in Hollywood, California.

PATRICK WOOD is vice president of Pipeline Associates, Inc., a software development, consulting, and training company. He is editor of a quarterly magazine, *The Postscript Language Journal,* and coauthor of several books on UNIX and C.

Library of Congress Cataloguing in Publication Data
The Personal computer / by the editors of Time-Life Books, Inc.
  p.   cm. — (Understanding computers)
Bibliography: p.
Includes index.
ISBN 0-8094-6066-1.
1. Microcomputers.   I. Time-Life Books.   II. Series.
QA76.5P39354   004. 16-dc 19   89-4665
                                               CIP
ISBN 0-8094-6087-X (lib. bdg.)

For information on and a full description of any of the Time-Life Books series listed, please write:
Reader Information
Time-Life Customer Service
P.O. Box C-32068
Richmond, Virginia 23261-2068

© 1989 Time-Life Books Inc. All rights reserved.
No part of this book may be reproduced in any form or by any electronic or mechanical means, including information storage and retrieval devices or systems, without prior written permission from the publisher, except that brief passages may be quoted for reviews.
Second printing 1990. Printed in U.S.A.
Published simultaneously in Canada.
School and library distribution by Silver Burdett Company, Morristown, New Jersey.

TIME-LIFE is a trademark of Time Incorporated U.S.A.